Women and
Culture Series

The Women and Culture Series is dedicated to books that illuminate the lives, roles, achievements, and status of women, past or present.

Fran Leeper Buss
Dignity: Lower Income Women Tell of Their Lives and Struggles
La Partera: Story of a Midwife

Valerie Kossew Pichanick
Harriet Martineau: The Woman and Her Work, 1802–76

Sandra Baxter and Marjorie Lansing
Women and Politics: The Visible Majority

Estelle B. Freedman
Their Sisters' Keepers: Women's Prison Reform in America, 1830–1930

Susan C. Bourque and Kay Barbara Warren
Women of the Andes: Patriarchy and Social Change in Two Peruvian Towns

Marion S. Goldman
Gold Diggers and Silver Miners: Prostitution and Social Life on the Comstock Lode

Page duBois
Centaurs and Amazons: Women and the Pre-History of the Great Chain of Being

Mary Kinnear
Daughters of Time: Women in the Western Tradition

Lynda K. Bundtzen
Plath's Incarnations: Woman and the Creative Process

Violet B. Haas and Carolyn C. Perrucci, editors
Women in Scientific and Engineering Professions

Sally Price
Co-wives and Calabashes

Patricia R. Hill
The World Their Household: The American Woman's Foreign Mission Movement and Cultural Transformation, 1870–1920

Diane Wood Middlebrook and Marilyn Yalom, editors
Coming to Light: American Women Poets in the Twentieth Century

Leslie W. Rabine
Reading the Romantic Heroine: Text, History, Ideology

Joanne S. Frye
Living Stories, Telling Lives: Women and the Novel in Contemporary Experience

JOANNE S. FRYE is winner in the Hamilton Prize competition for 1984. The Alice and Edith Hamilton Prize is named for two outstanding women scholars: Alice Hamilton (educated at the University of Michigan Medical School), a pioneer in environmental medicine; and her sister, Edith Hamilton, the renowned classicist. The Hamilton Prize competition is supported by the University of Michigan and by private donors.

Living Stories, Telling Lives

Living Stories, Telling Lives
Women and the Novel
in Contemporary Experience

JOANNE S. FRYE

The University of Michigan Press
Ann Arbor

For my mother, Emma, my sister, Eileen,
and my daughters, Kara and Adriane—
in gratitude for loving support

Library of Congress Cataloging-in-Publication Data

Frye, Joanne S., 1944–
  Living stories, telling lives.

  Bibliography: p.
  Includes index.
  1. American fiction—20th century—History and
criticism.   2. Women in literature.   3. American
fiction—Women authors—History and criticism.
4. English fiction—20th century—History and
criticism.   5. English fiction—Women authors—
History and criticism.   6. Feminism and literature.
I. Title
PS374.W6F69   1986   813'.54'09352042   85-24688
ISBN 0-472-10073-4 (alk. paper)
ISBN 0-472-08065-2 (pbk. : alk. paper)

Preface

"Men have had every advantage of us in telling their own story." With this assertion, Anne Elliot wins the assent of many women reading *Persuasion*. Men *have* told the stories and framed the cultural precepts; women, reading those stories and bound by those precepts, have too often found themselves living men's stories rather than telling and living their own. Like Anne Elliot, they have learned to mistrust the evidence offered by books.

Anne's rejection of the authority of men's stories comes in the context of a dispute over "woman's fickleness," and the ironies surrounding her conversation with Captain Harville distill the craft of Jane Austen's pen. But the implicit plea for a voice and narrative perspective of her own is Austen's as well as Anne's. For women writers, like women characters, have been denied the authority of their own stories as they have been denied the support of cultural precept. Their stories, when told, have been too often set aside as personal and feminine; their pens, when wielded, have been refused the authority of perceived truth. They, like their characters, have been denied the legitimate evidence of their own experience.

Yet women have been central to the history of the novel: as readers, as writers, as characters. Refusing silence, they have persisted in efforts to elude the male-defined labels and stereotypes. Indisputably loyal, Anne critiques the stereotype of female fickleness through her very behavior. Indisputably and brilliantly articulate, Austen reclaims a portion of women's right to speak and to offer their own evidence. Still, the tensions implicit in Anne's dispute with Captain Harville and in Austen's novels are the inevitable conditions of women's participation in the history of the novel: the tensions of living in a male-dominant culture while affirming the right to female voice and self-definition.

As an exploration of these tensions, this book, like many works of feminist literary criticism, is premised on a dual commitment: to the importance of affirming women's own perspective on female experience and to the power of literature in shaping our cultural awarenesses. Within these shared concerns, my specific focus is on the peculiar fruitfulness of first-person narration in contemporary claims to female voice and self-definition, the value of giving contemporary Anne Elliots the capacity to tell their own stories, their own lives. In exploring the generative possibilities of novelistic form, I am seeking to understand not only how female characters can tell their own experiences in new ways but also how all of us can perceive and alter the gendered construction of human experience. Telling lives, female protagonists find ways to subvert male-dominant patterns and to develop renewed representation of women's lives and self-definitions. Reading their novels, we explore the needs for personal redefinition, for narrative interpretation, and above all for positive cultural change. My analysis of the narrative process thus moves from what is specific to women toward what is enabling to women, and hence to all human beings, in the movement to achieve human equality.

My analysis is indebted to the work of many feminist scholars and to the cultural possibilities opened by the feminist movement in general: its energy, its insights, its intertwining of the personal and the political, its commitment to shared inquiry. The cross-disciplinary basis of feminist scholarship has also led me to explore the pleasures and possibilities of the interaction among such fields as narrative theory, cultural analysis, cognitive psychology, and the history of the novel. In the context of feminist understanding, the dialogic form of the novel then renews the interaction between women's lives and literary form.

The evolution of my thinking about women and the novel owes much to the students in my classes at The College of Wooster, especially students in Fiction by Women. I am grateful to them, to Independent Study students, and to students in courses on Jane Austen, Charlotte Brontë, and Virginia Woolf, as they have helped to shape my argument through their responses to trial versions of my central concepts.

To the Henry Luce III Fund for Scholarship at The College of Wooster, I owe particular gratitude for financial support and released time to give full attention to the writing of the first version of this book. To two National Endowment for the Humanities Summer Seminars, one at the University of Colorado in 1979 and one at Cornell University in 1984, I am grateful for a collegial context that shaped my initial thinking on the female *Bildungsroman* and renewed my theoretical convictions on women and narrative. The directors of these seminars, James Kincaid and Daniel Schwarz, both gave vital collegial support and critical interaction.

I owe special thanks to friends and colleagues at The College of Wooster who have shared in the intellectual discussions that make writing possible. For countless conversations on feminism, literature, psychology, history, and cultural analysis, I am especially grateful to Carolyn Durham, Arnie Grossblatt, Henry Herring, John Hondros, Rena Hondros, Brad Karan, Karla McPherson, and Jim Turner.

Finally, I am grateful to the women and girls in my family, who have taught me, in their living, the ways that stories work and the ways that gender is shaped.

Acknowledgments

Grateful acknowledgment is made to the following for permission to reprint previously published materials:

Alfred A. Knopf, Inc., and Weidenfeld and Nicholson Ltd. for excerpts from *The Waterfall* by Margaret Drabble. Copyright © 1969 by Margaret Drabble.

Alfred A. Knopf, Inc., and Victor Gollancz Ltd. for excerpts from *Violet Clay* by Gail Godwin. Copyright © 1978 by Gail Godwin.

Alfred A. Knopf, Inc., and Curtis Brown, Ltd. for excerpts from *The Stone Angel* by Margaret Laurence. Copyright © 1964 by Margaret Laurence. Reprinted by permission of Curtis Brown, Ltd.

Simon and Schuster, Inc., and Michael Joseph Ltd. for excerpts from *The Golden Notebook* by Doris Lessing. Copyright © 1962 by Doris Lessing. Reprinted by permission of Simon and Schuster, Inc.

Holt, Rinehart and Winston, Publishers, for excerpts from *The Bluest Eye* by Toni Morrison. Copyright © 1970 by Toni Morrison. Reprinted by permission of Holt, Rinehart and Winston, Publishers.

Virginia Barber Literary Agency, Inc., on behalf of the author, for excerpts from *The Lives of Girls and Women* by Alice Munro. Copyright © 1971 by Alice Munro. All rights reserved. Reprinted by permission of Virginia Barber Literary Agency, Inc., on behalf of the author. Published by McGraw-Hill Book Company.

University of Wisconsin Press for portions of "Narrating the Self: The Autonomous Heroine in Gail Godwin's *Violet Clay*," *Contemporary Literature* 24 no. 1 (Spring 1983): 66–85. Copyright © 1983 by the Regents of the University of Wisconsin.

Every effort has been made to trace the ownership of all copyrighted material in this book and to obtain permission for its use.

Contents

CHAPTER I

Women: Living Stories, Telling Lives

"What can a heroine do?" asks Joanna Russ in her incisive essay on the problems of female-centered plots. Very little, she responds, apart from falling in love or dying—and occasionally going mad. Even this degree of variety remains a function of the nearly single available plot for a female protagonist: the "Love Story" with its tragic and comic variants, concluding in death on the one hand and marriage on the other.[1] Her introductory list of (im)possible plots stands as an awesome reminder of how closely our plot expectations are linked to gender expectations: heroines do not kill bears or set out to travel the world; they do not prove themselves in battle or test the boundaries of human survival; they merely fall in love or fail in love.

An oversimplification, some say, but the history of the English-language novel yields few examples to contradict Russ's point. The paradigmatic plots based in the qualities of strength, autonomy, and aspiration seem reserved for male protagonists; the paradigmatic plots based in specifically female experience seem to confine women in domesticity and apparent passivity. Nancy K. Miller makes a similar point about the eighteenth-century French and English novel and the persistence of this pattern into the twentieth century as well: in her view, even the female-centered novel serves a male tradition because it is shaped by the "ideological underpinnings" of the erotic and familial plots.[2] It is hardly surprising that critics such as Carolyn Heilbrun and Patricia Meyer Spacks have bemoaned the difficulty of finding an autonomous heroine who escapes entrapment in plot expectations.[3]

We can feel the force of such plot expectations in nearly any female-centered novel from *Clarissa Harlowe* to *Pride and Prejudice*, from *Middlemarch* to *The Voyage Out*. We can see these expectations thwart the intelligence and sexuality and ambition of many a Maggie Tulliver and Martha Quest. We can witness innumerable protagonists being drawn by currents beyond their control to the only possible conclusions of their plotted experiences: Maggie to her death by drowning in *The Mill on the Floss*, Martha to the doomed marriage that concludes the first novel of the *Children of Violence* series, other heroines to lonelier deaths or happier marriages. But none of these protagonists can really *do* anything, none can act for herself or find in her intelligence and sexuality and ambition the resources by which to develop into complex adult womanhood.

At first this lack seems strange, for women outside novels do find ways to act, ways even to write novels and to perform public functions. Yet it is not so strange when we recall the cultural ideology that surrounds and encodes the actions of real women in much the same terms as those of novelistic plots. Perhaps it is an exaggeration, even of historical expectations, to say that the meaning of a woman's life lies in marriage and motherhood and that life without marriage must mean painful isolation, virtually the equivalent of death. But the underlying cultural ideology is not an exaggeration, and it continues to serve as the interpretive lens for understanding women's lives: male and female are perceived as polar opposites; male is equated with general human capacity; female is defined in terms of relational capacities and expressiveness. By this ideology—regardless of lived experience—women can find their "identities" only in terms set out by specifically sexual expectations, and such terms preclude them from agency and autonomy, qualities reserved for men and for the "generally human." Women, regardless of their other qualities, are ideologically defined through their sexuality and its attendant roles—wife, mother, sex partner.[4]

Within this sexual ideology, the conflict for women seems inescapable: love and work, sexuality and autonomy, body and mind are set in inevitable conflict. The internal dilemma yields the forced choice between being either an acceptable female or a nonfemale adult.[5] This is the dilemma that Simone de Beauvoir labels the conflict between woman's human "vocation" and "her role as female."[6] This is the dilemma that Adrienne Rich faced when, as a young wife and mother, she felt herself to be "both a failed woman and a failed poet," trapped between these two apparently irreconcilable roles.[7] And this is the dilemma that Rich has formulated more generally as the choice necessary for every "twentieth-century, educated young woman": "an inescapable either/or: motherhood or individuation."[8] Despite cultural changes and new possibilities for women's actions, the dominant ideology continues to force many women into the impossible dilemma of being perceived as either competent autonomous adult human beings or sexually relational female beings, but not both.[9] As we have learned to read women's lives through the "culture text"[10] of femininity, so we cannot simultaneously perceive femaleness and autonomy.

Grounded in the same femininity text, the limitations on female-centered novels mime the internal dilemma that continues to haunt women's lives. If a woman writer risks choosing a male paradigmatic story for a female protagonist, she needs to relinquish consideration of any specifically female qualities: she cannot, then, deal with problems of sexuality, with female socialization, or with reproduction or anxiety about reproduction. She cannot, in a male-defined "ambition text," address the problems of female sexual self-definition.[11] If, on the other hand, she chooses the alternative kind of paradigmatic story, based in specifically female experience, she is choosing a story that requires passivity and self-denial, a story with a prewritten ending: self existing *only* in relationship, with marriage and/or motherhood as the appropriate denouement, or the demise of the self. Her choices of narrative pattern are few indeed.

"Women can't paint, women can't write . . . ," mutters Charles Tansley in *To the Lighthouse,* and Lily Briscoe hears this refrain even in his absence.[12] Again the perceived choice: a woman writer, woman painter, is a contradiction in terms and must herself live the conflict that shapes the available female-centered plots. Hence the great difficulty that Virginia Woolf had in killing the "Angel in the House," the ideological phantom who whispers in her ear a message that reinforces Charles Tansley's message: "Be sympathetic; be tender; flatter, deceive; use all the arts and wiles of our sex. Never let anybody guess that you have a mind of your own. Above all, be pure."[13] Woolf must and does kill this phantom, for it insists that she can only be a woman at the expense of her writing or a writer at the expense of her womanhood; but the battle is fierce and distracts her from undertaking other more palpable adventures in the world at large. The same ideology that gives support to this persistent phantom also makes it nearly impossible for her to speak the truth about "the body," to address questions of female sexuality.[14] In order to be a writer, she must continually resist the cultural idea of womanhood. If woman *is* body, defined exclusively in sexual terms, she cannot write and certainly must not write of bodily experiences.

But for a man, body itself underwrites the literary gift. In the opening chapter of *The Madwoman in the Attic,* Sandra Gilbert and Susan Gubar analyze the force of male literary hegemony and discuss the frequent analogy of pen to penis—the male perception that creative force exists in very particular ways in the specifically male sexual generative powers. They quote Gerard Manley Hopkins with decisive effect: "The artist's 'most essential quality' . . . is 'masterly execution, which is a kind of male gift, and especially marks off men from women, the begetting of one's thoughts on paper, on verse, or whatever the matter is.' "[15] Unlike women, men can claim the resources of their bodies as participants in their capacity to write.[16] Masculinity and authorship merge in a culturally acceptable author-ity.

A similar merging explains the greater breadth of narrative possibilities for a male protagonist: it is not that the novel is any less conventional for a male writer but rather that the available sexual ideology does not set maleness in conflict with autonomy. For a male protagonist, maleness participates in his autonomy rather than resisting it; the ability to act includes his sexuality rather than being defined by it. As the conventional patterns for the female-centered novel—domestic or romantic—reveal the limitations on female autonomy, so the conventional patterns for male-centered novels reveal the *assumption* of male autonomy.[17]

This perception is fundamental to the traditional adventure novel, which traces its (male) hero's encounters with the larger world. But it is also apparent in the other prominent forms for male-centered novels: the *Prüfungsroman* and the *Bildungsroman,* novels of trial and of achieving adulthood.[18] Depending on the historical period, the content of the male hero's testing will vary widely, but each trial confirms or expands his self-definition; he will not encounter trials that force him to relinquish the one in an attempt to prove the other. Modern variants such as *Lord Jim* and *The Sun Also Rises,* which confront the loss of cultural absolutes and explicitly address the issues of male codes of honor, still do not set their protagonists' maleness in conflict with their humanity, even when they set issues of fundamental humanity in conflict with each other. Similarly, the expectations of the male *Bildungsroman* are for the protagonist's reaching adulthood as a simultaneous affirmation of his manhood and his autonomy, not a choice between the two. This is true even in the modern variants of the form, which are subject to a broader questioning of assumed values and a greater difficulty of resolution: whatever the difficulties of Stephen Dedalus or Paul Morel in finding a sense of vocation and adulthood, neither *A Portrait of the Artist as a Young Man* nor *Sons and Lovers* requires its protagonist to relinquish his sexual self-definition in becoming an "artist." Though each ends his novel in isolation, this is a triumphant isolation rather than a painful denial of a crucial portion of self.[19]

I am not, of course, claiming that all male protagonists escape death or painful accommodation to their social context—or even that their plots are never resolved in marriage. What I am claiming is that because the conventional assumptions of the novel as narrative form share in a dominant sexual ideology, they act to limit the possibilities for novels that explore women's full humanity. Women's actions are few because when women act they lose novelistic plausibility as women. Women's plots are nearly always "familial" or "erotic" because our cultural notions of womanhood require a personal context. Female characters lack autonomy because an autonomous woman is an apparent contradiction in cultural terms.

That, at any rate, is a provisional answer to one question that frames this book: why is it so difficult for women writers to create female protagonists who are both autonomous and affirmatively female? The power of a male-dominant sexual ideology entraps women characters and women novelists within outworn plots and outworn definitions; women in novels—and even in life—seem doomed to live within those old stories.

But for me such an answer must be only provisional, for it denies both the possibility of cultural change and the capacity of the novel to interpret experience in new ways. As Fredric Jameson says, "lived reality alters . . . in function of the 'model' through which we see and live the world."[20] Because the available models are resistant to change, the process of developing alternative models is slow and difficult. But it is not impossible. As the "imaginary resolution of real contradictions,"[21] narrative interpretation can make a distinctive contribution to this process of reinterpretation. And because the novel as form resists fixity and responds to its social context through interaction rather than simple ideological miming, its literary resources are peculiarly responsive to women's needs for alternative resolutions.

Although a male-dominant sexual ideology threatens to encode women as objects in paradigmatic plots, women are, after all, not objects but perceiving subjects, who cannot be fully contained within the femininity text. This is why Woolf was finally able to kill the Angel in the House and write with conviction rather than being herself "killed into art."[22] This is why women have been able to make significant contributions to the evolution of the novel despite the limitations of available plots. This is also why contemporary novels by women are able to develop further the possibilities for novelistic interpretations of women's lives.

The fullest escape from narrative entrapment can be found in women novelists' choice of the more fantastic narrative modes—supernatural or utopian or futuristic—as a way to free themselves from the power of current gender-based assumptions.[23] Charlotte Perkins Gilman's *Herland* provides an example early in this century of a fictional exploration of female strengths in a world apart from gender polarities, indeed an all-female world. Virginia Woolf's *Orlando* leaps across centuries and across sexual polarity itself in its exploration of the gendering of human identity and the possibilities for eluding the falsely imposed dichotomies of gender codes. Doris Lessing ends her *Children of Violence* series with the move into a fragile future in the epilogue to *The Four-Gated City:* here Martha Quest is finally freed from the gender restrictions and societal disasters of contemporary culture through an apocalyptic conclusion yielding new human social possibilities among a new generation of mutants. These and other feminist fictions—such as Marge Piercy's *Woman on the Edge of Time,* Ursula LeGuin's *Left Hand of Darkness,* and Joanna Russ's own *The Female Man*—point utopian directions for human development and illuminate the fallacies in current cultural assumptions about gender.

But the fantastic mode is only one kind of escape from narrative entrapment and cannot bear the full weight of our need for new narrative understandings. Though such fictions effectively dramatize "a rupture from the normal rules of the world"[24] and reveal alternative possibilities for imaged future hopes, they do not enact the possibilities for actively renegotiating the current "rules of the world" or adding possibility to present experience. For this process, we need fictions that interact more immediately with our own social context, fictions that make claim to speak of the world as we might experience it in the present.

Touching more directly on the contemporary social world, thematic attention to positive forms of distinctively female experience opens onto another possible escape from narrative entrapment, especially evident in the redefinitions of female lives in contemporary lesbian fiction. Novels such as Rita Mae Brown's *Rubyfruit Jungle* and Isabel Miller's *Patience and Sarah* show the present claiming of selfhood outside the patriarchal definitions of femaleness and in relation to other women. As Bonnie Zimmerman shows in her essay on the lesbian novel, this sense of freedom has not always been possible, but recent lesbian fiction is decidedly an affirmation of alternatives, "one reasonable outcome of the refusal to accept the limitations posed by some female novels of development or awakening."[25] The development of lesbian identity, then, yields "freedom, not defeat. Rejecting the outside world of heterosexuality, the lesbian recreates herself in a different mode."[26] This affirming identity is not simple, for separatism from the entire patriarchal culture is scarcely possible. Catharine Stimpson's analysis of the lesbian novel reminds us of some of the more sobering experiences of homophobia and stigmatization in lesbian fiction,[27] as do Zimmerman's references to "the violent attack of the homophobic social order on the emerging lesbian."[28] Nevertheless, possibilities for affirming femaleness and claiming autonomy are immediately evident in Zimmerman's description of the "lesbian vision of the individual in community"[29] and reside in an integrating and supportive context for female selfhood.

But, though vitally important, the lesbian novel is not alone sufficient response to the need for more complex narrative understanding of female selfhood in a social context: women also need to develop alternative life possibilities in a heterosexual social context. In some ways this narrative task is the most difficult of all. Because heterosexuality makes separatism into another kind of split identity for nonlesbian women, their social context cannot be so fully recreated to provide support for a strong female selfhood. For this very reason, the notion of heterosexual female "identity" is distinctively problematic and contradictory, and thus in particular need of narrative interpretation even as it is more clearly bound by the traditional paradigmatic plots for female experience. We need, then, not only lesbian novels in which women writers have not internalized "the patriarchal view of their subservience nor accepted, even superficially, their 'feminine role' and their ancillary position,"[30] not only utopian novels in which women writers explore alternative worlds and selves. We need also the possibility of heterosexual novels in which women are able to develop a capacity for complex selfhood in interaction with contemporary realities, resisting the old stories and telling lives in new ways.

In some sense, telling lives is what women novelists have always done—not literally telling their own lives, but finding in the flexibility of the novel form a capacity for conveying their subjective perceptions. And despite the persistent risks of narrative entrapment, contemporary women novelists are continuing to claim this novelistic capacity, going beyond historical limitations in order to continue to tell women's lives in new ways. From the historical flexibility of the novel form, they are developing fresh thematic and formal resources for narrative interpretation.[31] But one prominent strand of this multiple and complex undertaking seems, instead, to return to the historical resources of the realist novel and the historical participation of women in its evolution: telling lives, as novelists have often done, in a first-person female voice. Despite the difficulties of traditional narrative forms for women, this very traditional novelistic voice has also provided surprisingly fertile resources for a renewed interpretation of women's lives. In the work of contemporary women novelists, the narrating "I" finds additional ways, both thematic and structural, to avoid narrative entrapment, new ways to subvert the power of old stories.

Hence the second question that frames this book: why is first-person narration such a prominent and effective way in which recent women novelists have, despite the femininity text, created protagonists who embody a complex and autonomous womanhood? For within these novels, as they show us not only women living stories but also, quite immediately, women telling lives, we can perceive still more possibilities for overcoming the cultural contradiction between adulthood and womanhood.

In the six novels examined in this book, the protagonists are all confronting the conflict between culturally defined heterosexual female "identity" and the autonomous urge to self-definition. In each, the protagonist faces the temptations of traditional plots, of the expected cultural and novelistic explanations of their lives—precisely those expectations that have doomed their novelistic predecessors. But by contrast, each of these contemporary protagonists finds a way to engage the narrative process itself in rejecting fixed plot and especially in rejecting a teleological structure for her lived experience. In doing so, they all set aside cultural determinisms and claim personal agency; and they do so by examining the explanatory function of specifically female experiences and granting those experiences a place in a definition of personal agency rather than capitulation to passivity.

The specific novels to be considered illuminate the ways in which complex narrative can address and overcome the entrapment in traditional plot. Chapter 4 examines Alice Munro's *Lives of Girls and Women* and Toni Morrison's *The Bluest Eye* as they characterize possibilities for growing up both female and self-defined, the possibilities for taking a place as a woman in a community of adulthood without succumbing to culturally imposed femininity. Chapter 5 examines Gail Godwin's *Violet Clay* and Margaret Laurence's *The Stone Angel* as their protagonists redefine their own sense of adult womanhood through reassessing causality, memory, and narrative teleology. Chapter 6 examines Margaret Drabble's *The Waterfall* and Doris Lessing's *The Golden Notebook* as they show their protagonists immersed in a difficult present, using narrative projection to elude cultural fragmentation and claim complex selfhood. Though these are all heterosexual and predominantly white and middle-class novels—and partly bound by the specific demands of this cultural context—they are also evidence of a more generalizable process by which narrative and female selfhood can interact apart from these restrictions.

I have chosen these six contemporary English-language novels because they illustrate the form that altered novelistic conventions can take in redefining female experience and the ways in which characters themselves use the narrative process to change their previous interpretations of their own lives. I have chosen these novels, too, because each has been in some way specifically instrumental to my own recognition of the dynamic process involved in re-seeing both experience and explanation. Indeed, it is in large measure from these novels that I have developed the understanding of narrative process and of women's lives that gave rise to this book. And it is in large measure from these novels and novels like them that I have learned the essential features of my own poetics.

In order to suggest the relationship among these six novels and the shared implications of their narrative form, I want first to establish a theoretical context for the specific analyses and for the significance of first-person narration in novels by women. Thus chapter 2 identifies the issues I see as central to a feminist poetics of the novel: the qualities of the novel as form and its interest as a participant in cultural change. And chapter 3 considers the general usefulness of a first-person narrator-protagonist in the reassessment of narrative conventions: the narrating "I" as a claim to agency in developing new understandings of women's experiences. Throughout this initial and theoretical section of the book, my main concern is to identify both the ways in which the novel has been able to codify and falsify female experience and the ways in which it can participate, through narrative interpretation, in shaping a new perspective on women's lives as capable of embracing both autonomy and femaleness.

Finally, in chapter 7, I consider the woman reader as active participant in the processes of cultural change. As she interacts with the narrative form by which protagonists shape their lives, the woman reader herself becomes an interpreter: of the protagonist's experience, of her own experience. In learning to read differently, she also learns to see differently and in some sense to live differently.

This book, then, is an act of feminist literary criticism. Like all feminist acts, its writing has required continual questioning of "given" assumptions and has at times even threatened the very ground of its own argument. It borrows from and criticizes a diverse range of critical perspectives—formalism, structuralism, liberal humanism, deconstructionism, existentialism, Freudianism, Marxism—some of which give little credence to each other. I have learned from and defined my thinking against them all. Yet none of these definable orientations defines my own particular understanding of the interrelated concepts on which my analysis rests: narrative, language, self, experience, representation, "woman." I did not set out to be deliberately eclectic, but my efforts to assess these concepts in relation to cultural change led me to adopt eclecticism actively as one way to develop my own perspective while sustaining a critical stance toward "given" assumptions.

If my eclecticism has no definable limits, it does have definable goals. Most prominent are the goals I attribute to feminism in general: to understand women's lives—and hence men's—as they are shaped by a male-dominant sexual ideology, and to develop ways to improve those lives. Because I see literature as a powerful cultural expression, I also seek ways to make it more responsive to the needs of women's lives and the possibilities for cultural change. My pursuit of these goals owes an immense debt to numerous other feminist literary critics, whose work has challenged, provoked, substantiated, or contradicted my line of reasoning but always in the context of our shared enterprise.

My goals as a feminist literary critic have also led me to draw on the values and resources of disciplines outside what we usually see as the domain of literary study, especially cultural anthropology and cognitive and social psychology. A portion of my commitment to literature and to cultural change resides in an understanding—developed, in part, through the dialogue among these disciplines—that human beings live and see the world in relation to shared cultural precepts but that we also interact with our social world as conscious and responsible individuals.

Dialogue—between disciplines, between systems and individuals, between literature and life—becomes, then, a kind of definition for my eclectic perspective: a resistance to dichotomies through setting them in interaction with each other. Women need individual self-definition; women need a sense of shared reality. Selfhood is a function of systems; selfhood is a claim to responsible individuality. Literary form is crucial to our understanding; literary form obscures honest perception. Women must claim the distinctively female; women must resist definition by sexual difference. Each of these oppositions defines a node of tension in my analysis; each also suggests, as does the opposition between femaleness and autonomy, the importance of seeing oppositions in interaction rather than in forced dichotomies. As a cultural form responsive to individual perception and to evolving change, the novel becomes a particularly appropriate genre for feminist study: its dialogic form[32] itself encourages fruitful interaction between potential dichotomies.

Through the overall argument of this book, I have come to see novelistic narrative as both analogue of and medium for the general processes of feminist analysis. Like feminist scholarship, the narrative act is an interpretive process, an act of selection, ordering, and sense making; like feminist scholarship it too can yield alternative causal explanations, new interpretations of the past, and hence new possibilities for the future. And like feminist analysis, the novel evolves most fruitfully in dialogic interaction. A feminist understanding of the novel can thus help to develop new paradigmatic plots and new perspectives on women's lives. This book is my own effort to contribute to such an interaction; its ultimate goal is for women and men to find new ways to tell lives as they develop new definitions of human wholeness and new capacities for cultural change.

CHAPTER 2

Politics, Literary Form, and a Feminist Poetics of the Novel

Contemporary literary theory finds itself at a moment of crisis. Though theoretical work proliferates almost frenetically, agreement on the central issues seems to recede rather than come into focus: what is literature? what is criticism? why does either one matter in a world in strife? Terry Eagleton's recent *Literary Theory: An Introduction* characterizes the problem pointedly: offering itself as an "introduction" to literary theory, it asserts in its conclusion that both literature and literary theory are illusions and that his ostensible "introduction" is, in fact, "an obituary."[1] But, having proclaimed the death of literary study, Eagleton does not stop there. Instead he goes on to propose a recentering of concern in the question of "not *what* the object is or *how* we should approach it, but *why* we should want to engage with it in the first place."[2] And he identifies feminist and socialist criticism as distinctive "because they define the object of analysis differently, have different values, beliefs and goals. . . ."[3]

On first glance, however, feminist criticism seems itself to be at odds in attempting to answer Eagleton's crucial question: why should we want to engage with it? what is our interest in and commitment to the study of literature? Such uncertainty is evident even in the titles of recent theoretical work: "Dancing through the Minefield" or "Feminist Criticism in the Wilderness."[4] It is also evident in Elizabeth Abel's expression of concern as she introduces the special issue of *Critical Inquiry* titled *Writing and Sexual Difference*. On the one hand, she notes that the sophistication of recent analyses may "accord the feminist critic a position closer to the mainstream of critical debate" but, on the other hand, it may also "generate a litany of new accusations" that feminist criticism has retreated from its political origins.[5] Expressing a similar tension, Elaine Showalter speaks of "the current theoretical impasse in feminist criticism" and attributes that impasse to "our own divided consciousness, the split in each of us"; feminist critics, she suggests, find insight and value in contemporary theories, but they also feel the dangers in working within the constructs of male-defined theories.[6] As Mary Jacobus identifies them, the resulting polar options are all too familiar: "appropriation or separatism."[7] From all of these responses, it would seem that the proliferation of general theory both contributes to the growing sophistication of feminist criticism and exacerbates its internal tensions.

Nonetheless, feminist literary criticism—and I speak for the moment primarily of American feminist criticism—does have a history of its own, a history defined if not by a unifying answer, at least by the *need* to answer the question: why should we want to engage with it? Why should feminists be concerned with the study of literature? Threading through that history we can identify at least the potential for a unifying answer in a concern for the lives of women and the problems of gendered experience in literature. In American criticism this concern initially took the form of "a *feminist critique*," particularly the analysis of images of women in male texts.[8] Subsequently it shifted toward what Showalter has called gynocritics: analysis of the work of women writers, particularly as they characterize female experiences.[9] Most recently, this gynocritical process has turned toward analyzing the more complex interactions between women writers and a male tradition. Abel characterizes this recent phase as analysis that "translates sexual difference into literary differences of genre, structure, and plot."[10] For Annette Kolodny, what unites all of these efforts in an eclectic feminist criticism is a concern with "male encoding" and its consequences for women.[11]

Another way to look at this evolution of concern in feminist criticism is to note its similarity to a broad shift in contemporary feminist thought, as noted by many feminist critics, from the early focus on "sameness" toward a more recent valuing of female difference and the complexities of its definition in a male-dominant culture. Showalter concludes her overview of feminist literary criticism by tracing this evolution from the belief that all texts should be "sexless and equal, like angels" to the current affirmation of "the tumultuous and intriguing wilderness of difference itself."[12] For many feminist critics, this shift is an exhilarating one by which women are able to value femaleness and celebrate that which has been culturally devalued or denied. But the shift brings with it a new set of problems: how to celebrate femaleness while resisting the patriarchal definitions of femininity; how to refuse "sameness" without becoming trapped in "difference" as it is currently constituted. To acknowledge the shift is to return to the tension between appropriation and separatism: the need to speak despite male dominance and the threat of being absorbed into male-dominant constructions; the need to claim the specifically female despite the threat of being silenced and isolated within "difference."

Appropriation or separatism. "Sameness" or "difference." The Scylla and Charybdis of feminist analysis become most threatening when they challenge, from both sides, women's capacity to speak at all, to voice a specifically female perspective in a male-dominant language. Though the problematic relationship between language and experience is central to much twentieth-century thought, contemporary feminist criticism finds here a particularly acute challenge, a challenge at present complicated by cross-cultural misunderstandings and disagreements. Simply put, the current debate is between the dominant concern in American feminist criticism, with its experiential basis, and the dominant concern in much French feminist criticism, as evident in the commitment of *l'écriture féminine* to language, theory, textual femininity, and the female unconscious. As Margaret Homans describes it, this is an opposition between the view on the one hand that "experience is separable from language" and on the other hand that "language and experience are coextensive."[13] Although I think this characterization oversimplifies the two positions—an oversimplification aggravated by Homans's later claim that American feminists believe in "transparency between language and experience"[14]—I nonetheless find it a useful definition of the polar extremes and a useful presentation of the underlying problem for a feminist poetics of the novel: can available language elucidate women's lives or is it inescapably patriarchal?[15] Can women interpret their own experience or is experience itself always already interpreted? Is the novel bound into the status quo by its conventions of language and form or even by its very textuality? Or can it, through reshaping the language of a male-dominant culture, participate in a feminist commitment to cultural change?

Like Homans, I seek a way to bridge the two views of language, to escape the dangers that threaten from both sides, in order to reassess the possibilities of a feminist understanding of literature. Like her, I also see in a redefinition of "representation" the possibilities for affirming, simultaneously, at least some of the assumptions of both French and American feminists and for affirming the value of the novel in feminist analysis. The capacity that she identifies in four novels of double marginality is the dual *need* that I would place at the center of a feminist poetics of the novel: "representation, while undercutting the premises of representation. . . . Simultaneously appropriating and rejecting the dominant discourse, [these novels] formally duplicate the female experience that they thematize, the experience of both participating in and standing outside the dominant culture."[16] Following the lead of such novelists, a feminist poetics of the novel can examine the novel's capacity both to *represent* women's experience and to *redefine* the premises of representation. In recognizing women's experience as both participants in and outsiders of the dominant culture, a feminist poetics must not only identify the novel's formal and linguistic conventions as they nearly silence women's expression; it must also assess the novel's susceptibility to women's subversive expressions and the development of new conventions responsive to the experiences of women's lives and the needs of cultural change.

Indeed, I think this dual recognition can be identified in the work of a number of contemporary feminist critics. Despite Homans's attempt to distinguish her analysis from the efforts of other critics, her claim for the novels she analyzes is very much like Annette Kolodny's rereading of women's texts, Sandra Gilbert's and Susan Gubar's reading of text and subtext as palimpsestic, and Showalter's assessment of women's use of double-voiced discourse.[17] That is, all of these critics are developing alternative methods for reading women's texts and for identifying subversive representation of women's lives; all of them share an awareness of the presence of female voice and experience simultaneously with the powerful exclusion wrought by the dominant discourse. What Homans adds to the work of more overtly experience-based critics is the reminder that "representation" gains force in the *formal* enactment of the experiential or thematic concern.

My own perspective on the problem of language and experience then shares the general assumptions of a number of contemporary feminist critics: the dual recognition that experience cannot be absolutely separated from language but that language and experience are not fully coextensive either. Female experience and female voice *have* in many ways been preempted by male-dominant language, even to the point of the virtual silencing of women. But at the same time, women must be able to speak and to speak of their own experience if we are to claim a meaningful basis for feminist criticism or hope of feminist change. Without claiming a "transparency between language and experience," I *am* claiming a capacity for language to "represent" experience, even if this requires complex and subversive response, and for literature thereby to characterize anew the experiences of women's lives.

A concern for women's lives and for the power of literary form, then, does provide some kind of fragile unity to much contemporary feminist literary criticism, as well as the driving energy evident in the work of so many feminist critics. A feminist poetics begins to emerge not as a definition of the object in itself or as evidence of full agreement among feminist critics but as a shared inquiry into the understanding of female experience and its relationship to literature. And this inquiry can in turn illuminate the problems and possibilities of literary form as being both part of a complex system of conventions and simultaneously integral to lived experience. In its commitment to the analysis of gender, feminist criticism thus shares in the processes of cultural change as it recognizes in literature a powerful participant in these processes. This, at least, is my tentative answer to the question: why should we want to engage with it? Why should feminists be concerned with the study of literature? In studying literature, however we do or do not define it, we come to a greater understanding of women's—and men's—lives, of their relationship to the surrounding culture, and of the possibilities for living differently.

In my introductory chapter I posed the problem that provided the impetus for this book: the apparent irreconcilability of autonomy and female sexuality, not only in literature but also in much of lived experience. My particular concern in developing a feminist poetics of the novel is, then, a concern to develop an understanding of the novel by which it can participate in cultural change rather than reinforcing the status quo, an understanding that would enable new definitions of women's capacities to claim both autonomy and femaleness. In order to do so, I want both to address a specific version of Eagleton's question—why should feminists engage ourselves with the novel as literary form?—and to identify the possibilities in the novel for "representing" women's lives without becoming trapped in "difference" or silenced by the powers of male dominance. My first approach to a feminist poetics of the novel is thus to identify those qualities that make the novel peculiarly susceptible to feminist concern for cultural change: its capacity to "represent" the shared experiences of women's lives—"difference" as women experience it, whatever its explanation or cause—while simultaneously resisting external definitions of those lives as they have been encoded within male-dominant expectations.

I

As a genre, the novel is of initial interest to feminist critics because it has some rather direct links to the kinds of discourse used in people's daily lives and, therefore, to both interpretations and reinterpretations of women's lives. Four prominent qualities of the novel suggest its direct connection to life experiences: its narrative form, its flexibility, its popularity, and its concern with the individual. As a narrative form, the novel is closely tied to the multiple narrative processes by which human beings daily shape their experience. As a flexible form, it is rather immediately responsive to patterns of cultural change. As a popular form, it is capable of speaking to and for people in their ordinary daily living. And as a form based in individual experience, it is especially able to seek out new interpretations of experience that defy the "normal." Each of these qualities participates in an initial view of the novel as related to lived experience and peculiarly open to gender-based interpretation.

Consider, first, the centrality of narrative to both the novel and the daily storytelling by which people often make sense of their experience. As anthropologists have made us acutely aware, the need to narrate is an apparently pervasive human need: the need to tell stories, hear stories, read stories; the need to make sense of lived experience through setting events in narrative relationship to each other. We use narrative to assess cause and effect in a pattern of significance, to relate ourselves to a sense of purpose, to claim a shared reality with other people, and to identify a specificity and a continuity of self through memory. In short we use the process of creating narrative shape to identify our place in the world.[18]

The need children often feel at the end of the day not just to hear a bedtime story but also to tell the events of their own day is precisely this narrative need to give meaning and pattern to those events. Doris Lessing represents this life narrative situation vividly in her characterization of a conversation between Anna Wulf and her daughter Janet in *The Golden Notebook*. The familiar childhood plea, "Tell me a story," prompts Anna to respond, "There once was a little girl called Janet" and to proceed with the tale of "how this little girl went to school on a rainy day, did lessons, played with the other children, quarrelled with her friend." The sequence continues as, in Anna's words, "Janet eats dreamily, . . . listening while I create her day, give it form."[19] The entire process, giving form to an ordinary day, is crucial to Janet's evolving self-awareness: her attempt to place herself in the world and assess her experiences as part of a meaningful pattern.

Lessing thus draws on the common awareness of children's need for narrative pattern, their primary human relationship to storytelling. The significance of this form giving in the novel—Anna's knowledge that she creates Janet's day by giving it form—is doubly powerful because Anna herself, in recording this experience in her journal, is shaping her own experience as she tells of having shaped Janet's. Her journal serves for her the same function that the story serves for Janet. Through narrative construction, both Janet and Anna are assessing their personal experiences; through narrative construction they engage in the human process of meaning making. In doing so, they have "created" their experience as a part of an interpretive construct.

Such construction is accomplished in large measure through the identification of perceived beginnings and endings, for we assess our current situation in terms of its previous causes and its projected effects. People interpret and even choose their courses of action according to their anticipated ends: projected "conclusions" such as graduation, marriage, separations, departures, births, and deaths. All such demarcating events, in anticipation, shape the human choices prior to them and, in retrospect, shape the understanding of subsequent human experiences. Narrative construction, built as it is on the interpretation of cause and effect, beginnings and endings, becomes a primary means by which we decide what constitutes a cause or effect, a beginning or an ending. Ulric Neisser's assessment of the general process of cognition implicitly identifies how narrative becomes a cognitive instrument in our daily lives: "When we choose one *action* rather than another the embedding schema usually includes some anticipation of our own future situation; like a cognitive map it contains the ego."[20] We act, that is, according to our narrative construction of experience, future as well as past. As Barbara Hardy puts it, "In order really to live, we make up stories about ourselves and others, about the personal as well as the social past and future."[21] We create experiential narratives as a way of understanding or *making* a relationship among the events in our lives.

Narrative can thus be claimed as a crucial human means for understanding lived experience, what Louis Mink explicitly calls the "cognitive" function of narrative.[22] Although cultures vary widely in their perceptions of reality and in the symbolic systems by which they make experiences perceptible, there are no known cultures which lack storytelling as a participant in those systems. As Mink puts it, "story-telling is the most ubiquitous of human activities, and in any culture it is the form of complex discourse that is earliest accessible to children and by which they are largely acculturated";[23] like Janet, children learn how to interpret their experiences through the culturally available narrative patterns. Robert Alter makes a similar point: the human being "as the language-using animal is quintessentially a teller of tales, and narration is his [or her] way of *making* experience, or . . . of making nonverbal experience distinctly human."[24] Human beings, in other words, claim and define our experiences as our own—*make* them—through the stories by which we assign them meaning. It is in this process that narrative becomes, in Fredric Jameson's phrase, "the central function or *instance* of the human mind."[25]

Because "natural narratives and literary narratives are similar in both structure and style," as Susan Lanser reminds us,[26] the novel participates in this central human activity as both model and enactment of our daily stories. We see in the novel the kinds of interpretive patterning by which we narrate our daily experiences to each other; we learn from the novel the culturally available patterning by which to structure and understand the data of our lives. As the longest and most modern narrative form, the novel serves as a crucial exemplar for the process of interpreting and giving form to lived experience. In addition, as novelistic narrative is an agent of interpretation, it becomes as well a possible agent of *re*interpretation, not only giving form but also altering accepted forms—the process central to all feminist scholarship.

The interpretive process inherent in narrative is augmented by a second characteristic of the novel: its extraordinary flexibility as a form. Introduced as "the novel," it remains in many ways "the new." Although, as literature, the novel shares the conventional nature of all literary forms, it is incomplete to say, as Northrop Frye does, "Poetry can only be made out of other poems; novels out of other novels."[27] I would dispute such an absolute claim even with regard to poetry, but it is a still less accurate claim for novels. Quite simply, the language we use in our daily lives and in the stories we tell in our daily lives is the language predominant in most novels. As "a hybrid of narrative and discursive forms,"[28] the novel is continually bending its conventions to include issues at stake in the culture in which it was written. Walter Reed goes so far as to make this feature of the novel definitionally central: the novel, he says, is "a long prose fiction which opposes the forms of everyday life, social and psychological, to the conventional forms of literature, classical or popular, inherited from the past. The novel is a type of literature suspicious of its own literariness; it is inherently anti-traditional in its literary code."[29] He goes on to assert that the "novel explores the difference between the fictions which are enshrined in the institution of literature and the fictions, more truthful historically or merely more familiar, by which we lead our daily lives."[30] The literariness that encodes and encapsulates the novel is thus especially permeable to other cultural codes of its own time; its words carry a weight similar to the weight of words used in ordinary human efforts to communicate. It is true that the reader and writer share a sort of contractual agreement shaped by the conventions of literary genre,[31] but it is also true that they share a language coded as well to the experience of daily social life: a language with the referential impact of communication.

This is not to say that language in the novel *refers* in any direct or unitary way but rather to find in its flexibility a portion of the novel's capacity to interpret and participate in cultural change. Mikhail Bakhtin's highly suggestive analysis of the novel's development traces the historical evolution of this capacity to a developing consciousness of multiple languages—"heteroglossia"—and the resulting awareness that a given language must be seen as no more than "a working hypothesis for comprehending and expressing reality."[32] In Bakhtin's view, this human recognition that *all* language acts as hypothesis evolves into the novel's special dialogic capacity to interact with its contemporary surroundings: "an indeterminacy, a certain semantic openendedness, a living contact with unfinished, still-evolving contemporary reality (the openended present)" (p. 7). Thus does the novel reveal an "orientation that is contested, contestable and contesting" (p. 332). Thus, too, does its flexibility yield new interaction with social reality, new comprehension of cultural change. From a feminist perspective Bakhtin's analysis rings true: the novel has evolved in interaction with the social realities of women's and men's lives. But more crucially, the analysis points toward the significance of that flexibility now: the novel's dialogic capacity enables it to engage in "eternal re-thinking and re-evaluating" (p. 31) as it interacts with its social environment.

The incorporation of multiple languages in a dialogical form and the resulting openness to the languages and codes of lived experience have no doubt also contributed to the third characteristic I have claimed as vital to a feminist poetics of the novel: its evolution as a popular form in many ways prompted by and correlated to the rise in general literacy. In the eighteenth century, the century of its official birth in many literary histories, the novel was already a form available to a broad "social and educational spectrum."[33] Its growth and evolution over the subsequent two centuries, especially in its English-language versions, has depended on a broad readership and at least a partial incorporation of multi-class experience. Though its expressions have often privileged white middle-class experience and been shaped by male-dominant assumptions, its very multiplicity has opened its characterizations to a broader popular base, as its readership, at least into the mid–twentieth century, has incorporated a broad popular audience.

Many claims for the novel's feminist possibilities derive directly from the recognition of its popularity: its rise correlates with a rise in female literacy and middle-class leisure; its historical form is closely associated with varieties of personal relationships and the particularities of women's domestic and emotional lives; in comparison with other genres, a disproportionate number of prominent English novelists have been women, as have been a significant number of its most financially successful practitioners. Many historians of the novel have noted the primacy of women readers in eighteenth- and nineteenth-century authors' thinking about audience. Many feminist critics have noted the long and prominent association of the novel with women: as characters, as readers, as authors.[34] Decidedly, these correlations provide rich material for feminist analysis.

The correlations, however, are not without their attendant hazards for a feminist poetics. For if the novel has grown up in association with women, it has also grown up in association with the given cultural assumptions about women's lives. A tinge of irony colors feminist claims that the domestic novel freed women to enter literature as it broke down the limits of epic form: no longer defined by the feats of the (male) hero in a mythical world of fixed values, the novel now opened extended narrative to enquire into the complex and immediate experience of women's daily lives. The claims are crucial but not yet sufficient. For the realist strand of the novel, grounded in domestic detail and personal relationships, risks assault from both sides of the straits of feminist understanding of language: appropriation into the language and sexual ideology of the status quo and separatism into the world of female "difference." One assault comes from the recognition that the realist novel will not "seem credible" if it diverges radically from "people's beliefs about reality" and is redoubled in the formulaic expressions of many overtly "popular" novels.[35] The other assault comes from the claims, built upon assumptions of "difference," that women are especially good at writing novels because of their unique gifts for observation and relationship, qualities then trivialized by a male-dominant value system.[36] Obviously, the challenges can be inverted in the hands of women choosing to value difference and seek alternative ways of expressing it, but the risk still attends the novelistic perceptions of women's lives.

The potential for irony increases when we acknowledge that, as a popular form closely associated with women and often claimed by feminist criticism, the novel seems nonetheless to resist the most urgent feminist concern: the need for cultural change and the opening of possibilities in the lives of women. Thus, in contrast to a celebratory tone in some feminist analysis, a tone of resignation or despair pervades the work of a number of other significant analysts. Nancy K. Miller, for example, concludes *The Heroine's Text* with the statement that until the culture at large changes, we must either continue to read the old plots or perhaps "stop reading novels."[37] And Myra Jehlen argues that because the novel has its ideological base in the social structures of patriarchal society, it can be of little use to feminist needs for change and of little interest to feminist writers.[38]

These crucial warnings about the confinements of the traditional realist novel are joined by a warning implicit in the general academic study of the Anglophone novel: criticism of the twentieth-century novel has canonized far more male than female novelists and has simultaneously developed a more elitist view of the novel as form. On the one hand, the realist novel, with its assumptions of a popular audience, seems doomed to reinforce the status quo; on the other hand, developments away from the realist novel seem to resist women's full participation and to deny any vital connection with immediate lives of ordinary people.

How, then, can the popularity of the novel form be a resource, rather than a liability, to a feminist poetics of the novel? One answer derives from the kind of claim that Ann Barr Snitow makes for the realist novel in implementing cultural redefinitions: "The realist novel has always been the novel of such first phases. Since the inception of the form, novels have been 'how-to' manuals for groups gathering their identity through self-description."[39] Once a group has begun to redefine its beliefs about reality—once women have begun to reach new and shared understandings of their experience— the novel has the capacity to make those understandings available to a broad popular audience. But more than this: precisely because its flexibility interacts with its popularity, the novel is by definition disposed to incorporate developing perceptions and evolving kinds of discourse; its dialogic capacity, its openness to contemporary reality, its inclination toward a "decentering of the ideological world"[40] interact with its ties to popular and broad-based experience. It bears within its evolution as a popular form the protean capacity to resist cultural fixity and to reinterpret the lives of women. As a popular form, the novel has often tended to center in female characters and personal relationships; as a popular and flexible form, it has the capacity to criticize its historical limits and reassess the very lives it is sometimes accused of "fixing." Precisely as a popular form, the novel retains the capacity to evade the hazards of its popularity and help shape new understandings of women's lives.

A fourth characteristic, the novel's defining concern with individual experience, has similarly problematic but ultimately fruitful implications for feminist criticism, as it contributes to the novel's relationship to lived experience. The historical association of the novel with the notion of individualism has been noted by multiple analysts of the novel, with divergent measures of approval and disapproval: Walter Benjamin, Lucien Goldmann, Terence Hawkes, Edward Said, and Ian Watt, to name a few. Benjamin, for example, notes the birth of the novel in the isolated individual, as contrasted with the communal basis for storytelling.[41] More positively, Watt speaks of the subject matter of the novel as "individual self-definition,"[42] and Said calls the self the "primordial discovery of the novel."[43] This focus is, in part, because the novel, as an extended printed document, centers in the individual reader, alone with the book,[44] and in part because the idea of the novel has centered in the individuation of its characters.

An emphasis on the individual is decidedly troubling from a point of view, such as that of feminism, that views social forces as major determinants of human activity and that also rests on the need to claim a communal identity. Marxists, both feminist and non-feminist, are central in the critique of individualism, for clear ideological and methodological reasons. Mary Poovey's Marxist feminist assessment of "the promises of love" in Jane Austen aptly identifies the problem with individualism as the view "that the personal can be kept separate from the social, that one's 'self' can be fulfilled in spite of—and in isolation from—the demands of the marketplace."[45] Such awarenesses seem to argue against any possibility of seeing the novel as participant in feminist change. Indeed, that too is one of Jehlen's conclusions in her analysis of the novel: the novel's "organically individualistic" form, she argues, is posited on "the special form that sexual hierarchy has taken in modern times"; the form itself precludes female characters from "becoming autonomous."[46]

But while such an argument is provocative, I think it is not, finally, compelling. For it requires a relatively static view of the novel, which ignores its flexibility as "the new," its capacity for self-criticism,[47] its historically persistent incorporation of multiple perceptions. Indeed, I am convinced that the novel's very basis in individualism has rich possibilities from a feminist perspective, initially because feminism, like the novel, is intimately tied to issues of individual self-definition.[48] By social definition—in which the novel has itself been historically implicated—women have been denied individual selfhood, have been refused the right to autonomous action and self-definition. As outsiders in a patriarchal culture, women have also been held in relative isolation from each other and from a sense of social consensus. Thus the need for a sense of individual strength and agency and for the inclusion of female experience in the cultural definition of the individual becomes crucial to overcoming the cultural falsification of female experience. It is in this process that the novel's centering in the individual can be especially fruitful for feminist analysis. I share Jehlen's view that the achievement of female autonomy has radical implications,[49] as does any redefinition of individualism to include female autonomy. Through its individualism, the novel opens onto a capacity to offer new narrative interpretations of the female individual, not as isolated and self-serving but as a strong and complex human being in social interaction with other human beings.

Again this capacity is not simply claimed, for the notion of the individual often brings with it associations of unity, sameness, identity as stasis—associations that can be used to limit women to an essentialist concept of femininity. In feminist as in other literary analysis, the self-evident accuracy of Bakhtin's assertion that "an individual cannot be completely incarnated into the flesh of sociohistorical categories" (p. 37) is often overlooked in the urge to systematize the functional interaction between plot and character. But because the novel's distinctive narrative form is multiple and flexible, it can yield an alternative notion of the human individual as multiple and flexible, rather than unitary and fixed. If the novelistic individual extends beyond the boundaries of our sociohistorical and linguistic categories, it follows that what Bakhtin calls "an unrealizable surplus of humanness" (p. 37) becomes a leading edge onto new possibilities in the ever-reopening future. In a feminist poetics, this notion of the individual as a defining center of the novel's narrative form frees the idea of an individual woman from established sociohistorical categories of femininity and allows the possibility for a redefined individualism. Once more Bakhtin's terms, if not his male bias, point the way.

> The epic wholeness of an individual disintegrates in a novel. . . . A crucial tension develops between the external and internal man [or woman], and as a result the subjectivity of the individual becomes an object of experimentation and representation. . . . This disintegration of the integrity that an individual had possessed in epic (and in tragedy) combines in the novel with the necessary preparatory steps toward a new, complex wholeness. (Pp. 37–38)

The point to be taken here is the recognition that individualism in the novel, like the literary form itself, is a function of ceaseless and open-ended interaction. As the tension in an individual between external and internal—between established "categories" and a "surplus of humanness"—is inherent to the novel's dialogic form, so the notion of the complex and protean individual is an effect of that form.

In this sort of novelistic individualism, a feminist poetics can find a further expansion of the novel's capacity to speak to social concerns. Because the novel form is concerned with the lives of individuals, it opens immediately onto the social reality of both its author and its readers. Because it speaks from individual to individual—as Lessing says, "in a small personal voice" and "directly, in clear words"[50]—it affirms the possibility of social communication and of shared understanding. But because it is structured as process and shows us the "surplus of humanness," its individualism neither binds us to the known social reality nor limits its shared understanding to the absolutism that shadows the notion of "clear words." The novel's individualism itself can answer the feminist need to speak of women's lives and of the possibilities for changing women's lives.

II

This view of the novel as being closely linked to lived experience is what has attracted many feminist literary critics to it as a form of real interest in implementing cultural change. Much of the early feminist criticism of novels, in fact, seemed quite confident that, having identified the problems of sexual oppression, we had only to wait for and encourage the new and liberated characterizations of female experience in women's novels. But these new definitions of women's capacities were not immediately forthcoming. To return to the illustrative problem I initially set for myself, women writers have not provided us with a new wealth of strong autonomous female characters.

The recognition that such a "prescription" was not so easily filled and that literature could not be immediately claimed as an agent of cultural change helped to redefine the concerns of feminist criticism. Clearly, it was not possible to claim an interest in female experience as an easy basis even for a feminist poetics of the novel, despite its historical links to people's lives and to daily discourse. Although a view of the novel as dynamic and protean goes a long way toward establishing a more complex understanding of these links, such a view is not in itself adequate refutation of persistent male-dominant values in the novel form. In fact, the recognition that literary form often seems more recalcitrant than flexible provided one impetus for that recent phase of feminist literary criticism—the inquiry into women writers' interaction with male systems. Efforts to develop a feminist poetics have thus turned their attention to the powers of literary form and their grounding in male-dominant cultural ideology. But with this development—following upon an initial and perhaps naive optimism about literature's experiential relationship to cultural change—comes the threat that Elizabeth Abel pointed out: the withdrawal of feminist criticism from political concerns as it strengthens its theoretical concerns.

In part the threat of political withdrawal can be seen as a necessary function of the urge to develop a poetics or a theoretical construct, to develop understandings not bound by the particularities of lived experience. Properly speaking, a poetics is by definition concerned with the elements that distinguish a genre as form, its structure and constituent parts, not its relationship to human lives outside the literary text. This concern with form, relatively new to the study of the novel, provides source and direction for the contemporary explosion in theory of narrative and the novel, both feminist

and nonfeminist. And the development of taxonomies and mor-
phologies of narrative and the structuralist analysis of codes or literary conventions does give literary critics a potentially elucidating
framework for understanding the novel as genre. But it also necessarily threatens the feminist concern with changing women's lives
or reinterpreting the lived experience of gender, and it undermines
our concern with the central question of *"why* we should want to
engage with it in the first place." As Jonathan Culler asserts in his
introduction to Todorov's *The Poetics of Prose,* "poetics is not concerned with extraliterary causes or referents."[51] Poetics is not, in
other words, concerned with people's lives, not concerned with the
originating desire behind feminist criticism to understand and
change women's lives.

But feminist critics feel a legitimate need for a poetics, a definition of genre by which to assess its impact on those lives that remain the central concern. This need for an explicitly feminist poetics—a theory and definition that increase our ability to understand
women's lives—has found additional direction from a less absolute
version of the dominant interest in literary codes: Roland Barthes's
assessment of narrative as a *"performance"* dependent upon *"an*
implicit system of units and rules."[52] The insights available in narrative theory have thus participated in developing that sophistication of feminist analysis noted by Abel, and these insights have
pointed toward the possibility for a more complex politicization of
the study of the novel. The recognition has been crucial to feminist
criticism, for it is the enactment of literary codes that establishes
narrative expectations for women in the novel.

With this possibility of developing a more sophisticated political
base for a feminist poetics of the novel, however, comes yet another
threat of political withdrawal: the emphasis on the ineluctable silencing of women writers through the power of male encoding. In
the opening section of *The Madwoman in the Attic,* Sandra Gilbert
and Susan Gubar center their essay on feminist poetics in a concern
with such encodation and the resulting entrapment for women writers: "enclosed in the architecture of an overwhelmingly male-dominant society," women writers are simultaneously "trapped in
. . . literary constructs."[53] In its extreme form this entrapment
becomes the dilemma of irreducible "contradictions of genre and
gender" that can even strike the woman writer "dumb."[54] The

codes of the novel are thus seen to suppress both her female experience and her female voice.

The link to lived experience is present in the understanding, which Gilbert and Gubar emphasize, that the conventions of the novel gain force by being embedded in the conventions of a culture as lived out in its social system: literary constructs and social reality act as a double constraint. The link is present, too, in the recognition that these constraints do not act in isolation from each other; rather, they share in a dominant shaping ideology. The grounding of narrative in social expectation thus gives the literary text a double ideological presence: what Lanser calls its formal linking of "social life—ideology in the material sense" with aesthetic structuring— "ideology in the formal sense."[55] Its conventions, in other words, reflect simultaneously those that have governed past narratives and those that govern contemporary social reality. But though these are clear links to lived experience, they too threaten to suppress a concern for cultural change, not by refusing political awareness but by suggesting a resignation to inevitable oppression. In placing such a heavy emphasis on the doubly enforced constraint, Gilbert and Gubar and similar analysts verge on making feminist poetics into a poetics of victimization or exclusion: the novel seems to trap women irredeemably in patriarchal form. Although this is a perception of real use for a historical approach, as is evident in the fecundity of Gilbert's and Gubar's understanding of women's novels in the nineteenth century, it brings with it precisely the threat of political debilitation in any ongoing study of the novel.

But, interestingly, Gilbert's and Gubar's subsequent analyses of specific novels as "palimpsestic texts"[56] exceed the implications of their original poetics and point in the direction I find most fruitful for a feminist poetics. In powerful analyses of the works of nineteenth-century women, they identify not only women's entrapment in male-dominant discourse, but also the ways in which women writers eluded the full encodation of female experience in male literary constructs and began instead a process of female re-encoding. When explicitly claimed by women writers, such double-voiced discourse[57]—reminiscent of Bakhtin's view that the novel itself is double-voiced and hence always "internally dialogized" (p. 324)— illustrates the constraining power of literary structures, but it also expresses an active breach in the system of conventions forming one definition of novelistic discourse. The concern with oppression and repression—the power of material reality and of linguistic and literary form—thus again opens onto a concern with expression: the power of women to characterize their own experience.

Taking from this breach an alternative definition of literary codes, I see it as the basis for the second major shaping force in a feminist poetics of the novel. Without relinquishing the original concern with female experience and its representation in fiction through the evolving capacity of the novel to respond to cultural change, a feminist poetics must also be concerned with how the codes and conventions of the novel might be further broken down or redefined to give expression to women's perceptions and to accommodate new possibilities in women's lives. Since the novel, like all literary forms, is a conventional form, as well as one that is especially open to experiences of social reality, a feminist poetics also poses a different question: what might be the potential fruitfulness of the novel's conventional nature and how might it be turned to feminist effect? In a feminist poetics of the novel, the effort is to enable women to claim the explanatory possibilities of narrative, to develop new paradigms through which we can see our own experience rather than remaining within outworn structures that obscure and blind us to that experience. Because literary form in many ways does encourage us to interpret experience through what Nancy Miller calls the "grid of concordance,"[58] a feminist poetics needs to identify subversive techniques by which to develop alternative "concordances" about the lives and experiences of women.

I have already argued for a view of the novel as peculiarly susceptible to change. In addition, I think it is crucial to see all literary conventions and social ideologies as provisional understandings rather than static constructs. In Clifford Geertz's definition, ideologies are "maps of problematic social reality and matrices for the creation of collective conscience."[59] Similarly—and as expressions of a cultural ideology—literary conventions are socially created structures in the search for a shared reality. But since social reality is always problematic, never totally accounted for, groups of people are able to reformulate interpretations of reality, to shift perceptions toward a redefined "collective conscience." It is this shift in perception, being gradually worked out by the contemporary feminist movement, that offers new social ground for changing literary conventions and enables a feminist poetics to claim the fruitfulness of literary conventions as explanatory strategies rather than encoded systems.

All of the paradigms by which we interpret our experience—the plots, the expectations, the ideological frameworks—are not so much prior as they are interactional. In Neisser's explanation of the process of cognition, human beings receive information from the world around them according to available paradigms or schemata— "preexisting structures" of thought[60]—but are also able to modify the initial paradigm in response to discrepant information.[61] In this way, the conventions of literary narrative *can* act as an enclosing grid, a set of constraining interpretive paradigms that foreclose women writers' access to new interpretations of experience; but through the subversive voices of those same women, new conventions can also develop in response to the presence of discordant information in the lives of women. From the "emphasis added" that Miller sees in women's texts, from the subtexts that Gilbert and Gubar identify, from the muted expression that Showalter attributes to the voices grounded in women's culture—from all of these subversive possibilities by which women writers have claimed expression in resistance to the dominant culture, women's texts begin to develop new interpretive strategies for understanding women's lives. Made evident through the novel's protean capacity to interact with its social context, these strategies in turn gain interpretive power as women's lives respond to the "collective conscience" of feminist thought. As illustration, I will return to the original problem I set for myself: without literary conventions centered in female agency, we have difficulty perceiving such agency even when it exists; but the evolving recognition of women's activities outside the paradigm of the "love story" can force a breach in conventional literary paradigms and thus interact with the novel's openness to develop new literary conventions in response to and reinforcement of new possibilities in women's lives.

As cognitive strategies, both culturally and individually shaped, literary conventions, then, not only constrain but also enable both readers and writers in the process of changing cultural paradigms.[62] Although dominant literary conventions in the history of the novel, like the dominant cognitive strategies by which most human beings have interpreted their social reality, have been based in a male-dominant interpretive schema, emergent literary conventions participate in formulating alternative cognitive strategies. Through subjecting the conventions themselves to the dialogic process of novelistic understanding, we can discover in literary forms new ways of seeing women's lives.

The qualities of the novel that I have identified as links to lived experience—its similarity to daily narrative, its flexibility, its popularity, and its basis in individual experience—are thus given still greater import by a recognition that literary form itself can act either to constrain or to reopen interpretations of that experience. Rather than minimizing the political commitments of feminist literary criticism, a concern with form becomes itself decidedly political: to alter literary form is to participate in the process of altering women's lives. To return to Eagleton's question of *"why* we should want to engage with it in the first place," I will reiterate my initial response that feminist literary critics are concerned with the novel because it has close ties to the lives of women and the problems of gendered experience. But I would add to that the recognition that such concerns cannot, in fact, be entirely separated from those other concerns that Eagleton set aside: *"what* the object is" and *"how* we should approach it." For what the object is and how we should approach it are inseparable from why we are interested in it in the first place: it is our concern with cultural change that leads us to a concern with literary form.

III

What we often take to be the formal conventions of the novel are more precisely those conventions that evolved as a part of the nineteenth-century novel's concern to represent social reality in a world subject to rapid shifts in shared cultural assumptions. As "truth" was under seige by the rise in scientific, industrial, economic, and eventually psychological sophistication, so the novel evolved conventions by which to assess human experience in the midst of such complexity. But, as critics such as George Levine and Robert Alter have pointed out, nineteenth-century novelists were themselves self-consciously aware that their novels were not re-presentations of reality but rather representational fictions shaped by conventions.[63] We could even say that the entire history of the novel is defined by this same tension: the urge to speak meaningfully of human experi-ence in a social context coupled with the recognition that meaning is partial and equivocal. At any rate, the origin of the novel can be traced to this central recognition of uncertainty: a historical break with the univocal narratives of myth or epic, in which the old idea of narrative had been merged with an absolutist world view.[64]

From a feminist perspective, the break with mythic and epic vi-sions is manifestly important to an understanding of novelistic con-ventions, for this break provides the initial departure from a vision of a social world in which women are mere objects of exchange in the battles among men or one in which women's only power is mysterious or magical. To depart from such narrative traditions and to enter instead a narrative of social complexity is to open the nar-rative possibilities evident in ordinary human interaction. By defini-tion, the conventions of novelistic narrative initiate feminist under-standing as they reject the fixity of meaning.

The positions of the two sexes in the stories of epic heroes under-line the importance of relinquishing epic certainty: men fighting battles in which women serve only as booty or provocation. Helen of Troy, though most renowned, is scarcely alone either in serving this narrative function or in the mythic weight borne by the power of her beauty. Nor is Odysseus singular in encountering various and violent adventures that give shape and substance to his wanderings: as a hero of epic proportions he gains narrative presence through the completed actions of his series of conquests. Although I over-simplify to make my point, the pattern is decisive enough to need little illustration: men and women have clear sex-marked roles in the narrative forms of the epic, and for women, these roles are bound by the available images of female sexuality.

In myth and fairy tale, women are more likely to be significant agents of the tale, but here too the available roles are marked out by definitions of female sexuality and by the assumptions of uni-vocality. It is by now nearly a cliché, evolving out of early feminist work on images of women, that these patterns of myth, legend, and fairy tale have characterized women in one of two dominant polar patterns: saint or witch, virgin or whore, angel or monster. On ei-ther side of the polarity, the vision of woman, even when she does act, is basically an objectification through her sexuality, a denial of her own complex subjective reality, a fixed perspective on her as an outsider rather than an agent of her own reality.[65] She is either the good and passive Snow White or the wicked queen her stepmother; she is Eve the temptress or she is the virgin Mary.[66]

When the novel arises as a major narrative form, it breaks with these limitations in significant ways. As it develops what Bakhtin calls "the zone of maximal contact with the present" (p. 11), it breaks down the notions of absolute sameness in character and of absolute conclusiveness in plot.[67] In doing so it not only opens itself to notions of change and uncertainty; it also requires a reinterpretation of notions of gender. As men are no longer presented as identical with themselves, so women can no longer be easily presented as incarnations of sexually bound traits: their humanness exceeds the boundaries of sociohistorical categories.

This is why the novel's popularity, flexibility, and focus on the individual are all such powerful resources for new understandings of women's lives in the eighteenth and nineteenth centuries. This is also why the evolution of novelistic understanding turned naturally to personal relationships and hence to a more complex awareness of the dailiness of women's as well as men's lives. And this is at least one reason why women in the nineteenth century found in the novel a genre that was responsive to their own perspectives on human experience: Jane Austen, the Brontë sisters, George Eliot, and many lesser known women novelists claimed the resources of this narrative genre to convey their own human visions.

But the sociohistorical context for these novelists remained male-dominant. They could, to some extent, write of their own experiences and perceptions but the social realities continued to set boundaries to their novelistic world. The primary arena for women's actions, in the novel as in life, was by definition domestic; and the most favored plot—also by definition—was the cultural plot for a woman's favored destiny: the "love story."

This brief historical excursus provides some explanation of why the nineteenth-century realist novel is simultaneously in favor and under attack in contemporary feminist criticism. The realist novel gave women writers access to literary voice and hence shows us the experiences of women's lives, but it also constrained their notions—and ours—of women's lives within the assumptions and values of a decidedly patriarchal society. Its conventions were both those by which women gained access to literary expression and those by which we have come to see women's lives defined as primarily domestic and relational.

But, of course, the evolution of the novel did not stop in the nineteenth century, and a feminist understanding of its resources must also take into account the issues raised by novelists of the twentieth century in interaction with their own social context. Not surprisingly, we can find in Virginia Woolf's "Modern Fiction" a crucial moment in the evolution of novelistic conventions as she rejected what she saw as the limiting conventions of novelistic form: "The writer seems constrained, not by his [or her] own free will, but by some powerful and unscrupulous tyrant who has him [or her] in thrall to provide a plot, . . . But sometimes . . . we suspect a momentary doubt, . . . Is life like this? Must novels be like this?"[68] Rejecting the realist novel, Woolf, like many another modernist, was reacting to a sense of dramatic cultural change: the breaking up of many shared cultural values, the fragmentation of modern life, the inability to trust that one's own perceptions might hold true for anyone else. She felt, too, the inadequacy of literary conventions of the realist novel to the reality of subjective experience. With the cultural change, she felt the urgency for a new literary form to characterize the altered sense of life.

Current feminist interest in Woolf has emphasized the importance of reclaiming her identity as a socialist, a political feminist, a lesbian. This is work that is extremely important and restorative after half a century of denying or obscuring these parts of her life and work. But her concern with literary conventions—her efforts at formal experimentation by which she has achieved a place as a major modernist writer—are also of crucial significance to a feminist point of view.[69] For though her observations on form are cast in a generalizing "human" context—and share, as I have said, the concerns of male modernists as well—they are of particular use in a redefinition of the novel as a way of redefining female experience. Woolf's concern was with the reshaping of novelistic conventions in order that they might better "represent" the complexities of lived experience; the modernist recognition that "life isn't like this" joins the feminist recognition that though the historical premises of "representation" are inadequate, the novel's concern to "represent" lived experience remains fundamental.[70]

To represent by redefining the premises of representation: this, then, was the problem Woolf saw in her own relationship to her social context and to novelistic conventions, as it is the problem I have made central to a feminist understanding of the novel. As Woolf was well aware, the shifting of novelistic conventions can only be an ongoing process, not something that can be accomplished by feminist fiat. But novelists have always used literary conventions and been aware that readers bring conventional expectations to their novel reading; and the self-conscious play with these expectations has participated in our sense of the novel's malleability and its potential for portraying experience in new ways. With this knowledge, contemporary feminist critics, novelists, and novel readers can follow Woolf and find in the historical shifting of these conventions a peculiarly useful access to ways of redefining our cognitive strategies: not a feminist fiat but a feminist claiming of the culturally available strategies for change.

The premises of novelistic representation are not bound by strongly defined formal conventions, but our understanding of the realist novel is nonetheless structured by novelistic conventions in four broadly defined areas: plot, character, reality, and thematic unity.[71] The modernist breaking up of the codes and expectations in these areas was a clear refusal of the world view offered in the great novels of nineteenth-century realism and a denial that that view of "reality" had a special claim on the "real." Alain Robbe-Grillet's characterization of the "old novel" is indicative of what his predecessors in the twentieth century were rejecting before him: a "Balzacian character," "chronological plot," and "transcendent humanism."[72] Furthermore, like his predecessors, he also rejects the notion that reality is "already entirely constituted" and asserts that "not only does each of us see in the world his [or her] own reality, but . . . the novel is precisely what creates it."[73] Thus the conventions of representation in the nineteenth-century novel are seen as unviable for interpreting complex lived experience, especially in the modern world.

These "old" novelistic conventions are also the conventions that have been demonstrably problematic for any view of autonomous women characters and for characterizing female experience outside the assumptions of male dominance. Women have been bound by the anticipated resolution of plot difficulties in marriage, death, or painful isolation, by the definition of character in terms of the traits of "femininity," by the presentation of reality as the relational and domestic social context that the dominant sexual ideology presumes for women, and by the coherence of the love story. Thus a feminist poetics of the novel can usefully join modernists and postmodernists in rejecting such conventions. But since the necessity of a shared community, the desire for a meaningful place in the world, and the importance of assessing actual lived experience are also central to a feminist view, much of the postmodernist movement toward self-contained structures of verbal play or Robbe-Grillet's object-centered texts will not in itself meet the feminist need for a redefined capacity to represent. A feminist poetics of the novel needs, then, to understand, to subvert, and finally to reinterpret the formal resources of novelistic representation. If we understand these conventions as having only the pretense of stability or self-assurance, we can avoid reifying them and find instead their available resources as cognitive strategies, self-consciously invoked in the attempt to interpret and represent a social experience that defies a full representation.

Consider, first, the conventions of plot by which information takes its place in narrative. Even those theoreticians of narrative who are committed to its experiential significance recognize that such conventions intervene in any presentation of "reality" as story—that experience is not itself innocent. As Robert Alter says, "language can never give us experience itself but must always transmute experience into *récit*, that is, into narration, or if you will fiction."[74] Or, as Louis Mink says, "we cannot refer to events as such but only to events *under a description*."[75] And the initial selection process by which the simplest story is constructed is already a prior interpretation. For every narrative is based on a choice of which information is relevant and which irrelevant—based, as Hayden White says emphatically, on a group of facts "which *might have been included but were left out*."[76] Whatever information is included in a narrative is, in other words, always "infinitely filiated"[77] with other information. Experience, once perceptible, can never have naked presence but is instead always already a part of a narrative construction, always already interpreted.

In the conventions of the realist novel, this narrative construction emerges under the pretense of identifying accurate causal relationships: the plot is seen to work its way toward its inevitable conclusion through the interaction of experiential patterns; reality is seen to be manifest in the material world as if selection were not determinant of how that reality is seen. Even for women's experiential narratives, the initial process of emplotment, then, often becomes an imposition of the culture's dominant expectations for women's lives; their stories become an enactment of what White calls the iconic function of culturally available plot structures, "one of the ways that a culture has of making sense of both personal and public pasts."[78] If the anticipated plot *is* the love story, then events in a woman's life can only come into being, can only be voiced, under the description of her relationship to men and to the cultural text of femininity. If the beginning of her life is adolescence—as, for example, with Elizabeth Bennett—and the ending is marriage, then experiences outside this plot structure cannot come into focus, cannot share in the narrative structure. Though events are filiated in many directions, they are seen to have presence only as a part of the anticipated story. Thus, the traditional plotting that moves from possibility to probability to necessity through the selection and structuring of events is closely tied to the available paradigms for reading women's lives: we can only "see" the possibilities of women's lives in relational terms when we consider the pull toward the necessary conclusion in the progression of a plot. It is in this sense that plot is, to use Jonathan Culler's phrase, "subject to teleological determination,"[79] and it is from this recognition that women writers have developed strategies for what Rachel Blau DuPlessis calls "writing beyond the ending."[80]

In resisting the power of plot expectations, Woolf's development of a more associative form indicates her rejection of narrative teleology and cultural assumptions about cause and effect. Through brilliant formal innovations, her major novels elude narrative entrapment as they evoke the importance of internal complexity and disrupt the "naturalness" of cultural assumptions. But—apart from *The Years*—they cannot openly address issues of change in a social context because their associative form implies a more timeless view of reality. Similarly, the refusal of plot in, for example, Robbe-Grillet's novels can effectively defamiliarize our expectations but does not provide the possibility of narrative explanation and therefore denies access to the causal and temporal understanding we can hypothesize when we make sense of life "by imposing plots."[81]

A shift in the broad conventions of plot, which might allow the dynamic understanding developed through narrative while at the same time avoiding teleological determination, is thus an initial key to claiming the interpretive possibilities of novelistic conventions. One way to enact such a shift is to move from what Donald Marshall calls the "plot of history" to the "plot of discovery." The latter is defined not by its structured relationship of beginning and end with an emphasis on chronology, but by the "logic of interpretation."[82] In this way the effort is to assess possible meanings of events through the explanatory structures of narrative but to avoid a sense of their inevitability. Frank Kermode identifies a similar distinction when he gives priority to "fictions" over "myths"—to what he calls "agents of change" over "agents of stability."[83] The emphasis in either case is on temporary explanation in order to interpret experience, rather than fixing "reality" in a "true" telling, and is thus a renewal of the generative understanding that has always been a part of the novel's evolution. We are reminded that plot is a hypothesis about experience—to be tested against other possible explanations, both within the novel and in the writer's or reader's realm of experience—rather than an assertion about experience. As Kermode says in another analysis, sequencing is comforting because it meshes with "our notions of what life is like (notions that may have been derived from narrative in the first place)."[84] But the disruption of sequencing, the reminder that a given interpretation is hypothetical and partial, can lead us to recognize that life need not be what we thought it was: what we had taken to be inevitabilities through cultural expectations can be redefined into multiple possibilities. Even the past can thus be seen as indeterminate, or at least partially subject to our interpretive framework. Morag in Margaret Laurence's *The Diviners* recognizes this indeterminacy when she thinks that since we cannot know what really happened, we *can*, in fact, "change the past."[85]

This, then, is the view of plot inherent in the history of the novel and renewed in a dialogue between realism and modernism: plot based on process rather than product, plot as a possible interpretive schema for lived experience rather than the entrapment in a falsifying code. Change, rather than being foreclosed by narrative expectations—for example, of marriage or death—can instead be enabled. The refusal of narrative closure and of a determinate past becomes a way for the novel's plotting of events to show women's lives—like all lives—as ongoing process, not passive entrapment in romance or sexual destiny. A re-emplotment of lives becomes a way to shift the interpretive paradigm from explanations that denied women's autonomy and agency to explanations that include the breadth of human possibility as implicit in femaleness.

Like plot, character is central to the conventions of the nineteenth-century novel and yet has often been particularly destructive for women. Based in an idea of cause and effect in the development of a human being's life course, traditional character, apparently definable through traits, was visibly the source of "destiny." But as such, the concept of character also tended toward the notions of fixity evident in epic and myth and thus to reinforce cultural norms for women. Defined by traits, female characters were expected to match cultural expectations of what constitutes female identity: the virgin/whore dichotomy or the woman in love or the wife and mother. When the conventions of character interacted with limiting social expectations, feminine traits and female destinies often bound the lives of women characters into the grid of male-dominant expectations.

In the most absolute formulations of the conventions, feminists must then join postmodernists in the rejection of character as an enactment of the dominant culture's values. In Roger Fowler's definition, character is only "an illusion, a projection onto texts of the cultural expectations"[86] or in Jonathan Culler's phrase, only the "result of systems of convention."[87] Such are the views behind what Lucien Goldmann sees in postmodernist fiction as a *"radical disappearance of the character."*[88] Such are also the views behind a feminist critique of tbe conventions of character. But inasmuch as character is almost inevitably a gendered concept, the conventions of character are not only destructive to women but also of crucial interest. For gendered experience cannot be reinterpreted in literature unless gender is an available concept.

Again the modernist reassessment of character draws on the historical openness of the novel and provides an initial shifting of the conventions and an opening for feminist redefinition. Based on the perception that the self is all one can know, early-twentieth-century refusal of conventional character was evident in an increasingly subjective view of reality and a decreasingly delineated sense of

identity. Rather than acting as destiny, character became consciousness—the basis of perceiving and ordering processes in literary form. Rather than being consistently manifest in traits, character identity became, as Culler says, "relatively precarious."[89]

Evolving from these shifts in novelistic form—the centrality of
perception and the recognition that identity is a construct, not a
fixed reality—a feminist redefinition of the convention of character
can then claim modernist openness without relinquishing the possibility of gendered presence in the text. Though Fowler rejects the
idea of individuated character, his identification of defining
qualities provides a useful point of departure for the process of
claiming the concept of character while recognizing the inadequacy
of nineteenth-century conventions as they have been reified; a character, he says, is "an 'actant,'" "an assemblage of semes," "a proper
name," and is distinguished by "the language and thoughts that are
assigned to him [or her]."[90] Similarly, he says a "real person can be
seen . . . as a construction of roles."[91] By inverting and redefining
this correlation, a feminist poetics can renew the openness evident
throughout the novel's history in the "surplus of humanness" that
refuses to be bound by roles and always points characters toward the
future.

Drawing on but subverting Fowler's categories, the idea of character—and with it the idea of "person"—becomes most prominently the expression of agency, the capacity to act toward change—
an empirical being with experiential continuity over time, a proper
name, a distinctive set of remembered experiences, and a group of
attributes assigned to her or him by other characters or people and
by the perceiving self, but above all one who acts, even beyond the
limits of roles and labels. As with plot, and as in the renewal of
convention that we can derive from modernism, the assigned attributes must be recognized as temporary and explanatory, not fixed
and permanent, and they must be recognized as having been similarly attributed by an agent rather than being accurate descriptions of
definable traits. Character as agent, with impermanent characteristics, is thus a view of character unlike the traditional view and
yet able to participate in the process by which conventions of literature interact with lived experience. The emphasis on process, on
constant construction and reconstruction of individual identity,
opens the possibility of a female character *not* constrained by as-

sumptions of essential femininity but rather definitional of a new complexity embracing both autonomy and femaleness.

In the tradition of the realist novel, the possibility of belief in a comprehensible world revealed itself in the apparent claim to represent reality. Like an absolute version of the conventions of plot and character, this belief was always resisted by the novel as an evolving form in contact with its contemporary social context, and, again like the other novelistic conventions, it became even more untenable in the modernist vision. It is the loss of such belief that yields Woolf's anxiety that her perceptions could not hold true for anyone else and her rejection of what she sees as Arnold Bennett's "materialism."[92] Again, Woolf's concerns reflect not only the novelistic evolution in modernist form, but also a feminist conviction. For women have been historically excluded from visions of shared social reality, as is shown with special clarity in Elizabeth Ermath's analysis of how women characters are precluded—and thus extinguished—from the consensus that seems to underpin the traditional realist novel.[93] Such consensus, as it suggests dominant cultural assumptions, reflects an implicit acceptance of the male-dominant status quo, a definition of social reality denying possibilities of women's agency and self-definition.

Certainly, a key response in twentieth-century literature has been its increased subjectivity and unwillingness to try to define a social reality or to claim any "reference" to an external world. Such a retreat from a coherent "culture text" has, in a way, made women less excluded: if isolated subjectivity is everyone's reality, then women can have access to the dominant "reality." As in the earlier rejection of univocal epic, the further shift of literary conventions away from a relatively determinate and identifiable social world has also helped to open those conventions more fully to the private experience of women. The schematizing hold of an "accurate" view of reality, as seen through the dominant codes of experience, is loosened by the very process of subjectivizing reality. But in the effort to claim female experience as it has been denied by dominant assumptions, women have also needed the possibility of identifying a shared reality of their own and have thus required the possibility of portraying lived experience, the possibility that language can communicate something about "the real."

The modernist reassertion that there is no single "reality," as there is no unidimensional character and no one "right" plot, again assists in the feminist redefining of literary conventions. If reality risks becoming the chaos of sensations, undifferentiated and unpatterned without a human imposition of form and interpretation, then the interpreter achieves a special authority as providing one possible structuring of that chaos. But rather than accepting Roquentin's conclusion, in Jean-Paul Sartre's *Nausea*, that biography, history, and fiction create a *false* structuring of experience merely because they *are* a structuring, one can say that each structuring has a certain possible viability and reflects a similar process by which each of us lives our lives. The representational possibilities rest not on a belief in a fully comprehensible world—a belief the novel has always at least partially resisted—but on a recognition that interpretive structuring is a primary activity in life as in novels. As Geertz points out, humans could not survive without the symbolic structures by which we interpret experience.[94] Or in Sartre's terms, the human is "a signifying being" oriented toward the future.[95] A feminist poetics reemphasizes these human qualities as they participate in the evolving form of novelistic understanding.

In a feminist redefinition of the conventions, then, social reality derives from the recognition that the structuring activity is a shared human need and is the effect of the culturally available paradigms by which people interpret the world around them. For women writers and readers the claiming of subjective experience and the development of narrative explanations for what is specifically female in that experience becomes a crucial way of identifying an altered social reality. Through a paradigm centered in female experience (thus raising to visibility, among other things, the previously invisible qualities of women's strength and agency) the novelistic claim to portray a view of social reality becomes a means of access to newly shared experience and provides the possibility, through the writer-character-reader triad, for a sense of community in the new shared reality.

In this view, it is not that there is no reality, as in extreme versions of postmodernist thought, but that the novelistic constitution of reality is a part of the endless interaction between information and interpretation by which we all live. Adding the previously obscured information of explicitly female experience requires a new interpretive paradigm for social reality; the development of new paradigms makes accessible new information. In voicing their own multiple subjective versions of the world, women thus come to identify their reality not in the "femininity" of the dominant paradigm, but in a shared basis of female experience at the heart of the sense-making process. This is a commitment not to an unchanging reality but to a reality of shared interpretation in process.

Implicit in the dialogical form of the novel, the refusals of determinate reality, character, and plot are thus all a part of the process by which women can "extend the real rather than dissolve it"[96] through renewing novelistic conventions for feminist understanding. In this context, the conventions of thematic unity operate pervasively in our reading of all the other narrative conventions and in their transfer to our reading of lives. The principle of thematic unity is the governing principle for selection of events by which the plot—or even the "story"—is constituted, of characteristics by which characters are concretized, of objects and information by which the external world is made present. In each case, the selection process for the reader reading and for the writer writing is based on the anticipation of thematic unity. Clearly the reading at which we will arrive—either of the life experience or of the novelistic world—is crucially dependent on the governing principle by which these selections are made. In the traditional portrayal of women, it is almost inevitably the defining unity of the love interest; the narrative coherence depends on our assumptions that the novelistic lives of women will be centered in their relationship to men. But through altered novelistic conventions, the shift in thematic unity, and particularly the insistence on multiple thematic unities emphasized by the modernist refusal of determinate form, enables the perception that women's lives can have multiple centers. It thus becomes possible to construct alternative thematic unities based on female autonomy and informed by female experience. The emphasis once again is on process rather than product, a further evolution of the fundamental novelistic understanding: explanatory structures have referential power and value but must always be subject to alteration.

A key agent in this contemporary reopening of conventions to process is the presence of a feminist interpretive community. In her analysis of the functioning of interpretive conventions, Jean Kennard hypothesizes that "literary conventions change when their implications conflict with the vision of experience of a new 'in-

terpretive community.'" She argues convincingly that we must recognize the "nonliterary as well as literary influences" by which
literary conventions are changed, and she suggests that contemporary feminist perspectives have enabled us to read differently the
possibilities in earlier works such as *The Awakening*, even though
readers of its own time could not see it as an expression of "wom-
en's search for self-fulfillment."[97] She sees this convention as operating in more recent novels first as a development of the concept of
self-fulfillment and then as a convention that itself needed to be
broken.

Implicit in Kennard's argument, though not actually worked out,
is the recognition that such conventions create new cultural paradigms by which women readers read both novels and their lives and
by which women writers read their perspectives on life into their
novels. The feminist literary community thus provides a necessary
link in the dialogic process involved in literary and cultural change:
in perpetually evolving interchange, the culture and the individual
interact through the formation and use of interpretive paradigms
and with the intervention of newly evolved shared perceptions. The
dominant culture text, the grid of expectations, is changed by the
interpretive participation of individuals in the act of developing new
shared conventions: women gain cultural support from other wom-
en and thus gain the perceptual capacities for forming new literary
conventions and for reading lives in new ways.

In an early manifesto of feminist literary criticism, Adrienne Rich
gave powerful definition to its experiential basis: "A radical critique
of literature, feminist in its impulse, would take the work first of all
as a clue to how we live, how we have been living, how we have
been led to imagine ourselves, how our language has trapped as well
as liberated us, how the very act of naming has been till now a male
prerogative and how we can begin to see and name—and therefore
live—afresh."[98] In spite of the differences among feminist critics,
Rich's rationale for feminist criticism continues to define our unifying concerns: the affirmation of literature's interpretive power, the
recognition of language as both constraint and liberation, the need
to claim the agency of vision and voice in resistance to male dominance. Current work in feminist literary criticism seems most concerned with the difficulty of meeting these goals and with the recognition that language and literature continue to act powerfully as

constraint. But even these recognitions do not require the rejection of those early values or of the experiential basis for feminist criticism; they only require that our analyses are cognizant of the complexities of literary form as it both shapes and is shaped by experience. Mary Poovey has pointed out that ideology is enabling as well as restricting;[99] so, too, is literary form as long as we recognize not only its potential imposition of stasis, but also its enabling power in yielding new understandings of women's lives.

Through claiming the novel's capacity both to "represent" and to redefine the premises of representation, a feminist poetics of the novel, then, reclaims the historical potential of the novel and addresses precisely those political concerns that gave original impetus to feminist literary criticism: the fuller understanding of women's lives and the commitment to cultural change. Eagleton's claim for the distinctiveness of feminist criticism, from which I took my point of departure in this chapter, thus becomes a claim for the "life" of literary theory rather than the "death" he proclaimed in his "obituary." What is our interest in and commitment to the study of literature? Why should we want to engage with it? Enriched by the recognitions implicit in feminist literary criticism's new sophistication, the old answer reasserts itself: because it tells us something about how we live and how we might live. It helps give us that capacity "to see and name—and therefore live—afresh."

CHAPTER 3

The Subversive "I": Female Experience, Female Voice

Christa Wolf ponders, muses, narrates, analyzes, works her way through the "conditions of a narrative," the problems of giving voice to her narrator-protagonist, Cassandra: "Do people suspect, do *we* suspect, how difficult and in fact dangerous it can be when life is restored to an 'object'? When the idol begins to feel again? When 'it' finds speech again? When it has to say 'I,' as a woman?"[1] In finding speech, Wolf's Cassandra rehearses not only the problems of being a woman in a male-dominant society but also the problems of literary form for women writers. Despite the historical openness of the novel, even this form has not erased the fissures in this difficult enunciation: saying "I," as a woman, remains very nearly a contradiction in terms.

What is woman? The old unanswered question becomes a springboard for understanding this contradiction between "I" and "woman." For if we seek the meaning of femaleness in some "what" or essence, we have already submerged the knowledge of female subjectivity. "I" is enshrouded in "she," and "she" can only be understood by external definition. The difficulty of saying "I," as a woman, is the difficulty of separating subjectivity from presumptions of essence and at the same time recognizing that subjectivity is partially embroiled in, shaped by those presumptions.

Wolf's Cassandra understands the complexity of her claim to selfhood. Her narrative is her painful groping for voice in resistance to previous self-definitions, previous external impositions of definition. If she is to learn to say "I," as a woman, she must depart from her place as favored daughter in the patriarchal family; she must escape her father's image of her femaleness: "I knew him and he did not know me. He knew his ideal of me; that was supposed to hold still" (p. 50). Because she is attempting to escape the confines of that ideal, she will not hold still. But her alternative, in an epic world, is to become isolated within her subjectivity. Her painful disentanglement from the "we" that was Troy is her rejection of male priority; her search for an alternative "we" in the companionship of other women, her attempt to develop a new shared perspective, is smothered by the continued power of that male priority. Her narrative search underlines the fragility of selfhood in her world, as that world is defined by the public posturings—violent, cruel, often meaningless or hypocritical—of its male heroes. Its pretense to certainty makes all the more poignant the silencing of her cries to be heard, the denial of her voice and her experience. She learns to say "I," as a woman, only at great cost, only by discovering that painful isolation is the price she must pay for claiming her subjectivity. Wolf is right: to say "I," as a woman, is both difficult and dangerous.

But the dangers are not to Cassandra alone; they are also dangers to the privileges and restraints that attempted to silence her voice. For in learning to say "I," as a woman—even in isolation—she threatens the very assumptions of male-dominant thought. When she says "I" in full subjectivity, she disrupts that privileging as she disrupts external notions of essence, of sameness: the culture text of femininity, which has made her, as a woman, into an "object," cannot accommodate her subjective voice and presence. As the "I" speaks for itself and of itself, it necessarily insists on the contradictions between internal and external definitions of self and hence on that "surplus of humanness" that always provides an entry into the future, a resistance to fixity.[2]

Because Cassandra's context remains epic, her voice cannot directly threaten her social world (hence her isolation), but even her isolated claim to voice rends the wholeness of the social fabric in that epic world. And her speaking resonates even more profoundly in Wolf's own twentieth-century context, as it suggests the potency of female self-definition in a social context that cannot lay claim to seamless wholeness.

The literary dangers to patriarchal wholeness, then, originate in the woman's voice. Once the female "I" has spoken, the subversion is begun—even in novels embedded in a patriarchal context, even in novels by men. The moment Richardson's Clarissa Harlowe or Defoe's Moll Flanders speaks in her own voice she initiates a resistance to the femininity text. By virtue of speaking as a woman, any female narrator-protagonist evokes some awareness of the disjunction between internal and external definitions and some recognition of her agency in self-narration. To speak directly in a personal voice is to deny the exclusive right of male author-ity implicit in a public voice and to escape the expression of dominant ideologies upon which an omniscient narrator depends.

But, though they are part of a historical surge of interest in women's lives,[3] these early novels enact only a partial subversion of the femininity text, in large measure because they, like all novels, exist in interaction with the social context from which they arise. The male dominance of eighteenth-century English society, evidenced most prominently in the legal and cultural assumptions about marriage and economic life, inevitably informs the language and plot expectations of eighteenth-century novels. Clarissa's subjectivity exceeds the fixed image of the chaste woman but her choices are still limited by sexual expectations. And despite what Ian Watt calls Moll Flanders's "freedom from any involuntary involvement in the feminine role,"[4] despite her enactment of aggressive survival, her freedoms and actions can only be defined in interaction with the cultural limitations on a woman's possible goals: her success, however much it reveals economic changes of the period, must depend on her ability to manipulate the patriarchal institution of marriage and its relation to private property. And given the linear and episodic evolution of her adventures, Moll's tale evokes only a minimum of subjectivity: despite her "I," her narrative departs only minimally from an external vision. The disruption exists but does not extend its dangers.

In their far greater claim to subjective voice and presence, novels such as Charlotte Brontë's *Jane Eyre* and *Villette* come closer to enacting the powers of the subversive "I." But they, too, must remain partially bound by the assumptions of their social context. Though both novels press the limits of cultural definitions of female selfhood, female sexuality, female need for work and economic independence, both must also develop their perceptions in interaction with the knowledge that women of nineteenth-century England were bound by powerful economic and social constraints. Such novels find ways to encode alternative meanings and are aided in doing so by the manifest presence of subjective complexity in the novel's narrative voice, but their interaction with social reality by means of the novelistic conventions of realism set significant limits to their subversive power.

Throughout the novel's history both men and women have used first-person narration by both male and female protagonists to evoke narrative immediacy and mimetic conviction. They have given voice to a narrating "I" and subjective complexity to their individual narrator-protagonists. But, like Richardson and Defoe and Brontë, they have only been able to do so in interaction with the cultural assumptions of their own social context, and, of course, those cultural assumptions have always privileged maleness. Like Cassandra, the female narrating "I" could subvert notions of feminine essence but could still act only within the boundaries of her male-dominant world.

Few would argue that our own contemporary culture has escaped that male dominance: authority continues to reside more visibly and directly in male presence and voice than in female presence and voice.[5] But at the same time few would deny that the possibilities for women's lives now include a greater scope of action than in previous periods of history. It is in this cultural context—no longer a context of epic absolutes and not even a context of nineteenth-century patriarchy—that the contemporary possibilities for renewing novelistic conventions must be examined. It is in this cultural context that saying "I," as a woman, contributes an increased subversive value to the possibilities of novelistic representation.

I

Initially, the difficulties of contemporary novelistic representation seem to arise less from the social context of persistent male dominance than from the literary context of radical skepticism about the possibility or value of any representation. A significant number of contemporary first-person novels themselves resist the form's historical links to mimetic conviction and instead pursue its alternative capacity for self-conscious disruption of the idea of representation. This capacity, too, has always been present in first-person narrative; indeed it predominates in some of the earliest examples of the form, notably *Tristram Shandy* and *Don Quixote*. But in its contemporary expressions, the disruption extends still further and becomes an expression of radical skepticism. The narrating "I" dissolves into Samuel Beckett's tangles of contradiction and meaninglessness or Vladimir Nabokov's parodic withdrawal or John Barth's maze of mirrorings. Though such novelists play on the capacity of first-person narration to evoke presence, they instead choose the "I" as a kind of infinite regress into absence: not representation but a powerful disruption of our complacency about "the real." Similarly, poststructuralist critics are challenging any notion of correspondence between language and experience, challenging the idea that experience and selfhood are meaningful concepts at all, and thereby challenging us to a radical rethinking of our assumptions.

Such challenges—in fiction and in criticism—are raised by both men and women and suggest the difficulties faced by any contemporary novelist wishing to find in fiction a way to speak meaningfully of human problems in a social context. Such challenges are also a critical part of the contemporary ethos: novelists cannot naively assume an audience's suspension of disbelief or even an audience's interest in belief at all. But the challenges are particularly acute to women novelists who wish nonetheless to claim the novel's historical resources to interact with lived experience in meaningful ways, novelists who wish to use those resources for new understandings of women's lives. For at the same time that the contemporary ethos of skepticism challenges this capacity, the contemporary social reality of feminist change gives new strength to the novel's capacity to interact with cultural change in finding new interpretations for women's experiences.

Because the challenge of radical skepticism touches autobiography less directly and the possibilities of feminist narrative seem implicit in the renewed possibilities for feminist lives, one might expect to find in autobiography more immediate resources for "telling lives" in new ways. Indeed, this is the claim that Lynn Bloom makes: in her reading, contemporary women's autobiographies "present much more consistently positive images of women than does twentieth-century fiction by women writers, feminist or not."[6] On the face of it, this seems accurate: the lives of women like Margaret Sanger, Maya Angelou, and Margaret Mead can tell us much about women who are not trapped within the femininity text, women who have been able to claim autonomy. In Bloom's analysis, such an autobiographer "has a strong counter-normative sense of herself as an intellectually, sexually, economically, strong, independent, unique *person*."[7] The values here are precisely those values that have been problematic for female protagonists, precisely those that are of use in a search for female "role models."

But the operative word in Bloom's description reminds us of a different set of problems: if these women are, indeed, "counter-normative," then their lives can have little effect in an active critique or disruption of the prevailing sexual ideology. As Bloom also notes, these women avoid direct discussion of personal problems;[8] rather than confronting the conflicts they have faced *as women*, they tend to shape their narratives as "counter-normative" stories of achievement. In following a paradigmatic plot of strength and autonomy, they have suppressed the problematic issues of sexuality. Significant as role models, they nonetheless do little to revise the notion of what is sexually "normative."

Other analyses of women's autobiographies suggest a different usefulness of first-person narration for alternative understandings of specifically female experience. In identifying the importance of relationships in women's sense of self, Mary Mason implies a potential for greater inclusiveness in the narrating "I."[9] In identifying women's emphasis on dailiness and the life of the imagination, Suzanne Juhasz implies a renewed understanding of interior life through the narrating "I."[10] In identifying a predominance of fragmentary form in women's autobiography, Estelle Jelinek implies the capacity of the narrating "I" for a nonlinear multiplicity.[11] Like the rise of the domestic novel in the eighteenth century, such narratives give us access to previously obscured parts of women's lives as they draw on the resources of diaries and letters, with which women have long been associated. They critique the exclusive valuing of public achievement that seems to shape most male autobiographies, and they resist the problems of a "counter-normative" sense of female selfhood. But despite their sometimes innovative form, they risk imbrication in the femininity text through implying a definition of female as predominantly personal and through the necessary particularity of the lives that they, as autobiographies, must document. Instead of critiquing the prevailing sexual ideology, they risk confirming it precisely because they must assume a reality that is defined by what is given.

Nonetheless, from the general resources of the more personal autobiography, we can elicit the subversive capabilities of a narrating "I": an "I" that will draw on the importance of relationality and dailiness for women and on the value of nonlinear multiplicity. But by recognizing the limits and hazards of autobiographical form, we can understand more fully the generativity of the novel's dialogic capacity within which the narrating "I" achieves further efficacy: the capacity to engage the normative and simultaneously elude and critique it, to evoke realities at the same time that it interrogates our ways of defining them. Because they draw on these novelistic resources, a few contemporary feminist autobiographers—such as Kim Chernin and Maxine Hong Kingston—are able to expand these critical capacities in autobiography as well.[12] But their achievement rests primarily on their understanding of novelistic form: both give self-conscious consideration to narrative form itself; both invoke reality through dialogic interpretation; both subject our cultural notions of femaleness and selfhood to a similar dialogic understanding. It is not that the novel is the only narrative form capable of simultaneously invoking and critiquing cultural norms but that its formal evolution predisposes it to this critical interaction. Drawing on the complex resources of novelistic form in interaction with contemporary culture, first-person narration provides women novelists with an evolving access to subversive representation of women's lives.

II

For a number of contemporary women novelists, then, the narrating "I," with its historical ties to representation and its contemporary ties to disruption of complacency, provides an effective response to the challenge and a way to meet the need I made central to a feminist poetics of the novel: to represent while resisting and redefining the premises of representation. For these novelists, the narrating "I" not only subverts the externalized image of femaleness, as it has always done, but also gains the power to redefine the conventions of the novel for subversive representation beyond the femininity text. In using the "I" to undermine and redefine the historical conventions of representation, they find a new access to representation: their novels develop the capacity to say "I," as a woman, without yielding to the persistence of the cultural contradiction.

As a cultural icon, plot has historically enacted the femininity text in novels about women: its conventions have required that women's lives meet culturally anticipated patterns. As it enacts narrative skepticism, a narrating "I" thus begins the redefinition of plot by expanding the subversive capacity inherent in her subjectivity. Centered in an "I," plot becomes overtly a function of an individual human consciousness; as an openly subjective act, it necessarily loses some of its iconic force and can be presented as hypothesis rather than truth. The visible process of narrative construction and narrative selection, reinforced by a cultural context predisposed to notice literary self-consciousness, becomes an overt reminder of human agency and human fallibility: events must be selected and described *by someone;* stories must be told *by someone.* The story is presented as an individual perception that need not be evaluated as an expression of general truth.

When the protagonist of the novel is made her own narrator, she thus achieves a very immediate kind of agency and a capacity to renew our notion of plot. She is the agent by which events come into being as part of her story: she makes the selection as to which information is relevant to the plot she constructs; she sets the context for the causal links in her own life. She cannot, of course, claim total control—the fictional history posited by her author contains the material limitations on the information she can construe into narrative, and this history is always framed in interaction with her social context. But she does have the freedom of construction that lies at the heart of the human need to narrate, and in using that freedom openly, she subverts the convention of plot as an apparently inevitable unfolding of causal relationships.

In the conventions of plot, sequencing is usually presented as an external given, a "natural" chronology, but for the narrating "I" it too can be an overt function of narrative control. As the protagonist herself makes the connections over time that narrative inevitably involves, she claims the capacity for new understanding of her life and selfhood. The predominant narrative convention of past tense can be a way of fixing the story, giving it a determinate pattern. But in the claim to narrative agency in the shaping of event, the protagonist draws on the openness of human memory in interpreting sequence. Hayden White remarks that the "reality" of the data of the past consists in the fact that "they were remembered" and that "they are capable of finding a place in a chronologically ordered sequence."[13] As the needs of the present prompt narrative interpretation of the past, the narrator's memory can yield a different "reality," a different chronology: a subversion of fixity, a reopening of cultural "truth."

Thus the past, too, becomes subject to reinterpretation, not fixed in its pastness nor tied to the iconic function of culturally available plots. Virtually the entire project of Violet Clay in the narrative she constructs in her eponymous novel is precisely this redefining of the past in order to find in it a different path to the present and hence the future. It is not that she changes the information but that she places it under a different description and thereby identifies a different sequencing on which the interpretation of the past is constructed. The chronological order is established in a modified form by the change in narrative construction, the reintroduction of omitted information and the shift not in chronological facts but in the decision as to which facts are a part of which chronological sequence. In Louis Mink's words, "even though every memory claim is veridical, the truth of the narrative itself is precisely what is not remembered but constructed."[14] Through the narrating "I," the recognition of human agency in narrative construction reopens the interpretations of the past as it does the assessment of causality. For the narrative agent, the past exists in continual interaction with the present; memory functions both to shape the personal paradigms by which she orders and organizes present experience and to supply different information when she restructures her temporal paradigms for examining past experience.

As she shifts the narrative lens by which facts become events in a story, the narrator-protagonist changes the very nature of the "event"—its meaning, its place in a causal pattern, its temporal significance. When she shapes her story according to a female experiential perspective, even the events acquire new definition. This is the process by which Cassandra's externally labeled "madness" becomes her experientially defined withdrawal from patriarchy and thus a part of a new sequence rather than the conclusion of an old one. Through such redefinitions of narrative expectations, the narrative process becomes a powerful cognitive instrument for the understanding and ordering of women's realities. In claiming the right to narrate their own lives, female protagonists thereby claim the authority to name and construct their own experience.

In an ethos of skepticism, plot can never be seen as truth. But its efficacy as hypothesis can draw on that very skepticism. Through the narrative self-consciousness of the speaking "I," narrative encoding becomes an active structuration and thus a subversion of any rigid assumptions. When the narrating "I" openly adopts narrative conventions, she simultaneously resists their power. Consider, for example, the representation of life emplotment to which I referred in my discussion, in chapter 2, of the need to narrate: Anna Wulf's bedtime story to her daughter Janet. Beginning with "There was once a little girl" and concluding with Janet's own "for ever and ever," the story is self-consciously framed by markers taken from imaginary stories, the conventions of fairy tale narratives. These are conventions that threaten the lived experience with a kind of premature closure; the assurance that this narrative unit has reached its resolution closes off alternative interpretations. But the story reaches its "forever and ever" through Janet's interruption to correct her mother, to refuse the story line of the quarrel with her friend as yesterday's story rather than today's: "No mummy, I didn't, that was yesterday. I *love* Marie for ever and ever."[15] The acknowledgment that yesterday's story is not today's is thus integral to the narrative process itself. And in reminding us of the hidden threat implicit in the conventions of narrative and of the ways in which daily stories need daily to be remade, the narrative's self-conscious structuring underlines the tentativeness of all narrative pattern. Subversion derives from the immediate representation of the process of representing. As narrative reality is seen to be an interpretive construct, so it must be seen to be subject to reinterpretation.

Taking this capacity one step further, the narrator may not only critique available plot patterns but also generate new patterns from her own experience: emplotment in critical dialogue with re-emplotment. As a number of recent feminist critics have argued, women's use of palimpsestic narrative, of double-voiced discourse, has historically given them the capacity to subvert the dominant text and its emplotment of women's lives. In these instances, the critic is drawing from the subversive subtext the evidence for a re-emplotment of women's experiences in resistance to cultural expectations.

But the subversion goes still further when the novelist shows us a *protagonist* engaged in this process as the basis of her own narration.

If the narrating "I" is herself examining and rejecting cultural interpretations of her life experience, her own re-emplotment then becomes a double subversion. A narrator-protagonist can find in her life experiences those capacities that the culture text has denied and use them to develop an alternative narrative explanation. Or she can generate a store of experiential data from which she can select experiences falling outside the cultural expectations and thus retain the capacity to *re*interpret. Through developing a different plot structure, a protagonist like Violet Clay can reject her previous self-interpretation as helpless victim and redefine her experiences as a recognition of her own commitment to her work; through accumulating apparently conflicting interpretations of her childhood experiences, a protagonist like Del Jordan in *Lives of Girls and Women* can find a way of remaining open to alternative futures. As agents of their own stories, these and other narrator-protagonists are themselves engaged in the process of re-emplotment, raising to textuality the subtext of their own experiential interpretations. Because their plots remain open to change, they are able to use plot to interpret but still elude the femininity text with its teleological control over women's stories. And through their re-emplotment, they develop new ways of encoding the information of women's lives, new schemata to replace the old iconic function of plot, new stories by which to make sense of the past, both personal and public.[16]

As it makes visible the process of emplotment and re-emplotment, first-person narration also underlines the recognition that the narrative conventions by which we separate plot and reality are themselves based in a false distinction. As events are filiated in multiple directions and therefore subject to multiple narrative constructions, so the presentation of social and material reality is a function of selection and interpretation. And both are determined in large measure by the expectations of thematic coherence. Through her open acknowledgment of selection and construction, the female narrating "I" can thus draw overtly on the modernist recognition that both reality and story are at least partially subject to the perception and interpretation of the individual. Based in that recognition, her claim to descriptive control becomes a subversive rejection not only of the life text (or plot) that the dominant culture has presumed to be her experience but also of the social reality in which that life text is embedded.

Because the fictional creation of a social reality requires some presumption of agreement, the first-person narrator may seem to be most at risk in the redefinition of the narrative conventions of "the real." The threat that haunts much modernist and postmodernist writing is, after all, the threat implicit in first-person narration: individual isolation, the inability to escape perceptions that are merely personal, solipsism. But self-conscious narration, which is nonetheless committed to interpreting experience, can openly acknowledge the relationship between perceiving, telling, and interpreting; in doing so, it can also acknowledge that as reality is in part a social construction, so "the real" depends upon identifying plots and perceptions that have a shared interpretive power. The capacity of a narrating "I" to represent experience cannot be claimed through a single voice resisting the femininity text—that is why Wolf's Cassandra *is* finally isolated with her own hard-won understanding. Representation can only be claimed in a voice among other voices, a female "I" speaking to other women and building shared perspectives as mutual outsiders to the dominant culture. That is why Cassandra, despite her novelistic isolation, is able to communicate powerfully to Wolf's own contemporary audience.

Thus as the narrative voice becomes an openly communicative voice, the novel's individualistic form finds its communal value through the narrating "I"—an "I" speaking to an audience in the need to assess interpretations of lived experience, the need to develop a new perspective on social reality. Through a narrating "I" in the process of sharing narrative interpretations, a novelist shows her protagonist enacting one of the central ways in which people find a place in a human community and simultaneously responding to a powerful need that feminists feel acutely in the process of rereading women's lives: in telling each other stories, we reassure ourselves about our interpretations of lived experience or test the limits of those interpretations. As Janet provides her mother with the information of her day, she thereby attests to the overall pattern of her narrated experience: this is an interpretation of experience upon which teller and listener can agree. And from the overall process, its embeddedness in the relationship between the two of them, Anna reaches "the feeling of continuity, of gay intimacy,"[17] which is the governing tone of this section of her journal entry.

The shared structuring of experience gives access to human continuity: because we can explain our lives to other people or understand other people's explanations of lived experience, whether by telling a bedtime story or by writing a novel or by reading a novel, we gain an external confirmation that our lives have significance. We gain an enriched awareness that we are not alone in the kinds of experience we have and the kinds of perceptions we may formulate. Lessing, for example, has said that the passages in *The Golden Notebook* that she considered "hopelessly private" and that she was particularly anxious about including were the ones to which readers most responded, the ones in which "I spoke for other people."[18] Such experiences need not be specifically experiences of the author, but in drawing upon her knowledge of living as a woman, she can attribute to a narrator's personal voice the "naming" of female realities and thus open to readers the shared experience of redefined femaleness. This need to articulate "women's shared experience," which Margaret Homans calls "the touchstone of American feminist criticism,"[19] is central to the need and possibility for narratives of women's lives, and it underlines the importance of a partially receptive social context. Through disrupting the conventions of how we constitute reality and yet also speaking of her own reality, the narrating "I" enacts the process by which a claim to voice yields a redefinition of reality; as Adrienne Rich expresses it, "in breaking those silences, naming ourselves, uncovering the hidden, making ourselves present, we begin to define a reality which resonates to *us*, which affirms *our* being."[20]

III

Because the concept of female character has special importance for the literary representation of women's lives, I want to consider it at greater length than the other novelistic conventions. Only through an altered understanding of character is it possible to represent women's lives while refusing the assumptions of representation: to claim those female experiences that are denied by the femininity text and to develop a definition of female selfhood as embracing both autonomy and sexuality. As Rich implies, the feminist project—"to define a reality which resonates to *us*"—is impossible without that initial "breaking [of] silences, naming our selves." But to name our selves requires a still greater subversion of cultural assumptions, for in the femininity text, women are by definition the named, not the ones who name. Thus the narrating "I" finds its greatest power to escape the cultural grid through the narrative re-definition of female selfhood.

Not surprisingly, the interest in female identity and female character has been central to many feminist literary critics, particularly those concerned with women's lived experience. As Judith Kegan Gardiner indicates in the opening paragraph of her essay on female identity, critic after critic returns to the knotty problem of what Gilbert and Gubar call "the woman's quest for self-definition."[21] In Gardiner's summary, as in Gilbert and Gubar's analysis, achieving such a self-definition is complicated at best, for patriarchal oppression bears heavily on individual women's possibilities for self-identification. Gardiner concludes this brief overview by posing a question that is central to feminist criticism and central, as well, to my consideration of female character and to the problems of representation: "Who is there when a woman says, 'I am'?"[22]

Among feminist critics, the most frequent answer to this question is the reinterpretation of sexual difference as a basis for understanding female selfhood. This is Gardiner's approach as she adapts and revises male identity theory through Nancy Chodorow's "psychoanalytic insights about the differences between male and female personality structures."[23] In identifying the "difference" of female identity as rooted in early childhood experiences, especially in the mother-child dyad, she develops her way of addressing what is distinctive in the female characters of women novelists. Similarly, other feminist critics have found in psychoanalytic theory a way to talk about female "difference" and its "representation" in novels by women. Elizabeth Abel, for example, bases her work on a psychoanalytic model and finds female development in *Mrs. Dalloway* to be "a story of pre-Oedipal attachment and loss";[24] she also sees fusion of identity, in a psychoanalytic model, to be distinctive in women writers' treatment of identity and female friendships.[25] In a somewhat different vein, Annis Pratt, who sees women as precluded from "authenticity" of self[26] and examines women's conflict between being an authentic adult and an acceptable female,[27] rests her analysis on the unconscious and the locating of distinctively female archetypes. This process leads Pratt to see female identity as an interior movement toward spiritual wholeness rather than a claiming of an active selfhood in a social context.[28]

These understandings of female selfhood, and thus of what distinguishes female characters in literature, provide new ways of resisting male-dominant assumptions about female "identity." From them, we can learn to *see* female difference where it has previously been obscured; we can learn to interpret women's lives within the dynamics of what is specifically female. But, like more traditional assumptions and expectations for female behavior, these understandings must also be subject to continual questioning and redefinition. If, instead, they become fixed as new conventions of representation, they lose their efficacy in enacting cultural change. For a new convention of female character, defined by difference, would again interact with assumptions about "different" life plots for women and yield the circular reinforcement of the conventional assumptions of representation: expectations of plot distort female identity; expectations of female identity in difference limit the possible outcomes for characters' lives. As long as it retains its iconic power, the femininity text automatically encodes female difference within male dominance. As Gillian Beer argues in her instructive analysis of the ways both George Eliot and Virginia Woolf are able to escape from narrative determinism, there is a powerful relationship between plot and self, whose "ties" to each other can only be loosened through a number of complex restructurings.[29]

The need, then, is to avoid reifying any notion of female difference, and one powerful enactment of this need can again be found in the capacity of the narrating "I" to subvert novelistic conventions that themselves threaten to become reified. Implicit in the narrator-protagonist's capacity to say "I am" is her capacity both to claim difference and to refuse entrapment within it. As she claims her own voice and interpretation, she preserves the "surplus of humanness" that prevents her from ever being totally represented. Her "I" resists the notion that identity can be complete or that it is a unitary concept bound by her gender. In the contemporary narrating "I," the modernist view of character as perceiver and subjective presence opens onto the possibilities of female character present in the text but not bound by a difference: a narrating "I" who might "name" her own experiences, claim her own perception of femaleness, but still resist a sense of permanent identity in difference.[30]

The narrating "I" is not in any classical sense an "identity" at all. As contemporary autobiographical theory suggests, the act of narration itself resists notions of sameness. Instead of traditional autobiographical notions of personal identity—a "ghostly self which is absolute, ineffable, and timeless"[31]—contemporary theorists, like James Olney, argue that "by its very nature, the self is (like the autobiography . . .) open-ended and incomplete: it is always in process or, more precisely, is itself a process."[32] Identity as sameness cannot be the issue when narrative is a becoming, an open-ended "action-being-made" rather than a record of "life-as-fixed-reality" enacted by the author-ity of retrospective "truth."[33] The narrating "I" claims selfhood not in sameness or "coherence" but in voice, complexity, and experiential interaction.

The female narrator-protagonist, then, is particularly well situated to elaborate the definition of character as perception, subjective presence, and openness to change. As I defined it in my feminist poetics of the novel, drawing on the possibilities of modernist narrative conventions for a "new" representation, character can be seen as process rather than product. A character, I said, is an agent, an empirical being with experiential continuity over time, a proper name, a distinctive set of remembered experiences, and a group of attributes assigned to her or him by other characters and by the perceiving self—but above all, one who acts. Such a definition of character is not gender-specific but rather indicates the way in which a character may represent without succumbing to the conventions of representation, becoming gender-specific without being bound by current definitions of gender. Through enacting such a definition of character and hence of selfhood, a narrator-protagonist can show us new ways to restructure the relationship between plot and self, new ways to answer the question that I, like Gardiner, see as central to feminist literary criticism: "Who is there when a woman says, 'I am'?"

As this book argues in various ways, saying "I am" is itself one of the most powerful expressions of a woman's capacity to resist cultural definition: the narrating "I" both defines herself and subverts entrapment in difference. When we consider how labeling functions to reinforce assumptions about gendered experience, it is not difficult to see the immediate advantage of a narrating "I" for subverting the textual femininity of conventional character. If a female pronoun recurs throughout a text, it repeatedly reminds us of cultural expectations for what it means to be female; it reminds us, inevitably, of the femininity text. The "I," by contrast, reminds us only of a subjective narrating presence, a nameless agent; it asks us to remember only its subjective agency. The "she" can easily lull us into complacent and conventional expectations; the "I" keeps us conscious of possibility and change. Though his analysis denies the mimetic value of a first-person narrator—a value I have been claiming—Roland Barthes's comments on pronouns in *Writing Degree Zero* are pertinent here. In his terms, the third-person pronoun is "a typical novelistic convention; like the narrative tense, it signifies and carries through the action of the novel." Hence when the narration intends to disrupt convention, the narrating "I" is "the most obvious solution." In this view, the narrating "I" both resists the mythification of character and disrupts the novelistic expectation that the third person "he" or "she" is the one who "carries through the action of the novel."[34] As her own narrator, the "I" refuses containment in externally imposed femaleness. As the visible agent, the female "I" refuses objectification and assumes the capacity to act.

But if she is to be also female-specific, she cannot fully relinquish those initial identifying empirical qualities of literary character or human identity: experiential continuity over time and a proper name. In fiction, as in life, the name acts as a marker, and though names may vary or even change, they are an initial and relatively consistent way in which people present themselves to each other and by which literary characters are identifiable to readers. Similarly, experiential continuity over time as a physical being is an empirical given. Both qualities seem essential to a concept of character by which women might "represent" distinctively female experiences. But both also raise particular sets of difficulties, for readers seem able to find female characters plausible only when they match anticipated qualities of the femininity text; distinctively gendered names and physical experiences are both necessary and dangerous to the concept of female identity.

As is immediately evident, the use of name is minimized in a first-person narration. The character gains in the "I" that same capacity of the name as marker of continuity without having to reiterate a specific—and especially a gender-specific—label. This yields the kind of open identity that young protagonists are able to claim in the anonymous "I" without giving up that sense of continuity in name: both Del Jordan in *Lives of Girls and Women* and Claudia MacTeer in *The Bluest Eye* exemplify this capacity for subversion of female expectations without relinquishing experiential continuity. The "I" is also a way for a protagonist to retain visible continuity of character despite changes in name—as in the marriage customs that obscure women's claim to personal continuity through naming. This subversion is particularly evident in the "I" of *The Stone Angel*, who is able in the continuity of her narrating "I" to claim the correlation between her younger self as Hagar Currie and her present self as Hagar Shipley. The narrating "I" subverts the gender-specific implications not only of the textual "she" but also of the conventions of character naming, tied as they are to the conventional expectations of women's lives.

The narrating "I" is thus able to claim an empirical continuity without being confined by expectations of textual femininity. In the first person, the conventions of character are peculiarly susceptible to the reopening I suggested was central to a feminist poetics. But even more crucially, the narrating "I" participates in a redefinition of female selfhood beyond the empirical continuities. Through the subjective focus, the character's identity can be overtly developed as a construct, rather than presented as an invariable given—a *process* evolving through progressive reconstruction of the concepts through which she explains and interacts with the surrounding novelistic world. In looking out through the eyes of the narrator-protagonist, we participate in the recognition that she is not defined by character traits and that her identity is not her destiny, for we experience with her the choice making that is the basis of narrative construction. She can be made present in the act of formulating her interpretations of her world, critiquing the male-dominant paradigms of her novelistic context, and selecting female-specific information by which to redefine those paradigms. In choosing and interpreting, she is visibly a character in process.

As a character in process, the narrating "I" is not bound by character traits but instead redefines the premises of character representation: she is made present through suggested attributes, explanatory hypotheses about identity rather than unchanging qualities. Her narration is itself the process of ceaseless self-definition, the dynamic interaction between her hypotheses about who she is and her experience as she is living it. As a formulation of explanatory possibilities, self-narration calls upon a recognition that the self of the narrator is able to change and thus opens new ways of understanding female experience and female identity. This is the cognitive process that psychologist Ulric Neisser identifies in a particularly apt series of equations: "*Consciousness undergoes changes* throughout the course of life because we learn to *pick up new sorts of information in new ways.* These processes of change are called *cognitive development* in some contexts and *perceptual learning* in others; in political situations they have recently been called *consciousness raising.*"[35] As an expression of this ability to sort and interpret information differently, self-narration is able to participate in the representation of women without being bound by the premises of representation. In proposing that we alter the conventions of character as a basis for defining the self in process, I am not, then, suggesting the view present in Gardiner's hypothesis that "female identity is a process."[36] Rather, I am suggesting that we see all human identity as processual and that the understanding of self or character as process not only has peculiar usefulness for a feminist literary criticism but is especially available in a first-person narrative voice.

Because gender schemata are among the most culturally entrenched, they have been primary in the traditional definitions of character by traits. But when a narrator-protagonist is shown in the narrative act of interpreting herself and her experiences through the interaction of schemata and information, she gains a special ability to resist entrapment in a gender schema.[37] For she is able to examine her gender-specific identity as a hypothesis like her other narrative hypotheses and hence, like all hypotheses, as subject to change. Because she is engaged in the act of constructing meaning, she is able to assess her gender-specific experiences without reifying her identity in its current gender construction.[38] Through acting as her own narrator, she is able to make present a view of female selfhood as a conscious being making interpretive choices in interaction with available information and available schemata, only one of which is the cultural definition of femininity.

Those schemata, as I have said, are the attributes assigned to the self: in literary characterization, as in human existence, it is crucial to remember that these *are* attributions. Because the self as narrator is actively engaged in the attribution process, she is a continual reminder of the self as process, existing in interaction with a social context that attributes characteristics as explanatory hypotheses, not as fixed and defining traits. As I said in my discussion of character in chapter 2, the modernist recognition that "reality" is always in part a function of interpretation made apparent that character traits are always the function of an agent, not the function of an immutable truth. In Proust's words: "even in the most insignificant details of our daily life, none of us can be said to constitute a material whole, which is identical for everyone, and need only be turned up like a page in an account-book or the record of a will; our social personality is created by the thoughts of other people."[39] The act of seeing experience through the narrator's eyes is a reminder of the instability of human identity. As the narrating self is presented in process, refusing to be product, she reopens the conventions of female character and the assumptions by which women have been confined to a single social personality bounded by femininity.

Memory, too, can be seen to participate in a renewed concept of character as well as plot. A character acquires substance in part through a distinctive set of remembered experiences. But for a first-person narrator, these remembered experiences can readily become a resource for change rather than a defined and fixed personal history. Information from a personal past functions to specify selfhood and participate in a sense of continuity; everyone has a distinctive store of past experiences, which we use to specify, and from which we draw, in the interpretive interactions with our self-schemata. But as with current information, these memories are also subject to redefinition according to their place in an interpretive schema. Psychoanalyst Roy Schafer says that our self-histories change as a function of the questions we put to our past;[40] that is, the past is, in part, a function of the interpretive framework by which we sort through remembered information. Similarly, information from the past may be recalled to alter a current interpretive schema.

Because a narrating "I" can be both agent and text of her own novel, she has a special capacity—and even need—to reopen the narrative expectations for the power of memory in a character's identity. The dynamic interaction of present and past is thus often central to first-person novels and indicative of their capacity to reveal character as process. The narrator of Christa Wolf's *A Model Childhood*, who provides an intriguing example of this capacity, comments on the dynamic interaction between past and present: "The present intrudes upon remembrance, today becomes the last day of the past. Yet we would suffer continuous estrangement from ourselves if it weren't for the memory of ourselves." Slightly later she speaks of memory as "a process" and says, "an unused memory gets lost, ceases to exist, dissolves into nothing—an alarming thought."[41] In the act of narration, memory both specifies the sense of self and shifts in response to present experiences and concerns.

I am not suggesting, as some feminist critics do, that the forms of female memory are likely to differ from the forms of male memory.[42] Rather, I am suggesting that memory *operates* similarly in male and female, as a part of the ongoing construction of self, but that gender will be implicated in the *effects* of that process. When gender-specific self-perceptions are used to interpret remembered experience, memory takes shape in interaction with notions of gender. When present experiences and concerns suggest altered notions of gender and self, memory inevitably changes as well and thus becomes a renewable resource for self-interpretation—at least insofar as specific memories are not allowed, in Wolf's terms, to "dissolve into nothing" by being totally "unused." Because first-person narration foregrounds the capacity of memory to evolve in interaction with subsequent thought and experience, it can enact female selfhood in the process of renewal, interpreting what is female-specific without being fixed either by a unitary definition of femaleness or by an incomplete interpretation of past experience.

Consciousness and choice in a social context thus center the idea of self as process and the idea of the narrating "I": the formulations of interpretive schemata for one's own experience and behavior and the social participation in such formulation. These are the qualities that in some sense are defining of human beings: in existentialist terms, to be human is to go "beyond a situation," to be defined by what one makes of the given conditions.[43] Thus the emphasis on consciousness and choice becomes a part of the overall defining quality of my original definition of character and self: one who *acts*. To choose is itself an action and to be able to choose is the decisive characteristic of selfhood. Again in existentialist terms, to be human is to claim one's identity in *praxis,* in the projects, goals, and actions taken consciously toward the future.[44] From the point of view of cognitive psychology, the person experiences her- or himself in activity, in the processes of decision making. And from a moral developmental point of view, morality consists in "the exercise of choice and the willingness to accept responsibility for that choice."[45] Choices, of course, are always made in a context, but they are made.[46]

Such a definition of self, made available in the narrating "I," is not specific to women but can be enabling to women, opening the possibility of self-definition, the capacity to reconceptualize both experience and interpretive framework, the claiming of self-defined action as a way of eluding some of the constraints of an oppressive social context. This, as I see it, is the overall significance of first-person narration in novels by women: through the heightened consciousness and the narrative implementation of choice, the female narrator is redefining our conventional expectations for female character and, through them, for women's lives.

IV

Most of my discussion in this chapter has centered in the capacity of first-person narration to reshape broad novelistic conventions and thereby to represent women's lives while subverting the cultural expectations on which representation has historically been based. I want now to conclude by identifying a few of the specific areas in which a narrator-protagonist can develop new ways of understanding her life, new interpretive paradigms by which to claim female experiences in resistance to the femininity text. Refusing the "she" of male narrative encoding, such protagonists can reincorporate their femaleness into a narrative "I" in a schema that refuses the dichotomies of assigned "male" and "female" qualities.

Consider, first, how the biological sexual "polarity" of male and female grounds the femininity text: women *are* their bodies, their capacity for pregnancy and their sexual biological life stage. The female self examining her own experiences through such a paradigm feels trapped in her own body. Martha Quest, for example, is horrified at the anticipation of damage to her body through experiences of adult womanhood and thus feels alienated from any physical selfhood. Worse still is the perception that female biology is an *inescapable* liability, as it provides a necessary "identity." In the opening chapter of her autobiography, Maxine Hong Kingston reveals this threat to self-definition through her mother's illustrative story of a nameless aunt, denied identity or presence in the family history because of her illegitimate pregnancy. Kingston's mother's warning defines the liability of femaleness: "Now that you have started to menstruate, what happened to her could happen to you."[47] By such definitions, biological femaleness is a negation, a constraint, and an encompassing identity.[48]

But when, on the other hand, women shift the interpretive schema and see their physical capacities as only one explanatory framework—and one over which they themselves have some control—they need no longer be contained by a vision of biological vulnerability. In *A Proper Marriage,* as long as Douglas is absent, Martha is able to interpret pregnancy and motherhood as experiential possibilities rather than defining traits. This process is, in fact, *only* possible in Douglas's absence; Martha has far more difficulty even *experiencing* motherhood apart from its patriarchal institutionalization when Douglas returns. Martha's embeddedness in an omniscient narrative underlines the fragility of her self-definition: without narrative control, she lacks that basic sense of agency by which she might reinforce the agency achieved in experiential motherhood. In the end, she can only retain a sense of her self, still fragilely, by leaving the marriage and the imposition of identity—biological and relational—that marriage and motherhood enforce on her.[49]

Because Kingston's fuller reinterpretation of female sexuality is a part of her claiming narrative control over her own life, it has more lasting implications for resisting the cultural negations of biological femaleness while still valuing female "sexuality." In giving identity and story to the "no name woman" at the outset of her autobiography, she initiates the process of claiming narrative control over her own life; through her aunt she also gains access to a female heritage. In creating her aunt's story, she reaches both interpretive understanding and "ancestral help."[50] Her narrative control reinforces her reinterpretation of female biology.

Similarly, in *The Bluest Eye,* Claudia MacTeer refuses to place the physical realities of Pecola Breedlove's first menstrual period within the femininity text and instead makes them a part of the story of the three young girls' shared awe at coming of age. This experience, then, becomes a crucial marker in the story of their interwoven lives, acknowledged at the end by the symbolic seeds that Claudia and Frieda plant for Pecola's baby. Through her overall narrative construction, Claudia is able to claim those physical facts as simultaneously a part of Pecola's destruction and her own growth in shared female identity. By contrast, those same originating facts could scarcely be named in the culturally expected story of female coming of age, or could only be named as one step in the enclosing plot of femininity as it moves toward a limited womanhood. Under such alternative constructions of femaleness, biology is *not* destiny; it is, instead, one feature of an evolving selfhood and therefore subject to interpretive redefinition.

Like the cultural definition of female biology, the cultural definition of women through external appearance also threatens to contain and limit female selfhood, to prevent female autonomy. As Gilbert and Gubar see it, this " 'killing' of oneself into an art object—the pruning and preening, the mirror madness . . . —all this testifies to the efforts women have expended not just trying to be angels but trying *not* to become female monsters"[51]—trying not, that is, to exhibit culturally unacceptable autonomous control over self-definition. The obsession of the novel form with beautiful heroines is a case in point, as is the cultural anticipation that women will find narcissistic identity in mirrors and self-adornment. But the self as actor—as her own interpretive agent—is able to use mirror reflections and physical appearance differently. This renewal is the basis of two responses to be examined more fully in chapter 5: Violet Clay's comparison of psychological changes in herself as she compares her current reflection with a remembered one, and Hagar Shipley's ability to claim continuing selfhood in her eyes rather than in the physical negations of her aging body. Such an eluding of self-definition in physical appearance requires a resistance to the mirror of cultural objectification, a resistance that is assisted by first-person narration: external appearance is far less significant when one is looking out through subjective eyes rather than looking on through the claim to "objective" description.

To reconceptualize the place of biological experiences and physical appearance in one's own sense of self is an almost automatic effect of claiming one's own subjectivity: reading the subtext of experience, one recognizes the complexity that falls outside such cultural definitions. To tell one's own story yields a definition of self in resistance to external objectification. Though it is not a simple matter to reconceptualize biological experiences of femaleness, the recognition of personal agency in the telling of those experiences itself provides an initial reconceptualization and the basis for further rethinking.

Through claiming the agency of self-narration, protagonists can also take the social facts of female experience and redefine them as part of a different narrative configuration. Without her own narrative voice, Hagar Shipley might, for example, be confined within the cultural definition of her social experience; her lifelong anger and rebellion against the men in her life could easily be construed as part of the anticipated culture text for angry old women—the monstrous side of femininity. Instead, as Hagar tells her own story, she gives these same social facts a place in her story of female agency as she actively rejects the oppressive structures of her male-dominated world and reshapes her present selfhood. Similarly, in one reading of her life, Hagar's marriage to Brampton Shipley is "caused by" her willful rebellion against her father. But the redefinition of that event in the story of her developing awareness of her own agency shows a causal pattern connected to her current claiming of autonomous self-nomination. The information surrounding the fact of her marriage focuses an alternative causal understanding of the event both for her and for readers of the novel.

The broader definition of femaleness as relational and expressive is more problematic, for such a view is more likely to be integrated as a positive component of a woman's personal sense of self, as is evident in the claims made by feminist identity theorists. Indeed, some psychologists have found that women's self-esteem in general is no lower than men's because it is based in qualities that are culturally "appropriate" to women; they have also found that women in general have strong affiliative needs.[52] The problem in reconceptualizing the gender schema based in women's relational capacities, then, derives from the cultural view of dichotomized sex roles: "male" instrumentality and "female" expressiveness. This artificial polarization of human qualities is, in fact, the basis of the culturally imposed conflict between femaleness and autonomy with which I have been centrally concerned. But femaleness, even more than in biology and appearance, finds its positive cultural definition in the psychological qualities often associated with biological femaleness: nurturance, warmth, care, relationality. And so the redefinition of selfhood to include these qualities without being limited to them is both particularly difficult and particularly important.

Because this process is so complex, I will not here offer brief illustrations of how first-person narration contributes to overcoming the conflict between relationality and autonomy: that will be the major burden of the analyses in the next three chapters. For now I want only to suggest how the narrating "I" achieves this general ability. As it is freed from the limiting construct of permanent essence, the "I" effects an initial openness to multiplicity and hence an initial claim to multiple capacities. When the definition of self is constructed internally and multiply rather than externally and singly, her narration need not be defined by traits of nurturance *or* strength but can be instead an expressed capacity for both nurturance *and* agency, existing simultaneously. Because narrative enacts a contextual understanding of experience, a narrator can actively examine the enriching possibilities of human relationship without being bound by a concept of self-in-relationship as the definition of her femaleness. Through self-narration she can engage her understanding of friends, family, and lovers as a part of her self-interpretation without merging her "identity" with other people. Rather than being conceptualized as mutually exclusive traits, nurturance and autonomy are reconceptualized—through narrative itself—as mutually supportive capacities.

A culturally imposed fragmentation, then, loses power as the protagonist gains narrative power over the interpretation of multiplicity, sometimes even through deliberate self-fragmentation. The structural enactment of fragmentation by Jane Gray in *The Waterfall* and Anna Wulf in *The Golden Notebook* is a particularly vivid expression of this overtly claimed self-fragmentation as a means toward complex human wholeness. Escaping entrapment in the false wholeness of a culturally defined gender identity, Jane and Anna and similar protagonists show how a narrating "I" can go beyond a selfhood of diffusion and unmergeable multiplicity through learning to recognize her own agency in multiple roles and in complex self-interpretation. This, too, yields a wholeness that can incorporate both nurturance and autonomy.

Jerome Bruner talks of "the epistemologically impossible question, 'who am I?'" and responds, "there are many selves in a character."[53] Contemporary self theory indicates that everyone has a sense of "multiple selves" and that such a notion "represents a means of organizing one's overall self-concept"; furthermore, the "association of different self-views with different roles . . . represents *differentiation* rather than inconsistency."[54] Recent studies of women's feelings of "well-being" indicate, as well, that "the involvement in multiple roles" strengthens rather than undermines well-being.[55] The crucial narrative recognition builds on such perceptions and derives from the further knowledge that no list of roles, no quantity of sociohistorical categories, no number of traits can fully contain the complexity of human selfhood. There always remains, in Bakhtin's phrase, that "surplus of humanness" and there always remains the possibility of additional strengths and interpretations. With this knowledge, the narrative recognition of multiple selfhood—the claiming of personal self-definition through various explanatory hypotheses and roles—becomes a positive function of women's self-narration rather than a negative response to patriarchal oppression. It becomes a way to use the surplus of humanness to develop new sociohistorical categories, new understandings of women's lives.

The first-person narrator thus has a special capacity to subvert the expectations of a textual "she" and to open new possibilities for the representation of women's lives. She becomes the authority over her own experience as she is the agent of its interpretation; she opens new possibilities for conceptualizing her personal experiences, past and present, as they move toward the future. In the narrative process, we can see her actively rejecting received cultural schemata for her own experience through the dynamic integration of newly perceived experience into reformulated schemata. In an essay on Malcolm X as black autobiographer, Paul John Eakin describes a similar process of discarding "shapes for a life that are transmitted by the culture," in order in that "very process . . . to structure an apparently shapeless experience."[56] For women, the discarding of such "given" shapes involves the active process of using lived experience *as women* to structure new conceptualizations of what it means to be a woman. The goal identified by Jean Baker Miller—"feeling effective and free along with feeling intense connections with other people"[57]—is claimed in the process of narrating female experience, as narration becomes an active re-cognition of femaleness itself.

In giving their protagonists the right to speak in their own voices, women writers thus give them not only the capacity to tell their own stories; they give them also the interpretive power over their own reality and self-definition. The narration of the self resists the historical silencing of women's voices, develops new capacities for representation, and restores the interpretive processes to women's own agency. The speaking "I" claims her identity in process; in becoming the interpreter of her own experience, she also claims both her femaleness and her autonomous self-definition. Her narrating voice becomes her capacity for human wholeness in complexity and change.

CHAPTER 4

Growing Up Female: *Lives of Girls and Women* and *The Bluest Eye*

Narrative form has a special place in the growing-up process. On the one hand, storytelling seems particularly important to children as they leave behind the relatively embedded identity of childhood and develop a sense of self in a larger social context; as a process of contextual understanding, personal narrative is one of the ways children identify who they are and how they relate to the culture of which they are a part. But stories are, on the other hand, a primary tool of the culture itself, a way in which socialization takes place and a way in which a child learns the culturally defined roles of adulthood. In the growing-up process, narrative is both a powerful cultural tool for reinforcing the status quo and a powerful personal tool for shaping individual identity.

The implications for a growing girl are clear: she needs stories to help interpret her life and she needs to resist the patterns of the known stories, which define femininity as the goal of her growth. In a novel of growing up female, the dual need of female narrative both to represent and to subvert, then, has double urgency: not only the need for a recharacterization of female experience but also the need for a reinterpretation of narrative to resist rather than confirm the socialization process. Like the general need to represent while resisting the premises of representation, this need can be effectively met in those novels in which a narrator-protagonist has claimed control over the telling and interpreting of her own experience. As her own narrator, she can explicitly examine the destructive power of the femininity text into which she is supposed to be growing and then redefine the premises of representation in order to elude its power. Her narrating "I" itself becomes her ability to grow up in full complexity.

But even this process is not straightforward, and to explain why it cannot be, I want to begin my consideration of the growing-up novel with a consideration of its traditional form: the *Bildungsroman* as it both appeals to the need for representation and suggests why subversion is necessary. In the tradition of novelistic representation, the *Bildungsroman* has a central place. Its assumptions are the assumptions of realism: that "life" can be characterized in literature, that the patterns and possibilities of human experience are responsive to narrative treatment, that a character can represent human possibility and be understood through the interaction of individual choices and goals with the material realities of a social context. These assumptions are crucial to a novelistic representation of women's lives. But because we also know that "representation" easily assumes a congruence with present cultural values, it is not hard to see that women writers seeking new narrative understanding of the process of growing up must also resist the premises of *Bildungsroman* representation. A *Bildungsroman* that unquestioningly follows the "life" premises of its traditional patterns is very likely to show its protagonist succumbing to the cultural norms about adult womanhood: to grow up female within such a pattern is to succumb to the femininity text, to grow into the enclosing grid of the known social expectations. In order to resist such entrapment, a *Bildungsroman* seeking new definitions of female identity in a social context must also subvert the cultural assumptions about growing up female.

Ending as they do in the paradigmatic conclusions of death and marriage, *The Mill on the Floss* and *Martha Quest* are apt examples of the problems of a female *Bildungsroman* and its relationship to sexual ideology. For the process of growing up and attempting to find an appropriate adult role in a social context centers the structure of both novels, as it does the traditional *Bildungsroman*. But the traditional *Bildungsroman* is a male form, and the fates of Maggie Tulliver and Martha Quest indicate why this is so: there are few appropriate adult roles for women to grow into. As the traditional constraints on the female self focus in the opposition between femaleness and autonomy, so the *Bildungsroman*'s sense of linear development toward maturity is impossible when maturity itself forces a choice between becoming progenitive woman and becoming autonomous individual. As Patricia Meyer Spacks has observed, "the process of growing up, for a girl, is one of being curbed and tamed, of losing power."[1]

Nevertheless, the *Bildungsroman* is a form of particular interest to a feminist literary criticism. As a blatantly realistic form, modeled on biography or autobiography, it has a decided place for the experiential base of feminist criticism. And as a dynamic form, committed to the growth of a strong individual, it has a clear relevance to the urgency of female self-definition. Ellen Morgan suggests that the reason the form has been male is that "women have tended to be viewed traditionally as static rather than dynamic . . . ," but also suggests that the form is particularly useful to neofeminist novelists who want to offer strong positive images for women.[2] Thus the claiming of a focus on active expression of female selfhood in a social context would seem to be precisely the feminist potential of the form.

A recent collection of feminist essays on the *Bildungsroman* indicates both the continuing interest and the continuing difficulty of the form for feminist critics. *The Voyage In: Fictions of Female Development* shows the interest by its very existence but by the title immediately shows the difficulty of claiming a female identity in a social context. The paradigmatic novel used in the editors' introduction is, appropriately, Virginia Woolf's *The Voyage Out*, which despite its title is precisely a "voyage in," as Rachel, in effect, dies rather than marry.[3] Many of the essays in the volume similarly focus on the inner development of a self that must withdraw from a negating social context rather than find a place in it. The problem of self in society remains a problem.

The central goal for the *Bildungsroman* follows from Wilhelm Meister's life pattern: the development of self toward a balance between the ideal inner self and the adaptation required by the external world—what Jerome Buckley calls "accommodation to the modern world"[4] and what Georg Lukacs calls "reconciliation between interiority and reality."[5] In attempting to place the female *Bildungsroman* in the context of a strongly male tradition, the editors of *The Voyage In* develop a working definition that both correlates with this classic pattern and allows for specifically female development.

... belief in a coherent self (although not necessarily an autonomous one); faith in the possibility of development (although change may be frustrated, may occur at different stages and rates, and may be concealed in the narrative); insistence on a time span in which development occurs (although the time span may exist only in memory); and emphasis on social context (even as an adversary).[6]

This proves to be a useful definition, especially for the novelistic characterization of women's containment within patriarchal structures. But it may also indicate why the female *Bildungsroman* almost inevitably yields the destruction of its protagonist. For if the goal is the working out of a relationship between a coherent self and a developmental progression within a relatively fixed context, then women *will*, I think, collide with those expectations: the fixed social context can make no accommodation to a coherent female identity who is other than traditionally feminine.

As Woolf's first novel, *The Voyage Out* not only enacts this collision, but also indicates through its nascent modernism the human tension underlying the *Bildungsroman* form. Rachel acts out the novelistic choice between marriage and death, but she also reveals the inner dilemma that choice represents. In her resistance to Terence's jealousy of her inner autonomy, she reaches a temporary recognition: "she wanted many more things than the love of one human being—the sea, the sky. . . . she could not possibly want only one human being."[7] But shortly she decides that love, in its impersonality, is what can give her the larger world: "it was love that made her understand this, for she had never felt this independence, this calm, and this certainty until she fell in love with him, and perhaps this too was love. She wanted nothing else."[8] In both formulations of what she wants, she identifies the human need to be both single and relational, autonomous and in context—the need, in fact, that lies behind the *Bildungsroman* form. But, finally, in the form she gives both needs, she retreats inward: her expansion is a spiritual or metaphysical expansion; her independence is an inactivity. Rachel is enacting the impossibility of living fully in a world that denies meaningful action to women, and in doing so she reminds us not only that social constraints impose themselves, but also that the retreat inward is only a *reaction*, not a sufficient action.

Carol Gilligan offers a useful formulation of the problem that finally kills Rachel and that bounds the possibilities of selfhood for all human beings: "the paradoxical truths of human experience—that we know ourselves as separate only insofar as we live in connection with others, and that we experience relationship only insofar as we differentiate other from self."[9] Similarly Robert Kegan places the "lifelong tension" between autonomy and inclusion at the center of his view of human development.[10] The problem, then, is a human one, distorted for women by their confinement to *private* relational identity and their being denied autonomous selfhood in a larger social context; and the need is the human need for autonomous self-definition in a context that allows for private relationships but is not confined to them.

In what is to me the most nearly successful female resolution of this tension in the nineteenth-century novel, *Jane Eyre* further defines the parameters of the problem. Though the repressions that operate in all nineteenth-century fiction by women can be identified here as well—especially in the use of Bertha as double to enact Jane's anger and sexuality[11]—Jane shows most fully the possibility of a strong sense of self, a knowledge of social context, and the possibilities of a heterosexual relationship. She does this, as the editors of *The Voyage In* point out, by reaching "a balance between the developmental tensions of separation and relationship."[12] And she does it in continued resistance to external definitions of her identity. Initially, as Rochester proposes marriage to her, she insists: "I am a free human being";[13] then, playfully, during preparations for marriage: "I am not an angel . . . I will be myself" (p. 262); and then, departing from the false marriage she will not accept: "*I* care for myself. The more solitary, the more friendless, the more unsustained I am, the more I will respect myself" (p. 318). Her final marriage to Rochester, she tells us, is "perfect concord" because "I am my husband's life as fully as he is mine" (p. 454). We believe in the equality of this marriage in large share because we have experienced with Jane the long periods prior to her knowing Rochester and after her leaving Thornfield in which she is absolutely alone and self-sustaining. We also believe because we remember that Jane has always felt the need to be active and productive and now has a context for that need. We *know* she has an autonomous selfhood and we *know* she cannot live without feeling useful. By the end of the novel, Rochester provides both the useful outlet for her capacities and the willingness to recognize her strengths.

Such a life has its confinements: Ferndean is isolated and Jane's capacities must finally *all* be used in traditionally female relational activities. Her further connections—in the ongoing relationships with St. John, Diana, and Mary Rivers—are also limited to personal relational expressions. But clearly in the social framework in which *Jane Eyre* takes place, Jane has accomplished the most satisfactory balance between inclusion and autonomy that was available to her.

One of the special interests of *Jane Eyre* is its use of first-person narrative voice, and I think it is not an accidental choice for the development of an autonomous female character. In telling her own story, Jane can elude many of the external definitions of femaleness and claim immediately the agency of the narrative act. She uses narrative self-consciousness, through the internal use of tales to interpret experience and the overt concerns with memory and narrative time, to loosen the power of formal compulsions. And she makes use of the discursive possibilities of the form to address the reader and characterize her inner longings directly and powerfully, as in the famous outburst of anger.

> It is in vain to say that human beings ought to be satisfied with tranquility: they must have action. . . . Women are supposed to be very calm generally but women feel just as men feel; they need exercise for their faculties, and a field for their efforts as much as their brothers do; they suffer from too rigid a constraint, too absolute a stagnation, precisely as men would suffer. (Pp. 112–13)

She even reminds us of the parallel between the form in which she writes and the forms of unmet desire: "to open my inward ear to a tale that was never ended—a tale my imagination created and narrated continuously; quickened with all of incident, life, fire, feeling, that I desired and had not in my actual existence" (p. 112).

Thus the first-person voice implements her fundamental agency and identifies the complexities of her needs that lie outside the bounds of cultural expectations for women. And yet, in the end, she has instead met those cultural expectations and withdrawn from the larger world in which she might "exercise [her] faculties." I have already indicated that this compromise was a function of the social context of the novel, but I want now to hypothesize that the narrative form in which Brontë was working also interacted with social context as reinforcement, as well as in resistance. In doing so, I suggest two possible forces in that interaction: the linear structure of the narrative and the insistence on a firm and consistent identity. Though Jane tells her own story, she tells it from a definite beginning and toward a conclusion: if the beginning in isolation is to reach an acceptable balance with inclusion, the paradigmatic goal of the narrative will be marriage. And as Jane's identity is formed in initial resistance, it persists as the single coherent self, not open to multiple self-definitions or multiple roles. The final choice is thus guided into the form of either/or—isolation or marriage—and marriage, particularly "equal marriage," identifies the best available choice.[14]

My purpose here is not an extended analysis of *Jane Eyre* but an indication of problems and possibilities in a novel of female development. I use *The Voyage Out* and *Jane Eyre*—and recall *The Mill on the Floss* and *Martha Quest*—only to identify some of the issues in a female *Bildungsroman* in order to introduce some alternatives by which women novelists have used the first-person voice of their protagonists to break down further the confining expectations of both narrative and life. Beyond *The Mill on the Floss* and *Martha Quest*, beyond *The Voyage Out* and even beyond *Jane Eyre*, the first-person narrative process can help to shape female selfhood in a social context *not* bounded by traditional relational activities of marriage and motherhood. Narrative process itself offers one way to move beyond the *Bildungsroman* toward the enactment of the autonomous female self in society: through a disruption of linear form and a refusal of coherent identity, the narrative process becomes a still more positive enactment of agency.

I

As a growing-up novel, Alice Munro's *Lives of Girls and Women* can easily be seen in the *Bildungsroman* tradition. Indeed a number of critics do just that and at least one critic places it within a more narrowly defined strain of the *Bildungsroman*, calling it "a *kunstlerroman*" and comparing it to James Joyce's *A Portrait of the Artist as a Young Man*.[15] The two novels do have some interesting parallels. But within a genuine *Bildungsroman* tradition of coherent selfhood, Del's experiences in growing up female would be likely to force her sense of "identity" into a dichotomous choice between female selfhood and "artist" selfhood. I do not mean that Stephen Dedalus's identity omits address to other factors in his youth—religion, education, sexuality—nor do I mean that Joyce is neglecting modernist perceptions about subjectivity. What I do mean is that Stephen is able to shape his coming of age in relation to a relatively single-minded goal; because it embraces cultural notions of masculinity, his identity as artist does not preclude his identity as an adult male. Del Jordan, by contrast, must work toward her goal as an aspiring artist in a more circuitous way in order not to relinquish her female identity in attaining her artistic identity. She accomplishes this culturally denied task through self-narration, based on the recognition of selfhood in process and the centrality of interpretive perception.

In the course of her narrative, Del offers two particularly revealing statements about her sense of self, both of which identify an unwillingness to accept a fixed identity. Both are offered in a context of male/female contrast but neither contains her within her femaleness. In contrasting herself with Jerry Storey, she says, "he was what he seemed. I, whose natural boundaries were so much more ambiguous, who soaked up protective coloration wherever it might be found, began to see that it might be restful to be like Jerry."[16] Del's chameleonlike identity bears clear similarity to the idea of women's weak ego boundaries: the relationality that leads women to define themselves contextually rather than independently and to include in their identities a greater share of concern for those around them. But Del's *use* of this identity gives it a different dimension from its definition in psychoanalytic terms or in standard views of women's lack of "coherent self." For Del, this variable identity is a pragmatic response to her environment, a survival technique, rather than an internalized given. She is, in fact, acting much as Alice Munro says she herself did: "when I was growing up, I always operated in disguises, feeling if I do to a certain point what the world expects of me, then they'll leave me alone, and I can do my work."[17] Del's "protective coloration" is just that—protective—and makes possible her ongoing sense of self as a person who interprets her world and *acts* within her environmental context.

In the preceding section of the novel, titled as the novel itself is, Del articulates a more assertive version of herself as actor. This time the gender-based contrast is reversed and we can see more overtly the centrality of action, choice, and progression in her developing selfhood. The context is a conversation with her mother centered in the mother's assertion: "There is a change coming I think in the lives of girls and women" (p. 146). The mother is arguing, as she does through her own life choices, the need for women to have "lives of our own" rather than existing exclusively in "connection with men" (p. 146). But the mother's advice, like her life model, is conflicting: she assumes that Del will want children but argues that for a woman to have a life of her own, she must in effect give up relationships with men—give up, at any rate, an active sexual life, in order not to be "distracted, over a man" (p. 147). Del's response is complicated by her own conflicting feelings about her mother, but she takes from the conversation a view of herself in resistance to her mother's either/or choice between sexuality and independence. Unwilling to give up either "using her brains" or her sexuality, she rejects the advice.

> I felt that it was not so different from all the other advice handed out to women, to girls, advice that assumed being female made you damageable, that a certain amount of carefulness and solemn fuss and self-protection were called for, whereas men were supposed to be able to go out and take on all kinds of experiences and shuck off what they didn't want and come back proud. Without even thinking about it, I had decided to do the same. (P. 147)

This statement provides a powerful rationale for her flexibility: to test the boundaries of experience and continue to act strongly for oneself. Her chameleonlike identity is, then, not a function of weak ego boundaries or self-protection in response to being "damageable," but rather an assertion of her capacity to act for herself. Though her flexible sense of self—her assertion of a self in process—takes what seems to be a traditionally female form, she has in some ways modeled it on her view of masculine independence in order to claim a right to a self-defined identity as both female and autonomous.

This view of herself both draws on and distinguishes her from her perceptions of other women in the novel. Her view of her mother, for example and most centrally, is multiple rather than single and includes the present participation of her mother's past: "Inside that self we knew, which might at times appear blurred a bit, or side-tracked, she kept her younger selves strenuous and hopeful; scenes from the past were liable to pop up any time, like lantern slides, against the cluttered fabric of the present" (p. 62). These recognitions of past selves or self-constructs are often presented in the form of stories: narrative explanations of the personal past become narrative assessments of past selfhood. As both image and story, they are a way to claim previous interpretations of experience, but they are also a way to help interpret the present. The key for Del, however, is always to recognize them as constructions based on perception; the arrival of the mother's brother Bill in his current identity threatens her whole narrative structure of the past. Del says, "I kept looking at him, trying to pull that boy out of the yellowish man. But I could not find him there" (p. 74). The collision of past identity with present presentation is reinforced by the different stories Bill tells of their mother and their childhood. The stories do not cohere into an identifiable structure for the past, just as Bill's presence in his sister's memory does not mesh with his presence in her current home. Del's recognition that this is so and her knowledge that previous self-conceptualizations act as interpretive lenses on the present keeps her continually aware of the self as multiply defined.

The recognition that her mother is not just one thing gives initial grounding to Del's further recognition that she is both like her mother and not like her—a recognition that is important to most daughters as they develop a sense of what it is to be female. She can see her mother from her aunts' point of view as a "wild-woman" (p. 54) at the same time that she recognizes her mother's vulnerability in her commitments to her own activities and her attempts to explain and understand the external world. Del's perspective makes her want both "to repudiate her" and "to shield her" (p. 54); but more than that it makes her aware of her mother's conflicting identities as a woman within a social context. The knowledge Del reaches—"I myself was not so different from my mother, but concealed it, knowing what dangers there were" (p. 68)—is a preparation for reassessing her possibilities for herself living as a woman in a social context and a necessary ingredient in her social adaptability. She sees that the choices her mother has made have given her "her virginal brusqueness, her innocence" (p. 150) and knows that she will need to reach a different accommodation to her social environment, at the same time that she values her mother's share in her own identity.

The growing recognition of human complexity and change is furthered by Del's response to Miss Farris's suicide. Del must first separate her former teacher from her embeddedness in the teacher role and realize that Miss Farris had a life of her own that went on even after Del no longer knew her. The suicide also reminds Del of the multiple and conflicting hypotheses by which people attempt to interpret other people: hypotheses that are always based on partial knowledge and cannot adequately contain the complexity of anyone's lived experience. Del thinks back through her own discontinuous images of Miss Farris and concludes: "Though there is no plausible way of hanging those pictures together—if the last one is true then must it not alter the others?—they are going to have to stay together now" (p. 118). In recognizing that the images cannot cohere, Del is simultaneously recognizing the partialness of perception and the complexity of selfhood; she is also taking note of her own changing interaction with her experience. But above all, she is rejecting a single definition of Miss Farris as a woman devastated by loss of love and, in this rejection, rejects also the univocal definition of female identity as a function of sexual relationships.

This multidimensional view of self is crucial to Del's ability to develop as both aspiring artist and maturing female, seeking simultaneously a strong sense of herself and her capacity to belong in a social environment. She finds further support for such possibilities in the relationship she has to the projected media of her aspirations: words and stories. From her early childhood experiences, Del has a palpable sense of language, creating immediate and vivid mental pictures in response to unknown words: quicksand, confused mentally with quicksilver, becomes "a dry-liquid roll" (p. 2); birth canal becomes "a straight-banked river of blood" (pp. 33–34). The jarring of her literal images against her actual perceptions of experience makes reality both more vivid and less stable. Her "secret pleasure" in the "poetic flow of words" (p. 130) and her interest in rhyming also both open and affirm the relationship of language to experiential perception.

But the process of naming becomes also a way of knowing and controlling experience. When her Uncle Craig dies, she creates the literal image of heart attack: "an explosion, like fireworks going off, shooting sticks of light in all directions, shooting a little ball of light—that was Uncle Craig's heart, or his soul—high into the air, where it tumbled and went out" (p. 39). And then she proceeds to seek specific details of his death: "I wanted to know. There is no protection, unless it is in knowing. I wanted death pinned down and isolated behind a wall of particular facts and circumstances, not floating around loose, ignored but powerful, waiting to get in anywhere" (p. 39). Thus the process of naming becomes a way of actualizing and controlling experience.

Such a relationship with language has particular importance for her sense of being female. She is startled at the conflict between image and reality when her mother calls Madeleine a "bride"— "Her use of the word *bride* was startling, evoking as it did long white veils, flowers, celebration, not thought of here" (p. 13)—and thus early recognizes the tension between cultural identifications of women and their actual experiences. But she also feels the need to name and therefore claim as actual her own experiences with being female: witness, for example, her junior high school conversations with Naomi about menstruation and their later conversations about sexual intercourse and birth control. Even her wish to tell her mother about the "blood on the ground" (p. 189) after her own sexual initiation (though she pretends it has another source) is a part of this process of using language to externalize and control experience.

These uses of naming are then central in her uses of stories. As a child she encounters Madeleine's fury and wishes to "take this scene back to tell at home" (p. 15) and then finally joins the others in remembering Madeleine "like a story," almost like something "made up" (p. 23), but somehow integrated into their lives as their narrative version of her. Later, when as an adolescent Del is induced to watch Mr. Chamberlain's exhibitionist masturbation, she longs for the relief of making it into a story (p. 144) in order to release herself from the self-perception it locks her into. Indeed, her later relief in finally sharing this and other sexual experiences with Naomi (p. 195) is precisely the relief of gaining external control over her experiences in order not to be contained by them. And her ability to construe into a "Great Comic Scene" (p. 171) the humiliating experience of hiding naked in Jerry Storey's basement brings a similarly liberating relief. Stories, in other words, are a way of gaining an external perspective in order both to claim experience and to gain distance on it: a way to see the self as including those experiences without being defined by them.

Initially, then, Del's experiences of growing sexual awareness are implicated in her relationship with language. She becomes the agent of her own experiences by being able to name them and narrate them. This process is a way of claiming simultaneously her femaleness and her agency over her own experiences. But the integration must go further than this: it must also lead her to visions of self as autonomously female in a social context. On a larger scale, the entire novel is the narrative enactment of this process. Through its structuring of her experience she is able to claim that identity. The roots of this process can be first identified in her childhood sense of both separation and inclusion and traced through her continuing interaction with her environment as both interpreter and participant, while evolving a claim to complex female selfhood.

The novel's opening section centers in issues of inclusion and separateness as a part of Del's childhood chameleonlike identity. Initially, she seems to blend completely into her background, almost to have no identity at all: not only the unnamed "I" that Roland Barthes says is the pronoun of anonymity[18] but even an unnamed and undifferentiated "we."[19] Though the "we" breaks into "Owen and I" on page 2, the plural form recurs frequently in "The Flats Road," and we are not told sex or name for the "I" until the information becomes indirectly available in the novel's second section, "Heirs of the Living Body." This anonymity seems to argue an embedded identity for the novel's protagonist, a merging with her physical and material environment. The emphasis on material objects—the proliferation of material reality—adds to such a feeling. But even as objects proliferate, it becomes clear that their presence is a function of reality interacting with perception. The attempt "to name off the things" (p. 3) in Uncle Benny's house, for example, cannot succeed but shows the need to contain by describing, and the interaction of perception and objects yields here, as elsewhere, both the objects' intractable "thereness" in resistance to interpretation and their participation in interpretive process: "The things we remembered . . . were just a few things revealed and identifiable on top of such a wealth of wreckage, a whole rich, dark, rotting mess of carpets, linoleum, parts of furniture, insides of machinery, nails, wire, tools, utensils" (p. 3).

The apparent merging of self with environment, then, is not evidence of her *inability* to place herself, but of her *need* to place herself within her environment. Already she exhibits her need for multiple paradigms by which to explain her world and her sense that she is the interpretive center of those paradigms. Her self-indulgent gorging on the improbable sensationalist news stories at Uncle Benny's house is one way she tests the reality of her own family's views of the world. So too is her awareness of the contrasting worlds of Jubilee and Flats Road. As a representative inhabitant of Flats Road, Uncle Benny—"a steadfast eccentric" (p. 2)—helps especially to give her access to the knowledge that realities are, in part, a function of the perceiver.

So lying alongside our world was Uncle Benny's world like a troubling distorted reflection, the same but never at all the same. In that world people could go down in quicksand, be vanquished by ghosts or terrible ordinary cities; luck and wickedness were gigantic and unpredictable; nothing was deserved, anything might happen; defeats were met with crazy satisfaction. It was his triumph, that he couldn't know about, to make us see. (P. 22)

In recognizing these perceptual differences, Del indeed learns to "see," to interpret.

Because Del's initial "I" is given no identifying qualities or traits, it is doubly present as agent rather than identity: not only is she engaged in learning to "see," but also she is simultaneously presenting herself to us through her activities: she catches frogs, writes a letter for Uncle Benny, ignores her mother's warning in order to go and observe Madeleine for herself. Children's activities, they are still indicative of the child's claiming of her own agency. She also reveals the centrality of intellectual activity in her sense of agency, not only the reading to test the boundaries of reality, but also the active *placing* of herself in the world. Offering Uncle Benny a sample of her handwriting, she reveals the importance of mental geography in her own sense of herself: "*Mr. Benjamin Thomas Poole, The Flats Road, Jubilee, Wawanash County, Ontario, Canada, North*

America, The Western Hemisphere, The World, The Solar System, The Universe" (p. 9). The enlarging circles of the address are themselves the child's claiming of conceptual self-placement,[20] and the ensuing argument about the absence of heaven in her scheme reveals her commitment to empirical evidence, which exists side by side with her imaginative structuring of reality. In any case, she is claiming her own interpretive presence and is revealing herself through activity rather than traits.

The effect of the initial view of the protagonist—without name, without identified gender, and within a contextual "we" or at least strongly aware of surrounding relationships—is to see her as relatively free of all constraining labels and to sense a contextual embeddedness in family and place. Simultaneously, the effect of looking out through her eyes is to come to the gradual recognition of her interpretive agency. "The Flats Road" portrays the child, unconstrained by gender implications, self-defined in agency, and free to come and go easily in the interaction between individual assertion and embeddedness. And it portrays the child as active intelligence developing conceptual strategies by which to assess her physical and social surroundings.

The central human tension between autonomy and inclusion is thus enacted from the beginning of the novel as part of the narrative process of selection and interpretation. But it is portrayed as a dynamic interaction rather than a dichotomy; as such it establishes process as the novel's central mode of understanding and lays the groundwork for developing an adult female self capable of both autonomy and inclusion.

Following from the opening in "The Flats Road," each section of the novel exhibits a different version of the tension between inclusion and autonomy, as perceived through a different conceptualizing lens by which Del attempts to place herself. The sections are what Munro calls "almost self-contained segments."[21] Indeed, some reviewers of the novel argued that it was not a novel at all, but a collection of short stories. Though each section could stand alone, their effect individually would be very different, more the effect of an aim toward accurate perception of a set of events and less the awareness that experience is affected by the interpretive lens through which it is viewed. On the other hand, the cumulative effect of the sequential conceptualizations is the recognition of

complexity in lived experience and the necessity of continual reinterpretation.[22]

Thematic unity operates as a tightly controlling factor in each
section: death in "Heirs of the Living Body"; mother-daughter relationships in "Princess Ida"; belief systems in "Age of Faith"; and so
on. Though other issues inevitably cross boundaries, as in the concern with male/female differences in "Heirs of the Living Body" or
the resonating with the death theme in "Princess Ida," each unit is
governed by expectations of coherence. The balance that each section seems to identify between Del's sense of self and her sense of
belonging shifts with each conceptualization and reaches a temporary holding point in each altered framework. The reconceptualization of her mother in "Princess Ida," for example, yields that ten-
uous recognition of her mother's own capacity for pain and Del's
need to separate herself from identification with her mother as well
as from trust in her power; here Del's sense of self resides fragilely
between identification and distancing. The coherence of the section
marks the achievement of this balance.

But the balance is temporary, as are the integrations and separations she tests via the world of religious faith or the interrelatedness
of human lives both threatened by death and enacted by death. The
value of each balance is an achieved value for Del's increasingly
complex interaction with the world. Its expression in a single coherent unit underlines its inability to be complete. For each enactment of coherence has both a powerful distorting effect on interpreting lived experience and a claim to partial interpretive validity.
What is of particular interest here is that the *combined* effect of
multiple thematic coherences, with the same central protagonist
and the recurring concern with autonomy and inclusion, is precisely
the opposite of distorted containment. Like the self who can "take
on all kinds of experiences and shuck off what [she doesn't] want,"
the structure emphasizes choice and change in resistance to a total-
ized unity and participates in the revealed complexity of lived
experience.

This process is particularly important for the resistance to cultural definitions of femaleness, especially as they are overbalanced toward relational inclusion. Examined through the culture text, Del's
experiences would lead her precisely to the imposed choice between
femaleness and adulthood—inclusion or autonomy but not both.

This is the choice underlying her mother's advice to use her brains rather than getting "distracted by a man" and it is the choice undergirded by the continual opposition between male and female worlds in the novel. But examined through the multiple texts of partial truth, her experiences take on a more complex pattern and eventually lead her from such dichotomies to a recognition of simultaneity.

The primary task Del must undertake is, then, a reconceptualization of the external views of femaleness. Though she continually evolves through the narrative as a self in process, addressing needs of both inclusion and independence, the threat to these multiple balances is most powerful in the cultural definitions of adult womanhood. These pressures become stronger as she grows older and can no longer claim the apparently gender-free identity of her childhood. Though she is not precisely enacting the standard view of growth from primary identity to sexual identity to gender identity,[23] she does need to find a way to include sex and gender in her evolving selfhood if she is to interact with a social world as an adult female.

The most overt characterization of the femininity text in the novel occurs in a magazine article Del reads as an adolescent. The article, by a New York Freudian psychiatrist, claims to characterize "the basic difference between the male and female habits of thought, relating chiefly to their experience of sex" (p. 150). The difference that centers the article is presented emblematically as the difference in what girls and boys think of as they look at the moon: "The boy thinks of the universe; the girl thinks, 'I must wash my hair'" (p. 150). The damning generalization leads Del finally to rip up the magazine: "*For a woman, everything is personal; no idea is of any interest to her by itself, but must be translated into her own experience; in works of art she always sees her own life, or her daydreams*" (p. 150). Del's distress is intense, for the article clearly traps her in an unacceptable choice: "I wanted men to love me, *and* I wanted to think of the universe when I looked at the moon. I felt trapped, stranded; it seemed there had to be a choice where there couldn't be a choice" (p. 150). The choice is the one that I have identified as central to cultural views of femaleness; it is the choice that takes form in the novelistic endings in marriage or isolation.

Del perceives versions of this choice throughout her world. In junior high school, it takes the form of boys playing hockey and girls helping with sewing costumes (e.g., p. 108). In her childhood experiences with Uncle Craig and Aunts Grace and Elspeth, it takes the form of feeling his judgment to be "large and impersonal" (p. 25), while theirs, like her mother's, makes personal demands on her; or the form of absolute and unbreachable distinctions between "men's work and women's work" (p. 27). In her assessments of the boys at school, the distinction between the impersonal and the personal is similarly present: "Boys' hate was dangerous, it was keen and bright, a miraculous birthright, like Arthur's sword snatched out of the stone, in the Grade Seven Reader. Girls' hate, in comparison, seemed muddled and tearful, sourfully defensive" (p. 98). In later adolescence, she experiences the choice as between the "complicated feminine order" of household items and marriage plans (p. 161), underpinned by the sexually shady "life of the Gay-la Dance Hall" (p. 161)—both of which combine to form "the road to marriage"—and her own choice of retreat to read *The Life of Charlotte Brontë*.

Everywhere present in the novel, the dominant view of male/female difference—and the imposed choice it represents for women—reaches its peak in the penultimate section of the novel, "Baptizing," which shows us Del's sexual initiation and her sharpest conflict with the cultural expectations of women. In her relationship with Garnet French, the powerful currents of her own sexuality, and his, very nearly lead her to the choice against her own autonomous aspirations. Garnet's challenge to her—"You think you're too good for anything. Any of *us*" (p. 197)—makes clear the opposition: baptism, marriage, and children or action on one's own behalf. Though she has just said that she wants marriage and his baby, the enactment of commitment as he offers to baptize her in the river resurrects the other desires she had set aside during this relationship. In resisting his baptism attempt, she is convinced that she is fighting real drowning (p. 198); and the metaphorical drowning that she fights would equally destroy her: marriage and the relinquishing of her own aspirations. The power of the currents that nearly drown her is the power similar to the currents that pull Maggie Tulliver to her death and Martha Quest to her marriage: the need for sexual expression in a cultural context that says that is possible only in relinquishing one's autonomous goals. Del's early relationship with Garnet shows the implications of her own sexuality in the baptism: "Sex seemed to me all surrender—not the woman's to the man but the person's to the body, an act of pure faith, freedom in humility. I would lie washed in these implications, discoveries, like somebody suspended in clear and warm and irresistibly moving water" (pp. 181–82). The drowning that threatens her is the effect of the opposition between sexuality and autonomy: in the fight with Garnet, she would die either way.

But the escape from death—real or metaphorical—like the escape from marriage at the expense of selfhood, is prepared for by the novel itself. Del is not, as Hallvard Dahlie says, "saved 'in despite of herself' ";[24] rather she *saves herself*, through the enactment of possibilities that characterize the whole narrative process. Her self-characterization as one who takes on experience and shucks off what she can't use leads her continually to test available experiences, including cultural expectations of femininity, and to recognize always the need to reconceptualize so that she is not driven into an either/or choice. The narrative process, enacted through discrete and overlapping thematic unities that repeatedly undermine each other, with the self as active perceptual agent in each, prepares for this resistance to entrapment as it does for all the others.

In developing multiple perspectives on reality, Del has integrated the knowledge that each construction of reality is partial and threatening to other constructions of reality. Repeatedly throughout the novel she speaks of entering different levels of reality, different countries, different worlds. The entry into her love for Garnet was just such a shift of lens and hence of identity. The departure from that love is another, a reentry into "the world" with "its natural and callous importance." Similarly, she feels it as a return to her "old self—my old devious, ironic, isolated self" (p. 199). These shifts of the conceptual schema from "love" to "isolation" reenact the patterns of multiple reconceptualizations throughout the novel to free her from entrapment in love. But these shifts, too, reveal only a partial reality: as love was an inadequate narrative paradigm, so too is isolation.

Del experiences her return to her "isolated self" as paradox: "I was free and I was not free. I was relieved and I was desolate" (p. 200). Not surprisingly she also experiences a sense of distance on her self, feeling the pain of loss and simultaneously observing herself, constructing through self-distancing an alternative interpretation. Observing herself, she is both the person watching and the person immersed in suffering.

> Without diminishment of pain I observed myself; I was amazed to think that the person suffering was me, for it was not me at all; I was watching. I was watching, I was suffering. I said into the mirror a line from Tennyson . . . I said it with absolute sincerity, absolute irony. *He cometh not, she said.* (P. 200)

In observing herself and in structuring her experience ironically through the line of poetry, she is enacting the sort of process by which she has always retained agency in the midst of experience that threatened to submerge her, particularly that which threatened to submerge her in self-limiting definitions of femaleness. While in her dream world of loving Garnet, she had reacted similarly: "I talked to myself about myself, saying *she: She is in love*" (p. 192). And frequently throughout the novel she has both distanced and claimed her physical sense of self by looking in the mirror (e.g., pp. 127, 153).

Self-observation is one of the distinctively human qualities. The ability to gain a distance on immediate experience and simultaneously to recognize oneself as oneself—in a mirror or in a narrative characterization—is also the ability to recognize the human capacity of agency and change, to refuse to be defined by the mirror image of cultural femaleness. Like her mother, with her past selves stored up inside her, Del is able to look through an interpretive frame of identity and even through multiple frames of identity. But more than her mother, Del is able to see that the perceiver herself—and hence the capacity for multiplicity and for agency—is the fundamental identity that gives her continuity if not "coherence."

The novel's concluding synthesis in "Epilogue: The Photographer" is, then, not closure but reaffirmation of process, both in narrative structure and in personal identity; and it is an assertion of Del's selfhood in a social context that is not personal but does not refuse the personal. The focus of the epilogue—a novel Del had carried in her head during her youth, constructed imaginatively from the facts of the Sherriff family—plays on the whole relationship of fact to constructions of reality and the novel's persistent recognition that one cannot include everything. Even her Uncle Craig's historical manuscript, based on a proliferation of facts—which Del found too dull to consider finishing—was only a different kind of distortion from Del's imaginative constructions. As the child Del had attempted, hopelessly, to make lists of everything in Uncle Benny's house, now the adult Del, remembering Jubilee, tries to make lists of the material realities of the town in which she grew up: "And no list could hold what I wanted, for what I wanted was every last thing, every layer of speech and thought, stroke of light on bark or walls, every smell, pothole, pain, crack, delusion held still and held together—radiant, everlasting" (p. 210). Impossible, she knows, and yet she has identified what is possible: a valuing of material and social reality through multiple constructions of it.

Del's selfhood, then, exists as the agent of this process, in the narrative constructions of her growing up and in the resulting ability to enact her aspirations to be a writer. Her multiple narrative has participated in the multiple sense of self by which she claims femaleness as a positive part of her identity but rejects the cultural containment in femaleness. Her connection to Jubilee is powerful; her sense of herself as writer in a larger social context is possible because she can be rooted in her past without being determined by it. When Bobby Sherriff offers her his wishes for luck in her life, she responds, "'Yes,' . . . instead of thank you" (p. 211) and she does so with the knowledge that she has a connection to other people's lives but a claim on her own abilities. She has become an adult woman without denying either her femaleness or her aspiration, either her past or her future, either her self or her community.

II

The conflict between autonomy and femaleness as I have been defining it is most evident in its heterosexual white middle-class version: the version, in fact, that has dominated most of the history of the English and American novel. But in the black community in America, a view of the strong black woman who is both autonomous and affirmatively female is often expressed. Such a contrasting view of adult womanhood may be, in part, a cultural myth; research on black women's relationship to perceived female identity and autonomous self-definition is somewhat conflicting[25] and cer-

tainly the abuses of the image of the strong black woman as dominant matriarch are particularly destructive.[26] Still, the cultural issues are decidedly different for black women than for white women.
In affirming the multidimensionality of black women, Toni Morrison, for example, has asserted: "You see, I don't have to make
choices about whether to be a mother or whether to work. I do them
both because they both exist and I don't dwell on the idea that I am a
full human being. I know that."[27]

Nevertheless, the values of the dominant culture have a decisive
effect on the problems of female self-definition within the black
American culture as well. The concepts of the dominant cultural
definitions of female beauty and appropriately feminine relationality have their impact upon the black community even when
these concepts are not necessarily accepted. The culture texts of
both race and sex can interact with especially destructive power in
the developing self-awareness of black girls growing up in a white-
dominant society. In the literary characterization of black women's
lives, this destructive power is nowhere more evident than in Toni
Morrison's *The Bluest Eye*. At the same time, however, the qualities
of human complexity and the possibilities for female self-definition
in resistance to both of these culture texts are also given powerful
presentation in the novel's narrative process itself. Claudia MacTeer
narrates not only the destruction of Pecola Breedlove but also her
own self-formation; in telling of her participation in the human
complexity of the black community, she simultaneously creates her
self as an autonomous woman in the midst of human relationships.

The novel provides no decisive evidence as to the narrative agent
for much of its interior, but the initial memory of stunted marigolds
in 1941, which introduces the narrative as an exploration of Pecola's
destruction, makes clear Claudia's own need to engage in narrative
explanation. Further, the distance of memory and adulthood evident
in this passage ties it not only to the novel's concluding pages but
also to the complexity of voice throughout the novel. If not actually
the narrative voice throughout the novel, Claudia's is at least the
framing voice and the primary agent of our stance toward Pecola and
toward the novel's interwoven life histories. In its witnessing to
Pecola's destruction, the novel is simultaneously Claudia's claiming of voice and selfhood. Her narrative agency is a form of the
message Hortense Spillers takes from Morrison's *Sula*: "Through

the discipline and decorum exacted by form, the woman's reality is no longer a negation, but a positive and dynamic expressiveness—a figure against a field—shaped by her own insistence."[28]

The general problem for Claudia's self-definition is a version of the conflict between submission and self-assertion, which is the problem of all female authorship: "a life of feminine submission, of 'contemplative purity,' is a life of silence, a life that has no pen and no story, while a life of female rebellion, of 'significant action,' is a life that must be silenced, a life whose monstrous pen tells a terrible story."[29] But for Claudia the problem is framed by the additional issue of racism and by the recognition that self-assertion itself is inadequate when the needs of a community are crucial to any adequate possibilities of self-definition. As Claudia's friend and partial double, Pecola exemplifies the dangers in submission to silence, in withdrawal from self-definition. But the excesses of self-assertion are also destructive: Sula, in Morrison's second novel, acts in ways that both her grandmother and her culture define as "selfish," as she continues "floatin' around without no man"—nor children.[30] Her response to Eva is the culturally unacceptable one: "I don't want to make somebody else. I want to make myself."[31] And the culture's response to Sula is to reject her, to close her out. As Barbara Smith assesses Sula's resistance to cultural norms, "Self-definition is a dangerous activity for any woman to engage in, especially a Black one, and it expectedly earns Sula pariah status in Medallion."[32] More than that, her self-definition is in its very structure a chosen isolation.

Though framed very differently, the idea of self in community for Claudia MacTeer is, then, surrounded by dangers similar to those surrounding the female protagonist of the traditional *Bildungsroman*: the choice of female submission and silence, identity in purely relational terms, which is grotesquely and tragically mirrored in Pecola's reaching for love through madness, and the choice of female rebellion, identity in isolation—mirrored, too, in Pecola's final isolation as well as the more self-affirming isolation of Sula in the later novel. Claudia's eluding of these dangers is decidedly shaped by her cultural context but also bears intriguing similarity to Del Jordan's eluding of her community's imposed definitions of femaleness: the recognition of self in multiplicity but in community and the claiming of a complex and nonlinear narrative agency.

The expectations of the dominant culture provide the initial ironic framing device for the entire novel. The novel opens with the
staccato sentences of a first grade reading book describing house,
nuclear family, pets, and playmate. As the simplistic vision in its
simplistic language is then instantly repeated without punctuation
or capitalization and again without any spacing at all, it becomes a
visual enactment of the closely wrought and always tightening grid
that encloses human lives within these expectations. Such expectations in themselves leave no room for human growth.

In narrative interplay, then, the second brief section calls on the
voice of memory. Without name or sexual identity, the narrator
offers recollections of the concluding shape of Pecola's story, placing
it in a teleological framework, fatalistic and despairing.

> It never occurred to either of us that the earth itself might have
> been unyielding. We had dropped our seeds in our own little plot
> of black dirt just as Pecola's father had dropped his seeds in his
> own plot of black dirt. Our innocence and faith were no more
> productive than his lust or despair. What is clear now is that of
> all of that hope, fear, lust, love, and grief, nothing remains but
> Pecola and the unyielding earth. Cholly Breedlove is dead; our
> innocence too. The seeds shriveled and died; her baby too.[33]

We are told at the outset the losses that will define the story and the
lives it tells; the past seems as unyielding as the earth and as the
tightening grid of cultural expectations.

For Pecola this assessment is accurate. Some human events *are*
irretrievable and the double destructiveness of racism and sexism,
enacted as it is through the lives of people close to her, makes her
ending an overdetermined destiny. Irretrievable, too, is the narrator's innocence and the hope of magic incantations to overcome
destruction and loss. But the conclusion of this section establishes
an important alternative frame to either the cultural grids or the
teleological destiny: *"There is really nothing more to say—except
why. But since* why *is difficult to handle, one must take refuge in
how"* (p. 9). Narrative exploration of personal and communal experience is identified as, in fact, something "more to say." The constructions of memory and the empathetic projections into the lives
of the people involved become a kind of explanation of "how" and,

more than that, a formation of a "who" beyond the lost innocence and the irretrievable past.

At the center of this process is Pecola, visible victim of what the novel tells us are "Probably the most destructive ideas in the history of human thought"—romantic love and physical beauty (p. 97). She studies her image for hours, "looking in the mirror, trying to discover the secret of the ugliness" (p. 39). In feeling defined by what her culture has decided is ugly, Pecola accepts a sense of her own worthlessness and the incomprehensibility of getting "somebody to love you" (p. 29). For her, reaching puberty, experiencing her first menstruation, is both a terrifying—because unknown—experience and the initiation of the "wonder" (p. 29) of the possibility of having a child and being loved. But the only love she is able to gain is the destructive, though tender, love of her father; the only child she can have is the miscarried infant; the only adulthood is the flight into madness. In her childhood, Pecola experiences herself as both subject and object. As subject she is in love with the culture's idols: Shirley Temple, Mary Jane, the images of "cute" little girls, admired by adults and children. As object, she is denied humanity for her failure to match such expectations. At the candy store, Mr. Yacobowski looks at her without seeing and she experiences the "absence of human recognition," with which she is familiar: "She has seen it lurking in the eyes of all white people. So. The distaste must be for her, her blackness. All things in her are flux and anticipation. But her blackness is static and dread. And it is the blackness that accounts for, that creates, the vacuum edged with distaste in white eyes" (p. 42). Her response in anger momentarily reclaims her own subjectivity—"Anger is better. There is a sense of being in anger. A reality and presence. An awareness of worth" (p. 43)—but the anger is merely "a puppy," unable to sustain itself, squelched finally by shame. She turns instead to the Mary Janes—"to eat the eyes" (p. 43)—to reach destructively toward the pretense of subjectivity in a false cultural image.

The eyes remain for Pecola the locus of interplay between subjectivity and objectivity. Wanting to see and share in the cultural image of beautiful house with kittens, she accepts Junior's invitation and is instead tormented into an objectified identification with the dead cat: black face with blue eyes. And Junior's mother, Geraldine, sees her only as the little girl she has seen all her life: "Eyes that questioned nothing and asked everything. Unblinking and un-abashed, they stared up at her. The end of the world lay in their eyes, and the beginning, and all the waste in between" (p. 75). Eyes—needing to *see*, to participate in the culture's image of what life ought to be—again become, for Pecola, the negation of her subjectivity.

This destructive exchange of subjectivity for objectivity is even a process she enacts for herself, replicating what the culture does to her. When her distress with the miserable conditions of her life becomes unbearable, she wishes to disappear, limb by limb, portion by portion until all that is left is the eyes: "Try as she might, she could never get her eyes to disappear. So what was the point? They were everything. Everything was there, in them" (p. 39). Feeling herself to be culturally unacceptable, she decides that if only "those eyes of hers were different, that is to say, beautiful, she herself would be different" (p. 40). What ought, then, to be the active re-minder of subjective consciousness, personal presence—the human factor that cannot be made to disappear—becomes instead the basis of her objectification. And this is the objectification acted out in her final madness: looking into mirrors, in schizophrenic conversation with her "friend," admiring the blue eyes she can never have and worrying that they might not be the "bluest."

To see for oneself is to be able to claim a place in the world. This is what Pecola does on her way *to* the candy store; seeing dan-delions, experiencing them and "other inanimate things," she is able to interpret and possess her own experience: "owning them made her part of the world, and the world a part of her" (p. 41). To see oneself only through the negating and dehumanizing cultural definitions is to lose selfhood and have no place in the world: this is Pecola's madness.

Pecola, then, is fixed at the center of the narrative. Her ending is established from the opening pages. Her being is made "static and dread" by the images and eyes of the white world around her. Her sense of self is finally submerged in the objectification she located in the mirror. Though most extreme, hers is not the only instance of destruction through objectification. Her mother, Pauline, felt its impact when the white doctors denied her human participation in giving birth (p. 99). In her younger adulthood, she took from the movies false ideas of romantic love and physical beauty and structured them destructively into her life and the lives of those around her. Then, relinquishing those false images, she structured her life into a different coherence and her process of becoming was fixed, as she "assigned herself a role in the scheme of things" (p. 100). Her movement toward fixity was not so absolute as her daughter's was to be, but she nonetheless withdrew from the subjectivity of self-definition as she felt the power of cultural objectification. Her assigned place in the scheme of things gives impetus to one of the most poignant scenes in the novel when she turns from her daughter's hurt to comfort the little white girl dressed in pink in the white household that now claims her identity at the expense of her daughter's.

The destructive and objectifying impact of white dominant definitions of female beauty and female roles cramps other black women's lives into different molds. Geraldine is but one representative of a group of women who "come from Mobile. Aiken. From Newport News" (p. 67). These women, despising their blackness, "learn how to do the white man's work with refinement: . . . how to behave. The careful development of thrift, patience, high morals, and good manners. In short, how to get rid of the funkiness" (p. 68). In despising their blackness and shaping their femaleness into something false, they not only take on a narrow and self-defeating self-definition; they also participate in the cultural denial of black female subjectivity that destroys Pecola.

These patterns of objectification outline the apparent possibilities for black female selfhood in a white-dominant society. For Claudia they are doubly inadequate as they surround and participate in the destruction of Pecola: women defined negatively by false cultural objectification in appearance or romantic love; women narrowly confined in the few roles allowed to black women, as servants in a white household or as supporting actors doing "the white man's work with refinement." Each of these responses to cultural expectations is made understandable in the novel, as are the choices of the three prostitutes who claim some subversive freedom as well, though they are culturally defined as enacting only female sexuality. But each response is also inadequate to a strong sense of self as both black and female and participant in the strength of the community.

The most available resistance to objectification is enacted in the novel not by a woman, but by Pecola's father. Alone as a child, cut off from a sense of family or community, having suffered entrapment in the beam of the white man's flashlight during his first lovemaking, Cholly Breedlove chooses not the impossible hatred of the white man, but the possible hatred of the black woman (p. 119) and eventually the severing of his human connectedness. He chooses a course toward destructive freedom, inverse of total objectification but finally as harmful to himself and to Pecola. His experiences of joy, pain, anger, love can cohere only "in the head of a musician" (p. 125), and, paradoxically, only in his claim to freedom, his disconnection from continuity: "Cholly was free. Dangerously free. Free to feel whatever he felt—fear, guilt, shame, love, grief, pity. Free to be tender or violent, to whistle or weep" (p. 125). This freedom, then, is the basis of his love offering to Pecola, the basis of his participation in her destruction: "the love of a free man is never safe. There is no gift for the beloved. The lover alone possesses his gift of love. The loved one is shorn, neutralized, frozen in the glare of the lover's inward eye" (pp. 159–60). His freedom objectifies her, refuses to see her or allow her her own sight, as does Pauline Breedlove's refusal to see her daughter, and most guiltily, as does the pervasive cultural refusal to grant her subjectivity.

Claudia, then, recognizes that all these responses to cultural objectification are not only inadequate but also a part of the interlocking pattern that destroys Pecola. In taking on the narrative process, she is both assessing the damage to her friend's life and seeking a process by which to develop her own sense of self. The objectification of self is unacceptable, but equally unacceptable is the destructive freedom by which one is cut off from community. In Morrison's second novel, Sula enacts a female version of dangerous freedom very similar to Cholly's. She chooses an "experimental life" based on the recognition that "there was no other that you could count on; . . . no self to count on either . . . no ego. For that reason she felt no compulsion to verify herself—be consistent with herself."[34] In *The Bluest Eye*, Claudia is growing into a world where just such a response might seem appropriate. But her involvement with Pecola's life and her narrative assessment of that involvement enable her to find a different response to racism and sexism: a self that is not fixed in objectification but is rooted in community, able to address the human needs of both autonomy and inclusion.

The opening of "Autumn," the first narrative section of the novel, draws on the same apparent embeddedness of childhood with which Del Jordan's story opened: a narrating "I" of unspecified name and sex and often merging into a narrating "we." The embeddedness threatens destruction by a harsh environment, with its pain and sickness, its irritable adults who "issue orders without providing information" (p. 12). But it also offers an embracing warmth: "But was it really like that? As painful as I remember? Only mildly. Or rather, it was a productive and fructifying pain. Love, thick and dark as Alaga syrup, eased up into that cracked window. . . . So when I think of autumn, I think of somebody with hands who does not want me to die" (p. 14).

As a child, Claudia feels the simultaneous human needs for autonomy and inclusion and can already recognize the possibilities for both support and thwarting within this environment. Christmas, cultural emblem of children's hopes and desires, here becomes emblematic too of Claudia's claim to identity within her community. Her bemusement with the Christmas gift of a "blue-eyed Baby Doll" (p. 19)—"What was I supposed to do with it? Pretend I was its mother? I had no interest in babies or the concept of motherhood" (p. 20)—indicates an initial distance from cultural stereotypes of both female roles and female beauty. Her subsequent dismembering of the doll enacts her analytical curiosity and her distance from the objectification the doll represents: "I could not love it. But I could examine it to see what it was that all the world said was lovable" (p. 20). In such a culturally unacceptable act, she claims her right to be distinct from externally imposed definitions: her right to autonomous self-definition.

At the same time, she feels within her community the possibilities for inclusion that would sustain, rather than deny, her selfhood. Her real wish for a Christmas gift is "to feel something on Christmas day."

> "I want to sit on the low stool in Big Mama's kitchen with my lap full of lilacs and listen to Big Papa play his violin for me alone." The lowness of the stool made for my body, the security and warmth of Big Mama's kitchen, the smell of the lilacs, the sound of the music, and, since it would be good to have all of my senses engaged, the taste of a peach, perhaps, afterward. (P. 21)

Though this wish is unmet, it is indicative of a strong sense of self in sensory experience and within the context of a supportive community.

Claudia's needs and possibilities for selfhood are thus established in childhood. She tells us that she, too, eventually went through the process of accommodation to cultural norms—"adjustment without improvement" (p. 22)—and came to a "fraudulent love" for Shirley Temple and for the denial of her delight in the sensory. But the narrative enactment of the novel shows her differently. It shows her taking on the impulses to subjective assertion, shown childishly in dismembering the dolls, through dismembering the text of cultural expectations and re-membering the lived experience of Pecola and those who participated in her destruction. It shows her claiming the valuing of sensory experience through empathetically constructing the experience of others. And it shows her re-cognizing her own participation, through "adjustment without improvement," in the destructiveness of the culture texts and then finding instead the narrative agency to dismantle those texts.

The recognition of this possibility during her childhood is partial but becomes one foundation for the resisting agency that she is finally able to claim. Her hostility toward Maureen Peal, for example, provides a gauge of Claudia's evolving complex selfhood.

> Dolls we could destroy, but we could not destroy the honey voices of parents and aunts, the obedience in the eyes of our peers, the slippery light in the eyes of our teachers when they encountered the Maureen Peals of the world. What was the secret? What did we lack? Why was it important? And so what? Guileless and without vanity, we were still in love with ourselves then. We felt comfortable in our skins, enjoyed the news that our senses released to us, admired our dirt, cultivated our scars, and could not comprehend this unworthiness. . . . And all the time we knew that Maureen Peal was not the Enemy and not worthy of such intense hatred. The *Thing* to fear was the *Thing* that made *her* beautiful, and not us. (Pp. 61–62)

Valuing her identity in sensory experience, in personal capacity to engage her physical environment, she is able to locate her sense of selfhood there rather than in the negations of the culture around her. And she is able to know that the real evil exists in the text of that culture's expectations: "the *Thing*."

This perception, initiated in the childhood address to issues of inclusion and autonomy, becomes the basis of Claudia's narrative structuring of her life and Pecola's and the basis of her ability to act against the culture texts of both femininity and racial identity. Unlike Pecola, Claudia retains her capacity to look out through her own eyes and then develops the empathetic capacity to see the world through the eyes of others: the narrative construction of Pauline Breedlove's past or Cholly's and the overall exploration of the how and why of Pecola's madness attest to this capacity.

Morrison is very aware that each of us lives in our "own cell of consciousness," each of us making our "own patchwork quilt of reality—collecting fragments of experience here, pieces of information there" (p. 31). In giving to Claudia the role of narrative agent, she shows the possibilities for narrative understanding that goes beyond the teleology of culturally imposed madness or death, through a complex refracturing of experience showing the multiplicity of the ways each "cell of consciousness" creates its "patchwork quilt." The containing force of the cultural text is powerful— Pecola's irretrievable ending shows that—but reality itself is not absolutely fixed by this text. Claudia's examination of causes and effects and contexts reveals the human capacity for caring as one way to begin dismantling "the Thing."

Claudia's concluding invocation of her own guilt and participation is, then, a recognition of her participation in an overall cultural fabric. Her knowledge that it is "too late" (p. 160) for Pecola is a judgment upon that cultural fabric. But her narrative enactment of her own growing up and of Pecola's destruction is her use of memory and empathetic projection to claim a responsible place in a human community. In seeing her selfhood as implicated in the selves of those she writes about, she claims her multiplicity and her agency without the destruction implicit in the pure self-assertion of Sula's or Cholly's "freedom."

Claudia MacTeer thus enacts a different version of black female selfhood than either the acceptance of cultural expectations or the freedom that destroys others. The narrative process enables her to claim agency over her own interpretation of the world and to assume human responsibility within that world. Like Cholly's Aunt

Jimmy and the other old black women, she has grown up and learned to claim *her own* interpretation of experience: "Edging into life from the back door. Becoming. Everybody in the world was in a position to give them orders. . . . But they took all of that and re-created it in their own image" (p. 109). And in their old age they find some kind of freedom, as "the lives of these old black women were synthesized in their eyes—a purée of tragedy and humor, wicked-ness and serenity, truth and fantasy" (p. 110). Claudia, not old but now grown beyond childhood innocence, is able to share in this freedom of synthesizing lives and experiences, creating the world as she sees it. But more than that, she also incorporates her recognition of other people's subjective perceptions; in seeing people from the inside, as Morrison says she wants us to experience her characters,[35] Claudia achieves what Morrison says is her own goal for her readers: to expand individual "compassion" and "perception of life."[36] Claudia's expansion, then, is our own: a new recognition of the possibilities for black female selfhood—strong and compassionate, self-defined and responsible to others—and a more complex aware-ness of the relationship between individual and community.

Mary Burgher argues the near impossibility of autonomy for most black people in a racist society and the resulting importance of the idea of "collective liberation" in autobiographies of black women.[37] Certainly, Claudia's vision in *The Bluest Eye* of intertwined lives in the black community and especially among black women speaks to this need to claim selfhood within a shared social context. But it is important, too, to recognize that Claudia is also claiming a right to self-definition as a woman resisting the cultural negations often imposed on black women. In this sense she exemplifies what Mary Helen Washington calls "the Emergent Woman," a woman "whose consciousness allows her to have some control over her life."[38] Both autonomous and affirmatively female, Claudia is able to claim her place as a self-defined woman within a social context: her complex narrative construction of her own and others' lived experience be-comes her enactment of selfhood. For both Claudia MacTeer and Del Jordan, to grow up female means to grow against cultural expec-tations and toward the possibility of both autonomy and inclusion: female selfhood within a human community.

CHAPTER 5

Beyond Teleology: *Violet Clay* and
The Stone Angel

In order to represent female wholeness, the female growing-up novel must find ways to show its protagonist growing against cultural expectations, to represent her in the process of shaping an adult selfhood able to embrace both her femaleness and her autonomy. As I argued in chapter 4, the subversive capacity of the first-person narrator evolves from the narrative representation of her own agency in dismantling the culture text as she grows up in resistance to it. Because of the grounding of narrative expectations in the assumptions of the dominant culture, the narrator-protagonist must always remain alert to those assumptions as she shapes her own story in resistance to this anticipated power. But through her narrative agency, she is able to draw on the initial freedom of childhood, which gives some measure of openness to alternatives: just as her representation is not yet fully bound by the conventions of femininity, so the agency of her own narrative can open from the undefined quality of childhood. Since she has not yet enclosed her own self-definition within the cultural grid, she can use the narrative process to dismantle the grid and to interpret those female experiences that are not a part of it.

The subversive representation of adult female protagonists, however, raises a somewhat different set of problems. For them, the conventional assumptions about womanhood are already in place as a part of novelistic characterization: in the absence of support from the relative openness of childhood identity, the representation of adult women seems from the beginning to be confined within the femininity text. These problems would seem to be aggravated when a protagonist has herself shaped her life and selfhood to meet the expectations of cultural norms: her sense of who she is underwrites the novelistic conventions about female identity so that she seems fully enclosed within the grid.

Since few women are able to elude the grid completely, the representation of a female protagonist who has herself previously accepted cultural assumptions about women's lives and is presently in the act of new self-definition has real significance to a feminist perspective. As she examines her past embeddedness in the expectations of her social world, such a protagonist suggests ways to dismantle the grid retrospectively. And as she takes apart her previous understanding of her own past life, she develops, as well, a basis for reopening the future. Again the protagonist's act of self-narration provides a crucial access to such subversive representation: as she recognizes that her past life has been lived in relation to the cultural grid, her claim to narrative agency gives her the capacity to reinterpret her previous experience as a basis for new self-definition.

A critical component of this self-narration is the ability to subvert narrative teleology, to resist and redefine the power of the conclusion toward which a narrative moves. In the expression of the conventions of coherence, novelistic narratives are inevitably shaped in relation to expected outcomes. As Louis Mink expresses it, "The end reflects meaning back on the events leading up to it, but what in turn *counts* as the end is constituted by the intentions, choices, and actions referred to in the description of the events themselves."[1] It is, in part, through this process that female narrative paradigms based on the love story have come to require an ending in either marriage or isolation: given the selection and structuring of events according to cultural definitions of femaleness, the presence of experiences outside the love story can have no place in the narrative. Narrative coherence and narrative teleology both structure the stories of women's lives as a choice between sexuality and autonomy.

But, as I have repeatedly insisted, narrative has a powerful place in our sense of being human. Even from an existentialist perspective, which accurately identifies a reliance on stories with bad faith and inauthentic living, stories remain a human necessity: fiction is "deeply distrusted and yet humanly indispensable"[2] or " 'fiction' designates an apparently *unavoidable* tendency to reconstitute the self in more comfortable categories."[3] Though we know that we cannot expect our lives to respond to easy plotting, we nevertheless feel a recurrent need to narrate the events of our lives to ourselves and to each other, to give shape to the complexity of lived experience.

This need has, of course, participated in the entrapment of women's lives within the love story. In the urgency to give narrative explanation to female experience, women's lives become truncated by the expectation of known endings, misshapen by the reliance on the anticipated rather than the exploration of possibility toward an open future. The past—as events under description in anticipation of female "destiny"—takes on a power over the future and yields the premature closure that has held women's stories and women's lives within the confines of the femininity text.

In chapter 4, I examined some ways in which Del Jordan and Claudia MacTeer used the narrative process to keep their sense of selfhood open to alternative choices rather than being confined within the expectations of growing up female toward an exclusively relational identity. In this chapter, I want to examine some narrative possibilities for a re-cognition of the past rather than allowing its defined events to govern both present and future.[4] In Gail Godwin's *Violet Clay* and Margaret Laurence's *The Stone Angel*, Violet and Hagar both succeed in eluding the teleological grip of narrative expectation; they do so by developing alternative narrative schemata through which to examine past experience and by redefining those schemata to accommodate the altered information retrieved from memory. In this way they are able to retain the explanatory power of narrative form without becoming entrapped in previous explanations of their lives and selves.

I

The opening sentence of *Violet Clay* is the assertive self-definition of its protagonist—"I am a painter"[5]—but its narrative commitment is to a complex exploration of the significance of narrative design in the full claiming of selfhood. Though Godwin is writing through the voice of her painter-protagonist, she has cast the dominant problem of human perception and human choice not as a visual problem but as a problem of narrative design. The novel's characterization of this process gives new insights into the dangers and values of narration itself.

When *Violet Clay* was published in 1978, it seemed a disappointment to a number of Godwin's admirers. One reviewer attributed to it "the pep-talk quality of so many recent novels in which the heroine strides off the last page, her own woman at last."[6] The same review explicitly contrasted Godwin's previous novel, *The Odd Woman*, with the "narrow conception and general thinness" of *Violet Clay*.[7] Such a contrast has some validity, but I do not think it does justice to the actual complexity of Godwin's task in *Violet Clay:* with few literary paradigms, Godwin is attempting the creation of an autonomous female protagonist who defines herself by her relationship to her work without relinquishing her identity as a woman. For both Godwin and her protagonist, this process evolves through a complex reanalysis of the power of narrative structures and a careful reassessment of the past.

Godwin's preceding novel, *The Odd Woman*, provides an effective introduction to her concern with the significance of narrative pattern for arriving at a satisfactory self-definition: its protagonist is Jane Clifford, professor of literature, whose dominant mode of perception is through the identification of a literary parallel or a relevant narrative pattern in her own personal family history. There are clear dangers for Jane in this reliance on literary precedent, as Susan Lorsch has pointed out in her discussion of *The Odd Woman* and "the effect that literature—and the lies it often tells—has on those who believe it."[8] But even for Jane, those dangers can be partly averted by remembering that though stories do provide a significant pattern, they have only limited explanatory power.

> Stories were all right, as long as you read them as what they were: single visions, one person's way of interpreting something. You could learn from stories, be warned by stories. But stories, by their very nature, were Procrustean. Even the longest of them had to end somewhere. If a living human being tried to squeeze . . . into a particular story, he [or she] might find vital parts . . . lopped off. Even worse, he [or she] might . . . [be] unable to get out again.[9]

Prepared by this knowledge, both personal and professional, Jane makes an effective beginning at eluding the confines of available story lines. But her resistance to the love story and her strong identification with her work come close to leading her into the alternate denouement of isolation: her life provides no immediate escape from the sense of either/or choice.

As successor to *The Odd Woman, Violet Clay* gives new emphasis to these concerns with both the crucial defining power of narrative and its destructive self-limiting capacity. Through her central focus on considerations of narrative design, Godwin reassesses the need to hold onto possibilities while still making commitments, to have a defined selfhood without capitulating to the kinds of external self-denying self-definitions that Jane is struggling against. Significantly, Violet Clay is the first of Godwin's protagonists to tell her own story; she is both agent and recipient of the narrative process as she uses narrative patterns to gauge patterns in her own behavior, trying always to arrive at a self-definition continuous with the past and appropriate for the future and to work out patterns for her own sense of autonomous selfhood. In assuming this narrative control, she is better able than Jane to elude the threat of final isolation and convey a sense of active movement toward the future.

As Ian Watt has pointed out, the specification of the individual and the human understanding of causation are not only the central structuring elements of the novel but also the general human effects of memory.[10] Certainly memory serves these purposes in Violet Clay's uses of narrative toward self-definition and causal analysis. Much of the novel is concerned with her sorting out and discarding old self-limiting plots. She remembers and reevaluates the stories she has told herself all her life, and in the process she formulates another umbrella plot, looser and less familiar but nonetheless committed to the analysis of individuality and causation through the probing of memory for new information and alternative hypotheses.

This process of claiming and reclaiming past selves is never simple, particularly because a person may often wish to deny previous selves or to dissociate past actions from present self-awareness. Some of this confusion of continuity and discontinuity marks Violet's sense of herself and her structuring of her narrative. The core of the narrative time—a few short months of present time from an August day in New York to a mid-October day in Plommet Falls— provides the defining self-concept through which Violet probes past contributions to that self-concept and future implications of the changes it is undergoing. As she moves backward in time through her memories, she is exhuming her past selves and seeking areas of congruity between past and present; but as she is attempting to identify who she was in the past and who she is in the narrative present, she is also seeking the crevices in those apparently fixed self-definitions in order that she can simultaneously hold onto a continuous selfhood and yet understand the process by which she has broken free of those falsely constrained selves. As she strips away the various false labels and story lines she had previously imposed on herself, she moves closer to formulating a self that meshes with her narrating self without denying her past experiences and without foreclosing future evolution.

The narrative opens on a day that comes to be defined as Violet's "Day of Lost Options." Its significance cannot, of course, be evident to her or to us as we are embedded in her sense of present reality. But its events become the focus for her restructuring of her self-definition and as such they obtain a significance not present in the events themselves. Like lived reality, in other words, the day has no inherent pattern but assumes a pattern because Violet chooses it as the conceptualizing lens for her self-analysis. It is the day on which she loses her job and learns of her uncle's suicide, but more significantly it is the day on which she begins to shift responsibility for her life away from external forces and toward her own controlling sense of agency. Her assessment of her situation at that time, even before she has learned of her uncle's death, indicates how far she has to go in her redefining narrative: "I felt as though someone had canceled out all my own hope as well, taken away everything: my man, my livelihood, my youth, my promise, what looks I had, the roof over my head" (p. 72). In the midst of that day, she seeks pattern not in her own assessment but in the attribution of blame to external forces.

Nonetheless, that is the day on which, as she says in the opening paragraph, "my story begins in earnest" (p. 11)—the day through which she begins to view and review her own experiences. From the beginning, it is clear that while she has much to learn she also has much she can retain from that self. The first evidence of continuity is present in her careful interlacing of present tense with past tense as a way of identifying qualities that remain central to her: "I *am* a painter. I *like* to listen to music while I work" (p. 11, emphasis added). And then: "Even though I was doing hard work, I was in that rarefied state of consciousness I *like* best: submerged to a sensuous degree in my subject, yet allowing my thoughts to roam free. Today, they were striking out in many different directions, yet weaving a pattern, too. I was thinking of death and love and ambition" (p. 11, emphasis added). The self-definition she is formulating through her new narrative construct opens out from that continuous commitment to her work and from the developing need for a new pattern that can interweave her thoughts of death, love, and ambition.

As we proceed through this opening day, we identify additional techniques through which the narrative process addresses simultaneously the congruence and the alteration in Violet's selves. We become conscious not only of precise verb tense, but also of narrative superimposition of a past Violet on the present Violet. Consider, for example, the beginning of chapter 3; as Violet walks toward the interview with Doris Kolb that brings the loss of her job, she is discomfited by memories of a younger self: "I looked at my reflection in each plate-glass window I passed and recalled every detail of that younger version, getting dressed in a room by herself in the Martha Washington Hotel" (pp. 48–49). It is significant that the present reflection is directly superimposed upon the physical self-image of the past, but it is also significant that the past self, in this instance, is recalled in the third person: her present self seems cut off from that younger hopeful self. The jarring of the sense of connection against the sense of disconnection establishes the necessity of the circuitous narrative, for only in this manner can she safely acknowledge her past self and begin to seek out the appropriate continuities and establish narrative links.

In the narrative progression we become increasingly aware that it, in fact, is operating in three time schemes: not only the narrative present and the remembered past but also the narrative future. That is, we begin to recognize that our perspective is not submerged in the Violet of the present moment but is rather meshed with the perspective of the Violet who has lived through all of these experiences, past and present, and is assessing *both* from yet another temporal distance. Though we believe that the Violet walking toward Doris Kolb's office does indeed remember her younger self setting out to the galleries, we also begin to recognize the narrative implications of the juxtaposition: the false optimism of the one self and the jaded cynicism of the other reflect not only each other in inversion but also a continuous thread of self-observation and need for external confirmation in her sense of destiny.

Though the narrating self is not explicitly present in these juxtapositions, she provides the implicit presence of narrative selection and judgment here, just as she did in her opening use of present tense. In a later juxtaposition, she more sharply focuses the narrative lens through her present self toward a past self and thus emphasizes the concept of a continuous selfhood.

> But now, looking across the space of nine years at that evening, I understood its essence. There I had crouched in the shadows of my own potential. I had my feelings and I had my materials, but I didn't know how to make one work for the other. There I sat, waiting for something to happen, for the phone to ring, for help to come from outside. That something was happening inside, I never considered. That certain equations were being made, certain colors and tonal values being locked away in my visual memory which could later be opened by the right combination of accumulated experience, I never dreamed. And if I had been told, I would have replied impatiently, "But I want something tonight!"
>
> Now I saw the painting that might come out of all this. It would come out of that evening, but balanced by this one. "Violet in Blue" was how I thought of it. (Pp. 127–28)

The accumulation of such memories is assembled into coherent narrative not by the chronology of a past self yielding a present self, but by the constructed story of a present self growing into recognition of the future narrating self. Each juxtaposition aids in the gradual trust in a genuine sense of destiny, a destiny in the form of a goal to be grasped and shaped rather than a fate to be passively awaited: the existentialist shaping of identity through projected goals. Thus when Violet feels early in her stay at Plommet Falls that she is replaying "that same sense of destiny waiting in the wings" (p. 282) that she had felt the summer after graduation from college, we can recognize with the narrator that this belief is fraught with the dangers of past selves, but also pregnant with the possibilities of the future self. By this time in the narrative, we are increasingly aware that the shaping force for Violet's narrative is not mere casual memory but rather the conscious search for evidence by which to reconstruct her sense of self.

The narrative in which we actually share, then, is a different sort of narrative from the old story lines that had continually falsified

Violet's past self. This narrative refuses the containment of paradigmatic plot and seeks instead the possibility of explanation and coherence without that "lopping off" of significant parts of the self. In the final chapter, Violet speaks directly in the voice of her future self, remembering the closing episode of this part of her story.

> I like to remember that October morning. I like to go back into it from the "future," where I now live, and retrospectively paint into it all the prescient signs of my belated emergence. For years of my life I developed my negative propensity for time travel. At a moment's notice I could plunge into some awful moment of the past (or some awfuler fantasy about the future) and come back with enough material to take a lugubrious bath in. Now I am becoming adept in making the positive trip as well. I send my mental spaceship to points past or future and it frequently comes back with old buds of present blossomings (like that October morning); or sometimes a bold design for fruits to come. (P. 347)

The "buds," of course, were only there because they have yielded blossoms: she would not otherwise recognize their generative possibilities. What she is narrating is not a simple linear success story but rather the process by which she has reclaimed and redefined herself toward the possibility of success. As a process of selection, narration has provided her with a continuous selfhood founded in those past choices and past identities that she wishes to claim rather than in those that preclude the possibility of change and of committed work. Her opening label of herself as "a painter" thus becomes the defining thread for her continuous effort toward a destiny that is process rather than closure.

This overarching narrative pattern is very different from a rigid sense of plot: it indicates and identifies continuous patterns of choice rather than imprisoned self-limitation. But much of Violet's effort in her narration must be to remove the props of inauthentic use of plot to structure her selfhood, as is especially evident in her relationship to her work as illustrator of gothic romances. Because she is careful always to read the novel she will illustrate—a sign of the latent integrity in her relationship to her work—she has a large store of plots functioning in her thought processes. From these plots she has abstracted the obvious formula pattern that dominates essentially all of her cover illustrations: the heroine fleeing from the sinister-looking mansion, eventually to be retrieved by the villain who turns hero and comfortably ensconces her in the mansion turned benevolent. At the novel's opening, the formula has become a dangerously available self-defining pattern for Violet, who too clearly identifies with the heroines of these stories: indeed, in the first chapter, she is using a photograph of herself as model for the current illustration.

Even at the beginning of the novel, Violet displays a reasonable skepticism about this formula plot, particularly as she questions its conclusion—"we would belong to each other now and always" (p. 18)—and its failure to acknowledge any story beyond the "always." But her early skepticism is partial; as she goes on to create the story beyond the end of the story, she manages only to invert the gothic formula through series of questions and possibilities all couched in the need for formula definitions. The bemused cynicism of her projected story is very clearly linked to the fact that this is a thinly disguised version of her own marriage and divorce, which she then narrates for us undisguised in the second chapter. But the evident relishing of the pattern of gothic romance is clear enough in the conclusion of the inverted pattern in which she gives the hero a new bride who loves to listen to the story of the first wife, enjoying the "piquant" pleasure of sitting "in a warm, well-appointed place, listening in comfort and security to the tale of the wild ungrateful woman fleeing into the outside world, toward some sharp, shivery destiny of her own" (p. 23). Through such a transformation, Violet can simultaneously invoke the comfort of a defined pattern for her life and still hold on to the apparent claim to freedom of movement without genuine responsibility for her own "destiny." She can, even in the "freedom" of her role as artist rather than wife, continue to be an appropriate gothic heroine.

At this point in the narrative, the dangers of a fixed plot are very evident. She has chosen a label rather than making a genuine causal connection as she will later learn to do. At present, her dominant self-perception is that of victim, a label obviously related to her identification with the gothic heroine. She particularly likes to think of herself as "The Orphan" and thereby make herself eligible for "the currency of sympathy" (p. 12). True to this early pattern, her reaction after having lost her job is to wallow in self-pity and gin because the "grooves of my mind were more accustomed to the concept of Violet Clay as victim than as victress" (p. 73). Like her earlier attempt, her attempt to deal with the latest trouble is to develop a narrative line to the false semblance of significant pattern. First she rejects the narrative line someone else might have followed: "In someone else's story, the heroine would have embraced her setback" (p. 73). Then, she defines her own contrasting personal conclusion, through her integration of the gothic formula: "With the names and faces bobbed up phrases, fully formed and with an incontestable rhythm, like certain worn-smooth sentences that recurred predictably in the gothics I had illustrated: 'And then I knew that someone in that house wanted me dead' " (p. 74). After identifying the appropriate despairing refrains for her life as victim, she weaves her "own weird patterns of cause and effect" (p. 74) and defines the pattern once more as one of victimization, the fault of external circumstances beyond her control.

Though Violet claims to be doing only survival work in her job as illustrator, she has a decided emotional commitment to the gothic romance. So long as she can pretend to herself that she is responding to economic exigencies, she need not confront the realities or falsities of her own earlier ambitions to be a serious artist; but, further, in her work she is continually rehearsing her plot for her own life: the urgency to have an external destiny confirm her own identity, her own reality as part of a pattern. In another context, she identifies as the "perfect adolescent dream: freedom within safety" (p. 329). Similarly, what she wishes at this point from the externals of her life are excitement, validation, and achievement without risk: "that ecstatic sense of being dragged screaming toward one's destiny" (p. 20). In her commitment to the gothic formula and its implications for her own self-perception, she obviously runs the risks identified in Jane Clifford's thoughts: having "vital parts of [her] self lopped off" and becoming "unable to get out again" from the imposed self-definition that the narrative line brings. And with the commitment to formula plots comes a commitment to premature closure: a clear indication of the way in which she must learn new uses of narrative before she can become an autonomous self.

In part, Violet minimizes this risk by denying herself total commitment to any single plot: she simultaneously gauges her life against life patterns she attributes to people around her and thus creates at least the possibility for expanded interlocking life patterns. She has made a story out of her mother's suicide as a young grief-ridden widow—and she has had this fascination further emphasized by her uncle's fictional transformation of that suicide in his first novel. Similarly, she listens attentively and makes subsequent mental reference to her grandmother's narrative of her life story: the tale of the gifted young pianist who is subverted into marriage by the "tempting picture" of the "accomplished wife and mother who turns her gifts to the enhancement of Home"—the very image of the "safe and rich and beautiful" (p. 39). She creates a myth from her uncle Ambrose's life, as I shall discuss later at length, and she hears the life tales of Milo and finally of Sam with the relish of a story-lover searching out the patterns in another person's life. The risks in each of these patterns are less because no single pattern dominates: each would seem to bring with it a different sense of her own appropriate destiny and each can make some contribution to the larger flexible narrative so long as she refrains from making these lives into paradigms for her own. But it is only a fine line between narrative gauges and narrative models; she continually risks denying what the imposed narrative coherence inevitably leaves out. Hence she must learn not to make the implicit assumption that each story has an "ending," that each protagonist has a fixed defining destiny.

Each of the life stories that have particular appeal to Violet is founded in one or the other of her two major self-definitions: the artist and the woman. Indeed, the greatest conflict she faces in her application of external narrative lines to her own life is the conflict between these two dominant modes of self-perception. This conflict is evident from the beginning in her inversions of the gothic formula, but it becomes even more sharply defined as she reconstructs her personal past. Her memory of the decisive summer in Charleston yields the seeds of the conflict: she has just graduated from college, returned to her grandmother's for a summer's respite before taking on the art world in New York. But her stay is dominated by two stories: her grandmother's story of capitulation in femininity and her own projected story of "The Young Woman as Artist." Though she paints regularly and congratulates herself "for having achieved a modern girl's sexual rights without having to marry and ruin my career" (p. 33), she is also magnetized by her grandmother's repeated narrative: "some deeply feminine side of me loved this story of how the talented young Georgette had succumbed to a blitzkrieg assault on her vanity" (p. 39).

Her own abrupt capitulation to Lewis Lanier that very summer does not come as a surprise but neither does it resolve the conflict. She perceives her marriage as "captivity," but, worse, she values it as precisely that: "There was something sexy about having been captured, having been forced . . . to lie down in the sweet juices of traditional womanhood and abandon the hubris of an edgy, lonely struggle" (p. 42). She is particularly aroused by the perception of herself as a helpless "girl," and can even be brought to sexual climax by hearing Lewis murmur, "Poor little girl, I'll take care of you now" (p. 42). The false urge toward self-definition is easily satisfied on one level: all she has to do is think, "I am now a wife" and give herself up to her "senses, to Womanhood" (p. 43).

Even so, her abdication is incomplete because the story and the self-definition are only partial: in adopting the story of the wife, she has denied the story of the artist. And again, her abrupt rejection of one mode for another is neither surprising nor absolute. When she suddenly departs on the bus for New York, wishing to leave behind her self-definition as wife, she takes with her the possibility of pregnancy; in her final days with Lewis she adds to her sexual stimulants the chanted phrase: "Would you like a baby?" (p. 46).

The most direct confrontation between the two narrative patterns, then, comes after she has arrived in New York: graphically it takes the form of menstrual blood, the release from the possibility of pregnancy. But even then she does not know which pattern she wishes to define her. She recognizes that her departure had been tentative: "One foot in the door of the Unknown, the other still holding open its place in the Book of Old Plots" (p. 57). More, she half wishes she could have followed the plot of the "return of the prodigal wife."

Safe again within the bounds of just enough approval, I would have painted my way complacently through all the violets, then the roses and the lilacs, and finally become my very own Still Life with Lilies. My grandchildren would fight over my best paintings after the funeral. They would hang them in their homes and get busy tending the Legend. How She of the Untamed Spirit had once flown the coop but returned in plenty of time to cultivate her own garden—and make their lives possible.

Now here I was, in a run-down women's residence hotel, trapped in the chilly pink waters of my new freedom. And with no prospects—not even a biological one—of any legend to commemorate the fact that I had walked the earth, that I had once been special. (P. 57)

I recapitulate this section of Violet's memories at such length because it so clearly emphasizes both her need to fit into a narrative and her difficulties in doing so since she must always deny some part of her own reality. The problem, of course, derives from the inevitable falseness of the plots themselves, particularly from their insistence that as a woman she must make an either/or choice between her femaleness and her ambition. She has no available pattern for narrative connections that include both work and womanhood. It is not a problem that disappears even after she has ostensibly chosen her work; she continues to debate, in various forms, "the merits of perilous freedom versus stifling security" (p. 127). And her whole adoption of the gothic romance as a means of self-definition is merely a continuation of the same conflict: the urge to relinquish self-definition to the responsibility of someone else, if not a man, then at least an externally imposed destiny and self-definition. Having chosen art, she still refrains from actively pursuing it. For the moment, she continues to find it easier to remain within the confining but safe story line of the victim.

But that is to oversimplify both the choices that Violet makes and the implications of narrative structures for her self-definition. While she does not actually begin to take control of her own destiny until the day her story begins "in earnest"—i.e., nine years after she arrived in New York—she has worked out ways of preventing total self-victimization. And while her reliance on narrative patterns is certainly full of self-falsifications, it also provides her with her tentative tools of survival. The story of the young artist has to be altered and compromised, but it provides her with partial sustenance until she learns to make a more complex use of her need for pattern.

This story of the young artist, as both sustenance and foreclosure, is most fully explored through her relationship with her uncle Ambrose. As a novelist and a family member, Ambrose provides a model touching upon two of the most significant needs in her own search for narrative integration: the connection with a personal heritage and the idea of the successful artist. Through these connections she maintains a link to her own past and to her desired future; but simultaneously she uses that link to deny responsibility for herself. When she first arrives in New York, as we are told in additional extended memory sequences, she has a naive faith in his capacities and his commitment to Art. As the years pass, she is given ample reason for skepticism about this vision of him, but her need is too powerful: she requires his "story" as a model for her own and so she retains her personal myth about Ambrose the novelist as a sustaining base for her own personal myth about Violet the artist. When she risks confronting stray fragments of contradictory reality, she merely bypasses them: the fictitious narrative line that she and he have colluded in developing to explain his life is far too important in their mutual self-perceptions for either of them to risk the loss of its coherence. When he verges on admitting failure to her, she refuses even to acknowledge the admission and instead pushes him on with what he takes as a "recipe for salvation" (p. 95). Her superficial response is founded in her own necessity to believe his success story: "I wanted both to reassure him and be gone. To set him back on the road ahead of me in order to give myself a little more time" (p. 95). So long as he has not yet given up his destiny, she can feel secure in the future reality of her own. And while she does not thereby gain an impetus toward her own achievement, she does at least hold onto the possibility of a future.

Even later, when she has begun to realize that her image of Ambrose is distorted, she refuses to give up her sense that his life is a model for her own: regardless of his failings, he provides her with some sense of shared reality, mutual commitment to a goal. As she tells Milo the night of Ambrose's suicide,

> "I felt he was there for me to refer to, living his life a little ahead of mine, wanting the things I wanted. Even his flaws and mistakes have given me a certain comfort. I could sort of measure myself, judge myself, by him. I can't imagine not having someone between me and . . . I'm not sure what. Darkness? Hopelessness?

Where he has been for so long is it going to be just a dark, hopeless
space? I mean, you can't refer to a void, can you?" (P. 114)

Because his story has been so central in sustaining her, his death,
particularly the death of his paradigmatic story, is very threatening
to Violet: she is forced to confront a chaotic reality or a reality with
an intolerable shape. Or she must finally arrive at a new definition
of shape, a new assessment of her own self-definition.

Ambrose had experienced a similar confrontation himself; because he could not alter his own rigid story line or live with a
recognition of chaotic reality, his suicide was the only possible ending to his story. As he had made his entire life into a fiction, so he
had an obligation to his sense of an appropriate ending. But more
than that, the fiction he had made of his life was increasingly multiple and so risked having no appropriate ending at all. His "shape-
shifting" novel finally seems to have no shape at all; based on the
vision of "modern man awash in the flux of too many complexities
and possibilities" (p. 95), it loses all possibility of narrative design
and eventually disintegrates into the three speculative "outlines" of
his own last memory-fantasy constructions. In these, he seems to
have fused reality and fiction in a final effort to construct himself, to
establish a sense of coherence. Near the end of the third outline, he
writes: "Now at this juncture a resounding *dénouement* is needed, a
deep twist which would connect all the levels of his tale and free
him from his dilemma" (p. 343). Though he claims the protagonist
is interested only in living it, not in writing it, he ends the outline
with a direct address that merges not only his own identity and the
protagonist's, but also his sense of the fiction and the life: "How to
end such a tale of unaccomplished desires? You bankrupt rascal, this
has been your biggest caprice of all" (p. 343).

His suicide, then, is his final acknowledgment of the importance
of a shape. As such, it is extremely unsettling to Violet, not only
because she cared about him, but also because she too believes in
the power of narrative design, has believed in the design of his life as
a model for her own. She does not ever fully comprehend the reasons
for his death but through it she is forced to acknowledge that his life
had a reality beyond her own uses of it: "Angels, prods, warnings,
models, demons. With what variations we occupied one another's
thoughts" (p. 289).

In forcing herself to recognize that Ambrose existed apart from her own uses of him, Violet finally begins to come to terms with the major weakness in her uses of other people's stories to help formulate her own: she has created fixed myths rather than allowing for the fictitiousness and therefore instability of all narrative coherences. Stories do not become entrapments of the selfhood if they are temporary and explanatory, agents for change instead of specious attempts to capture reality. What Frank Kermode has said of cultural uses of fiction and myth holds true for individual uses as well: "Fictions are for finding things out, and they change as the needs of sense-making change. Myths are the agents of stability, fictions the agents of change. Myths call for absolute, fictions for conditional assent."[11]

Violet has an extremely powerful need for sense making but for most of her life she has attempted to satisfy that need through myth rather than through story. In her urgency to contain and define reality and her selfhood, she has relied upon false connections and epigrammatic labels that satisfy the explanatory urge but enforce a fixed identity rather than enabling her capacity for change. As she has conspired in Ambrose's mythologizing of his life, so she has risked mythologizing her own: "My life as I saw it then took on the aura of myth. I was not Violet Clay so much as I was the Penitent Who Still Dared to Aspire. In my solitary cabin I seemed to be always under the probationary gaze of someone who would not let me get away with a thing" (p. 268). Though she is by this time much closer to implementing her genuine commitment to her work, she has not yet assumed responsibility for herself nor learned the limitations of narrative coherence. The mythologizing and the labeling are remnants of the self-falsification in which she implicated her uncle Ambrose during his life and in which she continues to implicate him after his death. But like most of her narrative patterns, these falsifications provide partial sustenance and continuity as well as denial of full responsibility for herself.

So too with her need for external confirmation. Like fictions themselves, the human desire to be observed and validated by an external perspective—a desire implicit in the creation of stories— indicates a pattern of inauthentic living and yet is also central to the individual desire to overcome isolation. The reliance on the "probationary gaze" is an indication of Violet's continuing need for such confirmation. In her insecurity, she has often projected or sought out an external perspective as one way of shaping and validating her selfhood: playing out lovers' quarrels "while my cool self watched" (p. 17), externalizing her present activity "as though we were on a movie set" (p. 77), returning to the same place for a haircut "out of sheer need to be recognized for myself" (p. 166), and recurrently projecting the comments of future art critics upon her life and work (e.g., pp. 28, 30, 142). In their extreme form, these attempts are completely debilitating, as in her early days in New York when she seems unable to move without external guidance: "waiting for it to happen, waiting for my fate to begin shaping itself. I waited mostly for the phone to ring, . . . for some outside voice to explain to me what I was doing there and where I was to go next" (p. 126). And even in their less extreme form, they risk being inauthentic denial of her own isolation: in Plommet Falls, she softens her self-imposed solitude by doing her work before "some invisible audience" (p. 292). As she seeks confirmation and explanation, she relies on the audience, the "probationary gaze," the long-awaited voice of fate to provide a gauge for the self, a shape and purpose for an insecure identity.

But, though dangerous, these efforts, like the other patterns of her storytelling urges, are not entirely false. They are an immature manifestation of the genuine need that gives impetus to the larger narrative itself: the protagonist's need to step back from herself and identify patterns of selfhood, meaningful definitions of her own actions. As a personal assessment of her own past, her story inevitably requires a high degree of self-consciousness: she observes her own activities as she tries to link them together. But more, she invokes an immediate audience in the reader to help her define and assess her own patterns of selfhood: "you," she says repeatedly, as when she identifies "the morning on which I invite you to enter my life" (p. 13) or says, "In case you're worrying" (p. 65) and "perhaps you remember it, too" (p. 127). The effect of such reminders is complicated: the reader is drawn into the immediate process of the narrative and is even implicated as a participant in the structuring process. The narrator-protagonist is not telling us a finished tale but is rather requiring of us a recognition of her own sense of self, a validation that refuses to be a self-entrapment.

This need for recognition is closely linked to another of the human needs addressed by the process of narrating: the need to set one's own potentially solipsistic experience in a larger human context, the need to be not only unique but also similar to other people. This, of course, leads to one of the powerful risks Violet faces in comparing her own life to the stories she has made out of other people's lives: the risk of merging her own identity into the paradigmatic tale as a way of generalizing human experience. The story of her own marriage verges too closely on matching her grandmother's, and her own escape from that marriage is easily seen as an escape from her grandmother's fate, her grandmother's story. The drastic revision in Ambrose's story that his suicide requires similarly threatens her own story and forces her to rewrite both his and her own selfhoods. But despite such risks, the need remains and must be met in other less confining ways. In part, this need is served by the direct address to the audience, the involvement of readers in shaping and expanding the personal base of Violet's own narrative, particularly when she makes generalizations that deliberately embrace protagonist and reader: "As any of you know who have been there, there is a certain point on the road downward from your hopes . . ." (p. 73). The effect of such inclusion is a focused version of the entire narrative: my story is in significant ways congruent with your own; telling the story itself enables the sense of human connection without automatically denying the sense of individual identity. In the chapter titled "A Revery"—which is a sort of "spiritual retreat" (p. 121), a brief but decisive preparation for her later retreat at Plommet Falls—one of Violet's clarifying insights prepares her for the possibility of fruitful generalization: "Weren't we all involved in the contest between living and dying, between doing what we wanted and needed to do and not doing it?" (pp. 128–29). Her further exposition of this question invokes the sense of narrative coherence she has created for paradigmatic lives, but it shows a greater sense of open-endedness, a willingness to gauge the need for coherent individual stories against the possibility of altering the story line: she can accept her own conflicting urges as her individual responsibility and yet as part of a larger pattern of human need.

What Violet has begun to learn in the months following her "Day of Lost Options" is that she cannot rely upon the false shaping of narrative pattern. Order remains crucial to her. But she is learning to distinguish between order that falsifies and denies reality and order that helps to shape and give meaning to reality. The complexity of the total narrative design, then, is her way—and Godwin's—of retaining and validating her need for narrative coherence while still resisting its falsifications. She finally recognizes that the process of narration is closely linked to the process of self-victimization, both through the use of gothic patterns and through the reliance on external labels and definitions of self. Similarly, she recognizes that in both processes, the self risks avoiding responsibility for her own actions: on the one hand by requiring external confirmation and on the other by blaming external circumstances. But the narrating Violet has at last acknowledged these processes to be specious in the forms invoked by her younger self; and at the same time, from her retrospective assessment of her own development, she still knows how crucial the need is. Her final plunge into solitude marks the impossibility of living without some external context, and her entire narrative represents the healing of a self-defined selfhood through creating the narrative links for an audience and for her own self looking backward. The problem in seeking external confirmation evolves not from needing the involvement of some audience but from relying on that audience to define oneself: relinquishing the process of self-definition rather than claiming it. In using the narrative process simultaneously to claim her past self and to achieve a distance on it, Violet has renewed the process of external confirmation while retaining her obligation to self-definition.

In the course of structuring her life, narrating through the defining focus of her Day of Lost Options, Violet Clay has found a way of balancing existential reality against narrative form. Her predecessor in *The Odd Woman*, Jane Clifford, was obsessed with the Aristotelian concept of plot, moving "from possibility to probability to necessity"; at the same time she was very conscious that "you had to write yourself as you went along."[12] For Violet, the Day of Lost Options forces the knowledge that she must forego the sense of a necessary ending, forego a confirmed destiny—the knowledge, in fact, that her lost options were in some sense only "escape clauses" (p. 217, cf. p. 72) that prevented her from ever forging her possibilities toward a future. In formulating her new plot, stripped of escape clauses and shaped through a new knowledge of self-responsibility, Violet avoids the premature closure of false destiny and establishes a new sense of destiny that keeps her always at the point of possibility and yet defined through a commitment that integrates past decisions. She does not, as Ambrose does, become "obsessed by the *other* ways things could have gone in life" (p. 349); rather she claims the way things have gone and uses the narrative process to integrate toward the way she wishes things yet to go.

Her first major painting is in some sense the visual manifestation of this narrative process. The painting is a depersonalized portrait of Sam (Samantha), who comes closest to being an appropriate narrative model for Violet, not because Sam's life itself is paradigmatic but because she has learned ways not to deny the past—which for her has been particularly horrible—and yet still to claim the future: "She was like some hybrid woman, a composite of what had always been and what could be" (p. 345). The thematic focus of the painting is thus a new version of the old conception for "Violet in Blue" whose challenge Violet had defined as "how well I could capture the state of *precariousness*, how well I could evoke, through paint, choices hanging in the balance, the way different thicknesses (like different individuals) strove to impose their color against all that would go on anyway" (p. 128). This old challenge is refocused and renewed in Sam, "a subject that could be a match for my inner necessities" (p. 321). Violet realizes that Sam represents a refusal of the old gothic picture, a refusal of victimization, and a refocusing of the old questions for Violet herself: "There was something about her picture that intrigued me also. Sam had built her own house and was running in a different direction. Was there a choice to be made between these pictures or was it a matter of finding a new composition that could sustain a balance between them?" (p. 322).

The resultant painting, which will serve as the poster of an art show titled "Suspended Woman," becomes the affirmation of destiny that refuses closure: a reflection of Violet's own "inner necessities" (p. 321), a restoration of her commitment to her work, a renewal of an old conception, a claiming of herself as woman. The final two paragraphs of the novel give verbal play to the conception that takes visual form in the painting: "And there she is, and will remain, securely netted in layers of light. Meanwhile that limitless radiance which eludes us all spins on, taking our day with it, teasing and turning us for a time in its vibrant dimensions, continuing to spread its blind effulgence when we have gone" (p. 366). Its excessive language in part undermines the effectiveness of the statement, but at the same time it also mocks the possibility of concluding at all. Like the painting, the conclusion of the narrative pattern is fixed and yet resists conclusiveness.

Nearly five years before the publication of *Violet Clay*, Godwin wrote some notes on the concept of a "fully human heroine."[13] In the concluding section, she indicates some defining characteristics that are clearly a part of her thinking in *Violet Clay*. A fully human heroine would be, she says, "the subject of her own destiny, not the object of 'Blind Destiny' nor a character in someone else's destiny."[14] Such a heroine would also have a commitment to work and to growth and a sense of claiming her own identity and place. Having cited Jung's statement that "the larger problems of life are by their very nature insoluble," Godwin adds, "My heroine would not *solve* these problems, then, but she would be worthy of them."[15]

Violet Clay has not solved the problems of life nor has she found a way to resolve the conflicts between her sense of self as artist and her sense of self as woman. But in steadily addressing these problems, she has learned to use the process of narration itself to open the future and to affirm her autonomy and her self-definition rather than to deny and confine her. Through granting Violet the power of the narrative process to explore possibilities and to assess patterns, Godwin has given her protagonist the capacity to be "the subject of her own destiny": a destiny re-created and renewed with each new choice. Violet Clay has learned not so much the art of painting as the art of narrating the self and acting toward an ever-changing destiny.

II

As some readers of *Violet Clay* find her to be unappealingly passive and confined to a sense of female self as victim, so some readers of *The Stone Angel* find Hagar Shipley to be unappealingly cold and prideful, an enactment of the culturally stereotyped angry old woman.[16] Margaret Atwood refers to her as a "frozen old woman,"[17] and George Woodcock calls her a "choleric earth mother,"[18] who is dominated by her "black bile" until the end of the novel when she finally accepts "the blessings of another element . . . water."[19] Such characterizations point toward a vision of character defined by traits and confined within an external objectification of her self-hood.

Hagar's novel can also be seen as simply an enactment of such defined traits: the nineteenth-century vision of character as destiny. Toward the end of her narrative, she herself reaches a similar conclusion.

> When did I ever speak the heart's truth?
>
> Pride was my wilderness, and the demon that led me there was fear. I was alone, never anything else, and never free, for I carried my chains within me, and they spread out and shackled all I touched. Oh, my two, my dead. Dead by your own hands or by mine? Nothing can take away those years.[20]

Shackled by her own "nature," she seems doomed to enact the experience of her biblical counterpart—bondswoman in the desert—and to spread her lack of freedom like a contagious disease.

As character seems defined by qualities and labels, so plot seems initially to follow a fixed pattern from beginning to end. Though the flashbacks occur in alternating sections with the periods of the present time interior monologue, they occur chronologically and lead toward a conclusion that can only be inevitable; death, the eventual end for any life story, rounds out the narrative whose first flashback takes us back to Hagar's childhood. The pattern and the conclusion at least imply a coherent and closed form.

This encapsulated description of the novel would, then, make it an inappropriate expression of the process of women's self-narration as a redefinition of identity toward openness and in resistance to cultural objectification of femaleness. But this description of the novel does not do justice to its openness and complexity. Instead of being an encapsulated version, the novel is a narrative resistance to just such a version: an enactment of Hagar's redefinition of self and experience through the imposition of narrative form and the rejection of external definitions of her self. For Hagar, like Violet Clay, is the agent of her own story, the active source of selection and interpretation; though at age ninety she continues to "carp" (p. 3), her anger is not the choler of a humour-dominated character, but the legitimate rage of a complex person resisting the limitations on female identity and insisting on her personhood even at the moment of death.

The author's original title for the novel was simply *Hagar*,[21] and the entire narrative is indisputably Hagar's. Not only does it trace her mental processes in a first-person narrative of past and present, but also, and more importantly, it is her private exploration of identity: who she is and how she can interpret past choices as participant in present reality. In the counterpoint between past and present, the present experiences serve as interlocutors of the past, as Hagar seeks a narrative explanation for her life and identity. In "Narration in the Psychoanalytic Dialogue," Roy Schafer identifies the possibility of "changing" the past: "We change self-histories as we change the implied or stated questions to which they are answers."[22] Hagar's current life poses for her new questions that she can answer only by examining parallel circumstances in the past. The monologue is not psychoanalytic, but its effect is a narrative ordering of personal reality toward the kind of enabling self-history that Schafer claims for psychoanalytic narrative. She draws information from her memory to structure a narrative hypothesis that serves as both model and parallel for present experiences: a dialogue in creation of an altered self-history. Thus although the novel's voice is technically interior monologue, its form is governed by conscious narrative construction of the past as a way of reinterpreting both past and present, a way of using narrative form, in dialogue, to escape narrative teleology.

The structure of the novel is deceptively simple: a few days of Hagar's current life, told in the present tense, frame the periodic extended memory sequences, which fall in chronological order. Her present involves her difficulties as an old woman forced by age into physical dependence on her son and daughter-in-law, her decision to claim solitude and independence by running away to a deserted cannery by the sea, her conversation there with a stranger, and finally her return to the hospital where she dies. The present events, then, are sparse and prosaic. But much of their interest lies in the questions they pose to the past and the past-present dialogue that provides the restorative self-history through which Hagar orders her life and through which we recognize the legitimacy of her rage and the complexity of her sense of self.

The concern with complex identity is established early in the novel through Hagar's retrospective uncertainty about other people's identities. She remembers her father's three apparently contradictory responses to a piece of local news, responses she had not understood as a child: "None of the three made much sense to me then, but they stuck in my mind. I've since pondered—which was my father?" (pp. 15–16). Similarly, she recalls and then questions her childhood interpretation of her brother Matt: "Maybe he didn't feel that way at all—how can a person tell?" (p. 20). Such experiences of doubt about other people's "identities" and the need to reopen old interpretations set an initial context for seeing both the past and other people as, in part, a function of interpretation and therefore subject to reinterpretation.

The question of Hagar's own identity is posed most materially in her current relationship with her body. In its age and illness and pain, her body seems alien to her and beyond her control. This seems to be precisely the experience of aging that Simone de Beauvoir describes as a "feeling of depersonalization" that yields "a curious sense of doubling"—"this cannot be *I*, this old woman reflected in the mirror!"[23] Her "belly growls and snarls like a separate beast" (p. 34); she looks down at her body and sees "with surprise and unfamiliarity the great swathed hips" (p. 48); the mirror shows "a puffed face purpled with veins" (p. 68). And yet she knows that she is the same Hagar in the experiential continuity that ties all her experiences together: "I am past ninety, and this figure seems somehow arbitrary and impossible, for when I look in my mirror and beyond the changing shell that houses me, I see the eyes of Hagar Currie, the same dark eyes as when I first began to remember and to notice myself" (p. 33). Similarly, when still in Manawaka, after years of marriage to Brampton Shipley, she sought out a mirror: "I stood for a long time, looking, wondering how a person could change so much and never see it. So gradually it happens" (p. 117); and then: "The face—a brown and leathery face that wasn't mine. Only the eyes were mine, staring as though to pierce the lying glass and get beneath to some truer image, infinitely distant" (p. 118). In the eyes, she claims the "I," the self who persists through all the bodily changes. After all, the mirror reveals not an objectification of self, but an acknowledgment of subjective continuity. The physical assaults of aging estrange her from her body—especially because women's identities are supposedly manifest in their bodies—but the aging process also emphasizes the continuity of a selfhood residing in memory, intelligence, perception. And her rage directed at her own aging body is the resistance to a false entrapment of her intelligent and perceptual being rather than a static expression of a recurrent trait.

Hagar's selfhood, then, is not a fixed entity but rather the subject of a dynamic process of resisting false constraints and creating an enabling self-history, the informing dialogue between past and present. The first memory sequence is introduced through the concept of old age as a false objectification of selfhood and the recognition that children suffer a comparable objectification: "neither are human to the middling ones" (p. 4). Hagar's present feelings of denied humanity thus put the implicit question to her past: how was my childhood comparable? What can it tell me about myself and my approaching death? The responding sequence reveals a series of incidents that presented problems of interpretation and of exclusion to her childhood self: her surreptitious visit to the funeral parlor to see a dead baby; her chance witnessing of her father in an awkward sexual encounter that didn't materialize; the death of her brother Dan. In these and other circumstances she identifies the difficulty of interpretation and the impossibility of knowing with certainty the identity and yearnings of another person. At one point she characterizes her response as based on "the fury children feel toward mysteries they have perceived but been unable to penetrate" (p. 15); the past now provides her with a similar opacity except as she is able to control and interpret it in narrative form.

This initial sequence is dominated by memories of threats to her childhood sense of self: the knowledge that her mother had died in Hagar's own birth, the multiple sensations of self-consciousness, the recognition of threat and value in being similar to her father, and the denial implicit in his never calling her by her name. From this knowledge of self and the threats to female selfhood came her central refusal of this first sequence, the refusal to pretend to be her mother at her brother Dan's deathbed: "all I could think of was that meek woman I'd never seen. . . . To play at being her—it was beyond me" (p. 21). The whole series of memories could be interpreted as revealing failed sympathy. But instead it reveals to us her need to affirm her own sense of self as separate from female expectations, a valuing of life and integrity, a legitimacy of anger. The emphases on death, sexuality, and identity become explanatory emphases in the narrated memory by which she responds to the query put by her *present* feelings of denial. A rage at her helplessness and an insistence on her self-perception tie past self to present self.

In childhood she could not play the role of her meek mother and she reacted to uninterpretable mystery with a responding fury; in later memory sequences, she continues to identify in her narrated past a *resistance* to the attempts to confine and label her and an enactment of resistance through anger. The second major sequence tells how she chose her husband in anger at her father, who valued her matured femaleness only "as though I were a *thing* and his" (p. 37) and who persistently treated her as marriageable property. Her choice of Brampton Shipley, a virile and socially unacceptable farmer, was a choice against the confines of her *father's* definition of womanhood. It was a choice for her sense of self: "I was Hagar to [Bram] . . . he was the only person close to me who ever thought of me by my name, not daughter, nor sister, nor mother, nor even wife, but Hagar, always" (p. 69). And it is also a choice for sexuality, for she found in her marriage a sexual force that was compelling though it remained her secret, her response unknown even to Bram.

In marrying Bram, Hagar had again acted out of a kind of angry resistance. But her interpretive narrative leads her—and us—to an understanding that her actions were shaped by more than merely willful anger. This memory sequence was prompted in the present by a conversation about her background and a vision of herself as "Hagar with the shining hair" (p. 36), an integral self, a person of privilege, and an attractive female. Her remembered reaction against her father and toward Bram is revealed, then, as a legitimate urge away from the false confinements of the privileged daughter and toward a claiming of that strength of self and a validation of her sexual attractiveness. That her choice was fundamentally a sexual one speaks for the importance of her sexuality in her sense of self; that she kept her sexual responsiveness secret speaks for the cultural denial of any female sexuality beyond objectification as a marriageable daughter.

This narrative knowledge prepares her for further interpretations of her past, in which she identifies not only the integrity of her feelings for Bram, but also eventually the insufficiency of the choice based on those feelings. For the legitimate rage and the sexual need that motivated her marriage were, in fact, not granted scope within the marriage itself. Though he knew her as Hagar, as herself, he expected of her only that she meet his *own* expectations. He did not even suspect her sexual responsiveness because he did not expect it (p. 71): the interpretive schema was not available. What he did expect, as she discovered the night Marvin was born, was the production of male heirs. Again her resistance and anger emerged but again they were more than willfulness, for the primary motivation lay in her feelings of betrayal and denial. She remembers having broken a picture of a knight and a lady in fury as she felt how its false playing at passion had betrayed her (p. 73). She remembers the nights of sexual passion, her own arousal always kept secret, and the days of wrangling: the impossibility of integrating her sexuality with her daily reality, the impossibility of full selfhood while meeting the expectations of wife to Bram, mother to his heirs. From this knowledge of betrayed selfhood emerges the narrated choice once again to resist the imposed definition; the narrative segment identifies her refusal to be a function in Bram's scheme, her reclamation of her own sense of self, which had become shrouded over in a body and an image she could not recognize as her own. In an anger of hardened resistance, she chose to protect her subjective complexity by leaving Bram and by rejecting experiences of objectification through culturally imposed expectations of femaleness.

Through the narrative interpretation, Hagar's present self is able to recognize the strength and the necessity of that decision: "Each venture and launching is impossible until it becomes necessary, and then there's a way" (p. 120). And this knowledge, in turn, informs her present. The question she had put to her past had evolved out of a current feeling of trapped helplessness: "I've waited like this, for things to get better or worse, many and many a time. I should be used to it. So many years I waited at the Shipley place. . . . I felt something else must happen—this couldn't be all" (p. 98). And the answer the past has given her is the recognition that her current venture is both possible and necessary: "I've taken matters into my own hands before, and can again" (p. 123). From her past strength in taking action, she gains present strength to seek solitude, to go alone by bus to Shadow Point and its cannery by the sea.

Though she soon discovers that rather than having accomplished an escape, she has brought her loneliness with her to Shadow Point,

she also brings with her the enabling knowledge of the past informing the present. Her memories of arriving with her son John at Mr.
Oatley's house to begin her new life are again congruent with the
present arrival: "And here am I, the same Hagar, in a different establishment once more, and waiting again" (p. 141). Through identifying the similarity of past and present, she is able to expand her
concept of anger into a stengthening for the present. The legitimate
rage of resisting a falsely confining identity and the knowledge of
her own strength have prepared her for a more difficult resistance: "I
can't change what's happened . . . or make what's not occurred take
place. But I can't say I like it, or accept it, or believe it's for the best. I
don't and never shall, not even if I'm damned for it" (p. 142). From
her narrative interpretation of the past, she has gained *experiential
knowledge:* resisting the limitations of her identity as female has
pointed the way toward the strength for an honest rage against the
immutable.

Hagar's internal dialogue between past and present continues as
she narrates her son John's growing up, his return to Manawaka, her
own return to Manawaka as Bram dies, John's love affair and then
his death. The narrated memories are prompted by the natural surroundings at the cannery and then by the personal narrative of her
fellow solitary, Murray Lees. As the dialogue progresses, it continues to center in the integrity of her rage and the need to connect
past with present in a claimed selfhood. The most probing dialogue
between past and present is prompted by Murray Lees's narrative of
his son's death, which leads to her own narrative of John's horrifying
accidental death. The question both stories pose is the question
behind Hagar's entire series of memory sequences: "No one's fault.
Where do causes start, how far back?" (p. 214, cf. p. 162). This is, of
course, the question for narrative explanation, the assessment of
causal patterns. But it is also an implicit acknowledgment that the
answers are hypotheses, never the full assessment of the past.

From the unanswerable question to another unanswerable question, she continues to seek possibilities of explanation in the relationship of past to present. How does one live with the intolerable?
The question reverberates between past and present, John's death
and her own approaching death. Her reaffirmed rage is the answer to
which she returns: "It angers me, and will until I die. Not at anyone,
just that it happened that way" (p. 218). Though she agrees with

Lees that her anger is fruitless, she holds to it as an emotion of integrity in the face of the unacceptable. And, in fact, the strength of self she reveals as she faces her own death demonstrates that this rage is not fruitless at all: this is the rage that prepares her to interpret her ending as more than mere capitulation.

Through her retrospective narrative, she has also reexamined her relationship to culturally assigned roles of women: daughter, sister, wife, mother. Her relationship to these roles has been primarily a formal one, not an emotional one, so that her tension in relationship to the roles is not between emotional overinclusion and isolation but rather, as Harriet Blodgett says, between her withheld and socially proud self and her "urges toward emotional fulfillment." But her life is *not*, as Blodgett also says, "destroyed by the tension";[24] rather she has reached a time in the narrative present tense when she feels the need to reassess her relationship to them. Her narrative enactment of the past makes it possible to see, as well, her positive qualities in the way in which she interacted with these roles and to retrieve part of her experience of the past through its interaction with the present. This retrieval is most evident in her recovered ability to apologize to John—though he is represented by Murray Lees—and to cry tears of a grief she had been unable to shed at the time of John's death: "The night my son died I was transformed to stone and never wept at all" (p. 216). Her narrative enactment makes the past retrievable and frees her from a negated self played out in her role as mother.

Although a large portion of the novel is given to the narrated memories, their function, then, is to inform the present and to reveal the end as implicit not in a determinate past but in a continual reinterpretation of the past. In the opening pages of the novel, Hagar says she is "rampant with memory" but disavows any central concern with the past: "Some people will tell you that the old live in the past—that's nonsense. Each day, so worthless really, has a rarity for me lately. I could put it in a vase and admire it, like the first dandelions, and we would forget their weediness and marvel that they were there at all" (p. 3). Throughout Hagar's present, we see a valuing of sensory experience: she sniffs the air, watches the sky, listens to raucous birds and rhythmic slapping of water, decorates her hair with colorful June bug shells. She claims a special "feeling for any creature struggling awkward and unknowing into life" (p.

83), and after watching the clouds, she asserts, "How I shall hate to go away for good" (p. 105). When tempted to will her death, she finds that she cannot: "I can see as though in a mirror of never-ending depth that I'd not willingly hasten the moment by as much as the span of a breath" (p. 171). This valuing of life in the present is the end through which she now interprets the events of the past: the rage of Hagar's youth against being confined by other people's expectations of femaleness and the rage of her later adulthood against the immutable are both indications of her valuing of life and selfhood.

Hagar's preparation for her own death is, then, the source and the outcome of the whole series of narrated memories. Laurence's choice of the Dylan Thomas lines for epigraph underlines this central concern.

> Do not go gentle into that good night.
> Rage, rage against the dying of the light.

Hagar herself expresses this need in an early memory, when she tells of her brother Matt's death and wonders why he didn't fight his death: "Why hadn't he writhed, cursed, at least grappled with the thing?" (p. 52). Even when the drowning darkness tempts her, the temptation is only momentary.

> Now I could fancy myself there among them [the drowned], tiaraed with starfish thorny and purple, braceleted with shells linked on limp chains of weed, waiting until my encumbrance of flesh floated clean away and I was free and skeletal and could journey with tides and fishes.
>
> It beckons a second only. Then I'm scared out of my wits, nearly. Stupid old woman, Hagar, baggage, hulk, chambered nautilus are you? Shut up. (P. 144, cf. p. 200)

In pulling back from her momentary willingness to die, Hagar addresses her rage to herself and thus doubly reinforces the strength of her ongoing experiential self: she will not go willingly, nor will she relinquish that continuity of selfhood located in her anger.

As Hagar's narrative structuring of her past leads her to an increased complexity of self-awareness, it builds through the restructuring of multiple roles to a sense of strength in complexity. And it makes impossible the containment of her sense of self in the self-accusation that her "wilderness" of pride constitutes her personal continuity. Though this characterization could be made congruent with the narrative interpretations she has given us, the shackled self has become the interpreting self and her anguish emerges from the emotional reopening of that telling. The enabling self-history has *not*, in fact, confirmed her continuity in pride and fear, her denial of her feelings. Though she identified those qualities in her narratives of the past, the process itself has opened the altered interpretation that her rage was legitimate, that her actions revealed strength, that she was motivated by a value for life, and that she revealed a capacity to care, however thwarted. She has survived with dignity and "some human warmth."[25]

In Hagar's final days in the hospital, we can see these qualities emerge from the narrative structuring of past self to form the basis for her present strength. Her overpowering need to communicate it all cannot be satisfied: though she thinks with real intensity, *"Someone really ought to know these things"* (p. 265), she recognizes the impossibility of one person's ever fully knowing another. But she does manage to claim the strength of her selfhood rather than be bound by past negations.

> I lie here and try to recall something truly free that I've done in ninety years. I can think of only two acts that might be so, both recent. One was a joke—yet a joke only as all victories are, the paraphernalia being unequal to the event's reach. The other was a lie—yet not a lie, for it was spoken at least and at last with what may perhaps be a kind of love. (P. 274)

In her dying days, Hagar twice acts from personal strength and in freedom: she helps her hospital roommate to a bedpan—the joke on the nurses, the shared laughter of having acted from human sympathy for human need, against the rules—and she voices her love for her son Marvin. Both acts of freedom are small, inconsequential, and yet both are genuine victories of a self claimed and strengthened through her narrative reinterpretation of past and present. Though she is drugged and in pain and verging on incoherence, her narration shows her facing death with dignity and with an unwillingness simply to give in. Her final flair of anger, her final act of selfhood is to grasp the glass of water, insisting on holding it for herself. In this way, her death expresses her continued sense of strength rather than a helpless capitulation. It also expresses, in her two preceding acts of freedom, her participation in a human community. Even in death she is able to affirm both autonomy and inclusion, as she has claimed these possibilities in the interaction with the past. The narrative process has construed the interpretation of events to yield the ending in a death that redefines female selfhood in complex humanity rather than confirming the limitations of objectified femaleness.[26]

In an essay on "Time and the Narrative Voice," Laurence indicates that these two considerations are central to her own structuring of narrative fiction. The character, she says, is "an individual" with her own distinctive voice. In Hagar we see the enactment of this individuality, not as a group of identifiable features but as a subjective expression of voice in personal interaction with environment, both past and present, both social and natural. Laurence also indicates the centrality of the character's own choice of the relevant "personal past, the family past and the ancestral past." The character, that is, exists in the enactment of temporal relations: "the past and the future are both always present, *present* in both senses of the word, always now and always here with us."[27]

In Hagar Shipley, Margaret Laurence has given us a narrator-protagonist engaged in the complex process of ordering her past for the narrative interpretation of the self in the present. In her narrated memories, she seeks the answers to the questions posed by her present life: What will my death mean? Who have I been and how am I prepared to die? Though she is culturally cast in the role of angry old woman, such a description does not do justice to the positive force of her complexity or the legitimacy of her rage. In the end, she is not like the wounded gull trapped in the old cannery, battering against the floor "in the terrible rage of not being able to do what it is compelled to do" (p. 194). Rather she is a strong and complex selfhood, founded in rage and dignity: "for I'll be dead as mackerel. Hard to imagine a world and I not in it. Will everything stop when I do? Stupid old baggage, who do you think you are? *Hagar*. There's no one like me in this world" (p. 223). In this Hagar, Laurence shows the powerful uses of narrative as knowledge, the interpretive strategies available in the ordering of memory into experiential knowledge.[28] Hagar's rage is the human rage against the threat of objectification and against the ultimate threat of death, and her ordering of it reveals the fruitfulness inherent in the narrative process as enactment of both self and reality.

For both Violet and Hagar, the conventional expectations for women's lives provide real danger of entrapment, both textual and social. As women, they experience and even embrace the cultural definitions of who they ought to be, and they experience the powerful pull of narrative teleology toward the culturally defined conclusions. But as their own narrators, they also find the capacity to critique that teleology and to give subversive representation to their experiences as women. Through examining their previous life emplotments they are able to see them as only partial explanations and able to identify experiences and perceptions by which to find new explanations and new self-definitions. No matter how old or apparently entrenched in an old identity, they are able to claim what Simone de Beauvoir reminds us is the primary "justification for present existence": "its expansion into an indefinitely open future."[29] In their self-narration, they move beyond teleology toward human wholeness.

CHAPTER 6

Fragmentation, Complexity, and Wholeness: *The Waterfall* and *The Golden Notebook*

Because representation of women's lives is so closely tied to cultural expectations, most narrative form is in some sense based on female objectification: the cultural *idea* of femininity overtakes and obscures the lived *experience* of being female.[1] That is why women's ability to claim subjective experience in resistance to "idea" is a primary basis of subversive representation of female experience through a narrating "I" who refuses to be "she." A woman who speaks in her own voice of her own experience is a subject rather than an object, and as such, she is capable of self-definition and autonomous action. This is the resistance claimed by Del Jordan and Claudia MacTeer as they grow against the femininity text; this is the resistance of Violet Clay and Hagar Shipley as they re-emplot their previous experience beyond narrative teleology.

But as is implied by the nonlinear narratives of all four of these novels, the narrator's claims cannot be a simple rejection of objectification, for the cultural definition of femaleness is still as object. Simone de Beauvoir's classic statement of the difference in male and female sexual identity articulates, as well, the problem for the characterization of women in novels.

The advantage man enjoys, which makes itself felt from his childhood, is that his vocation as a human being in no way runs counter to his destiny as a male. . . . He is not divided. Whereas it is required of woman that in order to realize her femininity she must make herself object and prey, which is to say that she must renounce her claims as sovereign subject. It is this conflict that especially marks the situation of the emancipated woman. She refuses to confine herself to her role as female, because she will not accept mutilation; but it would also be a mutilation to repudiate her sex.[2]

Thus to refuse objectification is still to risk "mutilation": difficult as it is to claim her autonomous self-definition, a character who does so is then likely to suffer the mutilation of denying her sexuality.

An overt address to issues of female sexuality therefore raises special problems for the representation of women's lives. The female protagonist who wishes to address the problems of female sexuality in her adult present must again find a way to subvert narrative expectations. Like the narrative processes required to represent growing up female and redefining adult selfhood, this narrative process also draws on the open conventions of modernist fiction to reshape the possibilities of representation. But because of the more direct threat of mutilation, the narration of female adulthood in the present finds a particularly effective voice in the overt claiming of multiplicity: the protagonist's deliberate self-fragmentation as a narrative access to a fuller sense of complex selfhood.

The basis for this narrative process resides in the initial recognition that mutilation threatens a strong female selfhood. Based as it is on the culturally imposed tension between subject and object in female identity, the threat of mutilation is implicit in all female characterization. This is the threat Hagar Shipley feels in the tension between her living consciousness and her externally interpreted physical presence: a splitting of herself into mind and body, thinker or actor and perceived femaleness. Even more potently, this is the threat Pecola Breedlove feels in the judgment of the white world upon her ugliness, and this is the threat that eventually forces her to succumb to her own objectification as black and female: the mirror in which she examines her newly "blue" eyes is the mirror of a false and static view of female beauty, a mirror in which she has no selfhood. Or to return to *Martha Quest* and its enactment of Martha's acculturation, this is the threat she tries to ward off in her recurrent self-examination in mirrors, by which she claims sexuality through objectification in images that her social context requires of her as a female; and her response to this objectification is to succumb to the threat of mutilation as she feels continually obliged to deny parts of her own experience, torn between her sexuality and her sense of an "inner" self.

But the tension between self as object and self as subject can also yield self-projection—in mirror images and in narrative projection—as a basis for women's reclaiming agency over their own lives. While Pecola sees an empty sky in the mirror she holds up to herself, Claudia is able to see in Pecola a mirroring of a destructive culture and a way to interpret her *own* image outside its objectification: Pecola's objectified "she" prompts Claudia's "I" as sentient actor. Violet Clay's projection of herself into stories or into her self-portrait are objectifications of her identity but finally also prompting images for her sense of subjective agency. Del Jordan's brief narrative commentaries on her self as "she" and her experiences of self-observation are a way of freeing herself through self-distancing rather than entrapment within those images.

Evolving from the capacity implicit in modernist characterization—the capacity to be open and multiple, not bound into fixed or linear assumptions about plot and reality—self-projection thus becomes another crucial way in which the narrating "I" is capable of subversive representation. By integrating the experience of fragmentation into the structure of the narration, women writers can create a protagonist who resists mutilation as she writes both a self-objectifying narrative *and* an "I" narrative. One value of this narrative split is evident in its capacity to address the self-definition problems of characters like Violet Clay and Hagar Shipley: a female character's reassessment of her previous experience as a basis for present growth. Through a dual narrative voice, a narrator can further reinterpret and acknowledge her distance from her past sense of self, by keeping open her capacity to change. Nadine Gordimer's *Burger's Daughter*, for example, is split between "she" sections and "I" sections, a process partly explained by Rosa's distance from her adolescent self: "it's impossible to filter free of what I have learnt, felt, thought, the subjective presence of the schoolgirl. She's a stranger about whom some intimate facts are known to me, that's all."[3] Similarly, Christa Wolf's protagonist in *A Model Childhood* assesses her changing identity by referring to her childhood self as "she," and her present self as "you" throughout most of the book; giving narrative form to her dissociation of self from self, she gains the capacity of narrative self-definition and overcomes what Wolf's protagonist in *The Quest for Christa T.* calls the incredible "difficulty of saying 'I.' "[4] She develops, in other words, a new self-definition accomplished through self-projection and finally evident in her ability to say "I" at the novel's end.

But this capacity to assess identity through self-fragmentation has an even greater capacity for subversive representation when the narrator-protagonist uses it as a way to gain control over culturally imposed mutilation and to find in multiplicity the basis for human wholeness. Rather than becoming trapped in the false coherence of a culturally defined gender identity, or alternatively seeing her identity in diffusion and unmergeable multiplicity, an adult narrator-protagonist can claim the "I" as the agent of self-projection and self-fragmentation; in using self-narration to assess her relationship to sexual objectification, she can claim both sexuality and autonomy. This is the process by which both Jane Gray in *The Waterfall* and Anna Wulf in *The Golden Notebook* are able to develop their complex identities as adult women.

For Ellen Cronan Rose, these two novels share a concern for representation but reveal a fundamental difference in the rationale for this concern.

> Anna Wulf mistrusts art because its inherent order is false to reality as she perceives it in her experience. Jane Gray mistrusts art because the only art she knows is masculine, and it is false to her female experience. *The Golden Notebook* calls for a new kind of mimeticism; *The Waterfall* for a feminine aesthetic.[5]

But for me, neither of these novels is gender-neutral and neither is seeking a feminine aesthetic. Rather, both of them are based in the same essential concern: to represent women's lives anew, to speak honestly of female experience and especially of female sexuality. In this effort, both novels reveal a new kind of mimeticism grounded in female experience, and as their protagonists choose an enabling self-fragmentation instead of mutilation, both novels claim the capacity to represent women's lives while subverting the male-dominant premises of representation.

I

Jane Gray, the narrator-protagonist of Margaret Drabble's *The Waterfall*, prompts many readers of the novel to anger or disdain toward
her evident passivity, her retreat inward into agoraphobia, her lack
of clear identity. These readers complain that the protagonist's life
is either an indication of her madness or a function of her lack of
seriousness and her self-indulgent femininity. Jane, in fact, does
characterize herself as both passive and withdrawn; she even periodically refers to herself as "mad" or "schizoid." The label is reinforced by her repeated insistence that her sense of self operates at
multiple and conflicting levels, and further reinforced by her confused identification with her cousin Lucy, a kind of double, born
within two weeks of her and bearing a family resemblance.[6] And the
sense of split identity is pervasively evident in the narrative process
itself, the beginning in a third-person narrative and the frequent
shifts between first and third person that follow throughout the
novel.

This view is, in part, a function of the narrative schema by which
these readers perceive and integrate Jane's conflicting comments
about herself: cultural expectations and narrative expectations both
reinforce an anticipation of the femininity text. A novel that begins
with the protagonist's isolation in a self-enclosed and overheated
bedroom and proceeds to bring into her bed a lover—who is her
cousin's husband besides—is clearly susceptible to establishing narrative expectations based exclusively on female sexuality. Even
though the initial narrative situation is not likely to be familiar to
readers, the plot paradigm of romantic love as the appropriate rescue
from isolation is certainly familiar enough.[7]

In an interview with Nancy Hardin, Drabble herself reinforces
the idea that the novel reflects such a femininity text when she
accepts accusations that the book is limited and upsetting, based on
a rare human experience of "sublime, romantic passion."[8] She even
goes so far as to call it a "wicked book" and to acknowledge "respect
[for] the attack by people who say that you should not put into
people's heads the idea that one can be saved from fairly patholog-
ical conditions by loving a man."[9] In this view Jane is "saved" by an
act of "grace" embodied in an arbitrary and fateful encounter with a

rare sexual passion.[10] The protagonist becomes, indeed, a passive enactment of a destiny defined in purely sexual terms. It is this view, or one similar to it, that leads critics such as Elizabeth Fox-Genovese to see Jane as simply living out her fateful "nature": "Jane's natural masochism, victimhood, and suffering led her to an affair with her cousin's husband."[11] In more critical terms yet, Bernard Bergonzi dismisses *The Waterfall* along with *Jerusalem the Golden* as "disappointing, . . . embarrassing and unconvincing over long stretches" and, in his view most damning of all, essentially similar to "women's magazine fiction."[12]

Such statements have a legitimate correlation with the germination of the book. In the same interview with Hardin, Drabble characterizes the decision to write the novel in its dual voice as follows:

> It really wasn't deliberate, you know. It just happened that way. I'd been wanting to write the first section of that book for a long time and I wrote it and I was intending to turn it into a novel. When I'd written it, I couldn't go on because it seemed to me that I'd set up this very forceful image of romantic, almost thirteenth-century love. Having had the experience or describing the experience, one had to say what is this about? I thought the only way to do it was to make Jane say it.[13]

The origins in a "forceful image of romantic, almost thirteenth-century love" imply at least a kind of stasis—image rather than story—and, more, the knowledge that it is self-contained, distanced.

The germinal idea of the distanced Jane, enclosed in an "image of romantic . . . love," then, yields the opening narrative section of the novel: a highly self-conscious structuring of events to create the intensity of the love affair with James, what Jane later calls a "dialogue" between lovers, not a narrative.[14] The progression from such an image to the confusion of the first-person voice and then the repeated alternation may undermine such a pure image but—in a reading of the femininity text—can only yield an interpretation of Jane as mad, divided against herself.

Another possible reading of the self-division can be found in the familiar definition of the female split between mind and body.[15] In this reading, the third-person sections express Jane's sexual identity as the physical definition of selfhood, and the first-person sections express her analytical intelligence. The former remain in a kind of integral physical image and the latter provide supportive interpretations: seeking explanations in memory and context by tracing out the causal patterns in characters' lives and family backgrounds, and identifying the distortions and omissions that result from telling the story in terms of the narrative expectations of a love story. But, though it partially eludes the entrapment in the femininity text, this reading tends to establish two parallel texts and to reinforce the cultural split between mind and body. This, in fact, is a view Jane expresses as her experience of motherhood: "I felt a split between the anxious intelligent woman and the healthy and efficient mother . . . I felt that I lived on two levels, simultaneously, and that there was no contact, no interaction between them" (pp. 108–9).

The reading of the novel that I propose to develop evolves from such a view of Jane's split identity as evident in the narrative structure, but shifts from a dualistic interpretation to a sense of the self as multiple and shaped by the interaction among narrative constructions of identity. In this view, Jane's manipulation of narrative paradigms leads her to reject any single sense of self or reality for a recognition of self in process, able to be both strongly sexual and autonomous.

Drabble's statement about the germination of the novel provides an initial impetus for this reading as well. As she says, once she had written the opening section with its "forceful" and "romantic" image, she "couldn't go on" because the concluding image requires no more narrative explanation: in the paradigm for romantic love, the narrative concludes when the protagonist has found that love. It is, then, in Drabble's decision "to make Jane say it" that she shifts the center of the narrative from romantic passion to interpretation; in doing so, she gives to Jane the agency and control she claims to have denied her. But more than that, this narrative agency reveals that it is not James who saves Jane, but *Jane* who "saves" herself through retrieving her capacity to act in narrative construction and finally beyond narrative construction.[16]

As I have repeatedly argued, the claiming of a woman's right to speak for herself is central to feminist redefinition of female experience. It is this process of claiming her right to speak that governs the novel's narrative interplay between first- and third-person voices, a process by which Jane learns to distance and control the cultural definitions of femaleness, and then to include, as contributing strands of her sense of self in process, the decisively female experiences that do not prevent her capacity to act for herself. Though I do not entirely agree with Carol Gilligan's illustrative use of *The Waterfall* in her analysis of women's morality, I do, like Gilligan, see the novel as the process by which Jane reformulates issues of selfishness and selflessness and "identifies herself with the first person voice," thereby arriving at an ethic capable of including "activity, sexuality, and survival without abandoning the old virtues of responsibility and care."[17]

Since the body has been the primary basis for cultural objectification of women, it is not surprising that the dominant concerns of the third-person sections of the novel are centered in female biology. In the initial third-person sections, of course, we are given the novel's motivating image in which the body is source of sexual passion: not the affirming sexuality of female experience but the objectified sexuality of romance. In this view, sexuality is a succumbing, giving in, yielding up of selfhood. The novel's opening line—"If I were drowning I couldn't reach out a hand to save myself, so unwilling am I to set myself up against my fate" (p. 7)—ironically tricks us into believing we are reading a first-person novel and then immediately withdraws the impression: "This is what she said to him one night" (p. 7).[18] The withdrawal of first-person agency from such a statement underlines the passivity of her immersion in the physical and joins her to those female protagonists who have been drowned by their inability to gain control over their lives, including their sexuality. Both the drowning imagery and the actual expression of passion in these first sections make clear the total passivity of such a notion of romance: initially James merely lies beside her in bed, joining her in the cocoon of isolation she has created around herself. Required by such a view of female sexuality to be mere bodily presence, Jane seems indeed to retreat from any consciousness except sensory receptivity.

As preparation for such a passive passion, her preceding labor and childbirth seem equally passive. Rather than requiring "labor," in fact, the birth seems merely to happen, like an extension of passive immersion in her own solitude. Warmth and dampness provide the primary sensory experiences and together lull her in an underwater world without sound: "Everything was soft and still: the whole night, and Jane's nature with it, seemed to be subdued in a vast warm lull, an expectancy, a hesitation, a suspension and remission of trial. The snow fell outside the uncurtained window, and she could feel the blood flowing from her onto the white moist sheets" (p. 9). Even her physical surroundings, including "the violent colors of birth," are "resolved into silence, into a kind of harmony" (p. 10). In such a trancelike state of passivity, she is very much without a self; her immersion, isolation, and peaceful relinquishing of connection are even reminiscent of Virginia Woolf's characterization of self-dissolution in death in *The Voyage Out.*[19] Jane describes these feelings as similar to being "with somebody one loved—to be wanting nothing, to be desiring and suffering nothing, to be without apprehension, loss, or need" (p. 13). Love, in this view, *is* related to death: an absence of selfhood, a total relationality by which any need for action is precluded. Her withdrawal from external connections is, thus, an appropriate preparation for that sort of romance: "The room softly surrounded her; she could tell that there was no dissension in it, for all dissension came always from herself, and having removed it, having removed herself, everything else could but fall gently into its own place, as the snow fell" (pp. 13–14). Sleeping Beauty, Snow White under glass, she is a cultural objectification, ready to become James's "prisoner," asking only, "And in the end, then, will you rescue me?" (p. 38).

In the initial third-person narrative section of the novel, Drabble, through Jane, has thus created a classic association of femaleness with body with passivity and dependence. Love and sexual expression are not actively chosen but rather exist statically in the drugged quality of immersion. This does not mean that female sexuality is itself passive, only that woman as body has no active control. In fact, the other side of culturally defined female sexuality—its active dangers—does not so much belie this passivity as *require* it. At one point the narrative even indicates that the self-isolation in which Jane has placed herself is a kind of handicapping process: "She had once thought herself a dangerous woman, and it was in fear of such knowledge that she now lay where she was, . . . harmless, weak" (p. 29). Similarly, she sees her "sexual beauty" as "a menace and a guilt and a burden . . . a cruel and disastrous blessing, a responsibility, wild like an animal, that could not be let loose" (pp. 37–38).

Jane's passivity and her knowledge of the power of sexuality become the two major supports for the novel's enactment of the love story and its locus in the body. In the "she" sections, Jane spends most of her time with James or waiting for James, withdrawn into an inner space either domestic or sexual; even their minimal excursions into the world outside her home are given the aura of her passivity under his guidance. To this inner world, sexuality seems to set the boundaries and drowning continues its correlate.

As a powerful biological urgency, sex is then granted the momentous quality of birth or death. Within this intensely sensual self-enclosure, Jane's initial drowning—in passivity and in succumbing to powerful sexual currents—is reenacted in sexual experience, bringing together birth and death as did her initial isolation for Bianca's birth. Her first orgasm confirms both the power and the passivity, both the birth and the death.

> her body about to break apart with the terror of being left alone right up there on that high dark painful shelf, with everything falling away dark on all sides of her, alone and high up, stranded, unable to fall. Then suddenly but slowly, for the first time ever, just as she thought she must die without him forever, she started to fall, painfully, anguished, but falling at last, falling, coming toward him, meeting him at last, down there in his arms, half dead but not dead, crying out to him, trembling, shuddering, quaking, drenched and drowned, down there at last in the water, not high in her lonely place. . . . (Pp. 158–59)

The intensity of this physical/emotional experience, coming as she says from "such depths of need" (p. 158), leads her to grant it that momentous quality, "like death, like birth: an event of the same order" (p. 158); and to experience, then, her sexuality as the enactment not only of drowning but also of birth: "Her own voice, in that strange sobbing cry of rebirth. A woman delivered. She was his offspring, as he, lying there between her legs, had been hers" (p. 159).

As both birth and death, her orgasm epitomizes the tension inherent in the love story. Birth, here, is a restoration of one's body; the release of the caged "animal" of sexuality yields a physical wholeness not otherwise possible. But the "drowning" means relinquishing both the "high" and "lonely place" *and* the perception of oneself as a separate being. For the drowning is a (sub)merging, again a succumbing to forces that overwhelm, and a loss of one's sense of self outside of relationship. In the love story, a woman finds "herself" by losing "herself": Jane's initial dissolution in passivity and her subsequent dissolution in sexuality are ways of "finding" herself within the love story.

But this self can exist *only* within the love story and the inclusion she seems to find in such merging is at the price of a self outside the love story. As the opening third-person sections showed her as having banished her "self" as the source of dissension, so her continued inclusion in the love story requires a repeated banishment of a dissenting consciousness. This is the view that centers cultural definitions of femininity: to be fully a woman one must exist relationally; to choose otherwise is to choose isolation and to remain "alone and high up" in a preorgasmic state of unrelieved tension. For a woman in the love story, the choice is between inclusion and autonomy. She cannot have both.

In some ways this view seems to fit with the psychoanalytic view of women's weak ego boundaries and even to play upon the correlation of weak ego with female biology. In her analysis of "Family Structure and Feminine Personality," Nancy Chodorow points out this correlation between women's difficulty in establishing and maintaining a "consistently individuated sense of self" and the biological experiences of femaleness: "Women's biosexual experiences (menstruation, coitus, pregnancy, childbirth, lactation) all involve some challenge to the boundaries of her body ego (me/not-me in relation to her blood or milk, to a man who penetrates her, to a child once part of her body)."[20] Similarly, we see Jane dissolved and blurred in the novel's opening section's concern with the fluid world of childbirth: blood and dampness. And we see her in her experience of orgasm "drenched and drowned"—both "half dead" and newly born.

Initially these experiences are clearly events under description within the femininity text: Jane would seem to be trapped by the expectations of what constitutes female sexual identity. In both instances of biosexual experience, she claims her physiology and in doing so seems to lose her sense of conscious selfhood. Her body, in other words, seems to enact her loss of self: her drowning, whether the passive succumbing or the release of sexual power, seems biologically destined.

The third-person sections of the novel, then, are constructed on this correlation of physical and psychological in the cultural expectations of femininity. To be female is to be defined biologically, to be passive and dependent, to be sexual at the expense of autonomy. The life of "she" is constructed to meet these needs of the love story and destined to a choice between femaleness and autonomous selfhood. From such a narrative, the "I" is actively excluded.

But the love story is only a part of the novel—only about one-third of the pages are third-person narrative—and the judging, questioning mind cannot be indefinitely repressed. Though she defines herself externally as female passivity and sexual power—and, as body, must drown in her female physiology—Jane as narrator cannot permanently repress the assertive "I": the banished source of dissension in her initial self-dissolution and the critical intelligence that had to be put to sleep in her release of the "animal" of her sexuality. This assertive "I" has no place in "an image of romantic, almost thirteenth-century love," but given her own voice, she will proceed to the assessment Drabble assigned her: "what is this about?"

The first intrusion of the first-person voice on the self-enclosed wholeness of romance is thus a breaking through of the agent-self from the falsehood of narrative containment as "she." Significantly, the last words in which a reader might contentedly believe her- or himself to be immersed in romance—"now she lay there, drowned in a willing sea" (p. 46)—achieve the total passivity that makes the continuation of the "she" narrative nearly impossible. In order to leave behind image and move into narrative, the novel requires some breach in the coherence of the femininity text, and the recentering in a speaking voice of subjectivity provides both agent and breach.

It won't, of course, do: as an account, I mean, of what took place. I tried, I tried for so long to reconcile, to find a style that would express it, to find a system that would excuse me, to construct a new meaning, having kicked the old one out, but I couldn't do it. . . . I cannot judge myself, I cannot condemn myself, so what can I make that will admit and encompass me? Nothing, it seems, but a broken and fragmented piece: an event seen from angles, where there used to be one event, and one way only of enduring it. (P. 47)

The effect upon the preceding image is explosive: the "I" has broken through the enclosure in external definition as body and fractured it into irreconcilable pieces. The readmission of "self" as active presence to the concept of femaleness, in effect, destroys that very concept.

The entire preceding narrative thus becomes merely an event seen from *one* angle, no longer a coherent and full account. In admitting that it is no longer "one event," Jane unravels her carefully woven world of passion and reopens the welter of lived experience, for she recognizes that any narrative account is inevitably partial, that events are always under description; and facts are always filiated in multiple directions not relevant to a given narrative account. Indeed, she goes on to acknowledge that "the ways of regarding an event, so different, don't add up to a whole; they are mutually exclusive: the social view, the sexual view, the circumstantial view, the moral view, these visions contradict each other; they do not supplement one another, they cancel one another, they destroy one another. They cannot co-exist" (p. 47). In developing what she calls "that sequence of discovery and recognition that I would call love" (p. 47), she has thus omitted those facts and interpretations that could not fit into the love story, and created a vision in contradiction with other possible accounts.

The import of this bursting out of her previous narrative is multiple: the shattering of the vision of romance, the discarding of the female-is-body-is-passive equation, the assertion of subjective complexity, the foregrounding of narrative as construction. And through all of these, we must recognize the resurgent complexity of lived experience. Although the "she" can be contained within the love story, the "I" lives in a more complex world. It is this "I" then who not only claims narrative agency but also seeks new interpretive processes by which to assess her lived experience and identifies herself as actor rather than recipient of action.

I must make an effort to comprehend it. I will take it all to pieces, I will resolve it to its parts, and then I will put it together again, I will reconstitute it in a form that I can accept, a fictitious form: adding a little here, abstracting a little there, moving this arm half an inch that way, gently altering the dead angle of the head upon its neck. If I need a morality, I will create one: a new ladder, a new virtue. If I need to understand what I am doing, if I cannot act without my own approbation—and *I must act, I have changed, I am no longer capable of inaction*—then I will invent a new morality that condones me. Though by doing so, I risk condemning all that I have been. (Pp. 53–54, emphasis added)

In claiming her own voice and rejecting the false image of femininity by which she first places herself in the love story, Jane identifies not only the need to analyze life experiences seriously, but also the centrality of *form* in arriving at an interpretation. She finds, too, the capacity to *act*, as narrator and as responsible agent, in constituting and living the events of her life.

Such control does not lead her to abandon the "she" narrative entirely, but rather to invoke it as one kind of narrative explanation. Once asserted, the "I" remains a presence even in the "she" sections, for we know Jane to be agent as well as object of the narrative in subsequent third-person sections. In fact, the only section of the novel revealing that purity of focus on image and body is the first section, before the initial intrusion of the "I." Though Jane's experience of orgasm is a similar expression of passivity and sexual objectification, it is not that pure and motionless world of the opening sections. It is different in part because active sexuality cannot be motionless, cannot be fully objectified, and even more because we as readers are aware of the "I" sections that frame it. We know Jane to be actively constructing this explanation, not passively submitting to it.

Similarly, Jane's naming of biosexual experiences can be seen as her claiming of narrative control over them. Though they occur within the "she" sections, these experiences provide an initial distortion of the anticipated femininity text by introducing facts not likely to occur in a thirteenth-century image of romance. The structure of the third-person sections enacts the femininity text of passivity and dependence, but in them Jane is nonetheless *naming* female experiences that have historically been silenced and denied visibility. Though the sense of childbirth as an expression of fluid self-boundaries is a question of interpretation, the fact of multiple fluids associated with childbirth is not; and it is a fact rarely named in literature. Similarly, Jane's experience of sexual orgasm may be shaped by the narrative paradigm of "feminine love" but it also presents an experience rarely named and here given to metaphoric expression in terms with physiological correlates. From this capacity to name her female sexual experiences, Jane achieves—even in the "she" sections—a kind of narrative control over them and makes them available for future assessments of her sense of self.

Once we sense the pervasive presence of Jane as narrative agent, we, then, come to take a different view even of the third-person sections. Rather than being trapped in the narrative paradigm they enact, these sections become a kind of mirroring process by which Jane uses one pattern of explanation to examine experiences that are particularly problematic for her. We know, as she does, that this explanation does not convey her actual experience, but with her we know, as well, that her writing about that experience is a way of examining it and opening it to alternative interpretations. It is in this context that we recognize her naming of biosexual experiences to be a claiming of narrative control over them. So too with the description of passionate love: as a falsification of experience in the self-objectification as "she," this narrative pattern can still serve as a temporary explanatory pattern by which she protects herself from the overwhelming sense of guilt that threatens her outside that narrative. As such, the "she" sections are not fixed and static but rather available for interaction with the I-in-process.

It is significant that each of the first two sections of "I" narrative ends with Jane's expressed wish to retreat to the enclosed world of the love story. At the end of the first "I" section, she says, "I will go back to that other story, to that other woman, who lived a life too pure, too lovely to be mine" (p. 70). Near the end of the second, she reiterates this need: "I want to get back to that schizoid third-person dialogue. I've one or two more sordid conditions to describe, and then I can get back to that isolated world of pure corrupted love" (p. 137). Her own commentary on its "purity" and impossibility, its distanced imaging, thus reminds us that it is structured *by her*, to meet her needs. In the subsequent "she" sections, we are aware simultaneously of the complex experience she has omitted in order to create this self-enclosed world and of her need for its safety as a way to elude and contain her sense of guilt.

Similarly, each of these "I" sections begins with the recognition that the preceding narrative had falsified experience. The "I" as conscious agent recognizes and rejects such falsification even as she continues to use it as an interpretive schema: "Lies, lies, it's all lies. A pack of lies. . . . What have I tried to describe? A passion, a love, an unreal life, a life in limbo, without anxiety, guilt, corpses" (p. 89). Repeatedly, she engages her sense of guilt and her knowledge of human complexity as she tries to dissect her experience, analyze its constituent parts. And she seeks ways to explain her behavior without either being entrapped in the love story or giving up her belief in her love: "Perhaps love can't survive a contest; perhaps it dies if it admits the outside world, or crumbles to dust at the breath of coarse air. But that air is the real air, I know it. I can't make the connections; I can't join it up. And yet love has a reality, a quotidian reality . . ." (pp. 89–90).

Making the connections finally is the effort of the whole novel: the "I" sections, the "she" sections, and the interaction between them. The connections must acknowledge the complexity of experience but must also somehow acknowledge and include her experience of loving James; they must claim her autonomy and her relationality, her questioning mind and her female body. The connections, in other words, cannot be the connections of the love story, based on its required repression of the autonomous "I". Instead, they will be under the control of the autonomous "I," who uses narrative self-consciousness to elude narrative entrapment.

The proportions of the novel are instructive for how Jane proceeds in this effort. Having begun in the extended image of "pure" and distanced love—the longest "she" section in the novel—she moves increasingly toward a more complex view of experience. Once the breach has been opened by the first-person voice, the narrative proceeds in an alternation of the "she" and "I" sections of substantial length until a little more than halfway through the novel. But increasingly, as the "she" narrative cannot sustain its purity, it cannot be sustained at all, and the "I" narrative begins to take over. The "purity" and distinctness of the love story break further and further apart: the movement of narrative and the knowledge of an agent "I" make such an image impossible to sustain.

The controlling "I," then, is responsible for the entire narrative, not just one portion of it, and she uses the narrative split to develop a sense of self in complexity; the complex self brings with it a rejection of thematic coherence and an ability to use multiple coherences in order to retain her complexity. In her initial section of "I" narrative, having acknowledged her "lies" of omission, she goes on to document the areas she has omitted. She says, for example, "I omitted, too, my feelings for the baby; I regret that this was necessary, as they were good feelings, pure emotions, but I could not find a place for them in my narrative" (p. 48). She explains further that this omission was caused by her sense of guilt: "one man's child in the story of my passion for another man" (p. 48). So, too, with Malcolm and Lucy: "There was no way of thinking of [Malcolm], just as, with James in my arms, there was no way of thinking of Lucy" (p. 50). She claims that these omissions were caused by guilt, but her initial explanation that she "could not find a place for them" in the narrative also holds true. For once she has raised them to consciousness, introduced them as a part of the information from which events have been selected and constructed, these other parts of her life begin to participate in a criticism of the love story. She repressed thoughts of them in order to create a coherent love story— to deny her sense of guilt; having broken that narrative coherence, she becomes increasingly unable to return to it. The breach in the narrative becomes a part of the eventual restructuring of the experience as well.

Similarly, her self-consciousness about narrative causality aggravates the breach. Wanting to see her love as absolute, she sees the past as leading inevitably to the present: "The narrative tale. The narrative explanation. That was it, or some of it. I loved James because . . ." (p. 70). What follows in her series of causal assertions, however, is precisely a construction from her memory, which she has searched for information to forecast this love. She finds "forecasting shadows" because "they are always there" (p. 62), but in doing so she demonstrates that the narrative structure of causality is a retrospective imposition—a "narrative tale"—not, in fact, an inevitable causal sequence. The *ending* determines what she sees as causal rather than the causes yielding the ending.

Conclusions, then, are also an imposition on experience that takes its hold on how one proceeds to live. Having reached one kind

of conclusion at the end of the first section of "she" narrative—
"drowned in a willing sea" (p. 46)—she finds this stasis to have a
kind of hold on her sense of that relationship. When she enters the
love story, she feels the narrative compulsion to repeat the direction
toward that ending. It is only as she increasingly withdraws from
the "she" narrative by drawing experiences from it into her "I"
narrative that she begins to elude its teleological pull toward repeated "drowning." Toward the end of the novel, she sees conclusions
differently because she sees her experience differently, beyond the
confines of the love story: "It's odd that there should be no ending,
when the whole affair otherwise was so heavily structured and or-
chestrated that I felt, at times, that I could see the machinery work,
that I was simply living out some textbook pattern of relationship"
(p. 249). To the extent that she acted in relation to her created story
line, she was doing just that: "living out some textbook pattern."
The story into which she originally wrote her love *did* have a kind of
power over her. At the same time, her acknowledgment of the complexity of experience led her to break out of that pattern rather than
enact a conclusion her narrative might have predicted.

Jane's structuring of her experience and her resistance to a self-
enclosed narrative paradigm are assisted by her recognition of other
narrative patterns[21]—especially a tradition of women's literature.
In rejecting and claiming various definitions of herself, she uses the
fiction of Jane Austen and Charlotte Brontë as parallels. But the
most obvious and significant parallel is *The Mill on the Floss*, invoked both explicitly and implicitly in the triangular relationship
with her cousin Lucy. When Jane draws the parallel, she claims not
to have Maggie's "superego," to have instead succumbed fa-
talistically to a Freudian view of sexual passion: "Since Freud, we
guess dimly at our own passions, stripped of hope, abandoned forever to that relentless current. . . . We drown in the first chapter. I
worry about the sexual doom of womanhood, its sad inheritance" (p.
162). Indeed, her initial enactment of the love story *is* a drowning in
"the sexual doom of womanhood," a modern acting out of Maggie's
repressed sexuality, reaching the same "doomed" conclusion. But
for Jane the "drowning in the first chapter" becomes only the
closure of one kind of narrative; the gauging of her life against Maggie's shows precisely the ways in which Jane refuses that doom. For
by moving outside the love story, introducing experiences that do

not "fit" in that narrative, she rejects the closure that is inevitable within its confines. Through her own narrative agency, she is able to act on her sexuality, claiming it positively, but also able to refuse it as the definition of her selfhood. Her recognition of Maggie's experience serves as a way to structure her resistance to the love story and reopen the conclusion posited in the first section of the novel.

Jane's sense of herself as "nothing, nebulous, shadowy, unidentifiable" (p. 148), coupled as it is with the recognition that others must see her to be clearly defined, takes on a new significance in the context of narrative enactment. She has written herself into a third-person narrative but that is only a way to see herself from the outside. The external view is inevitably more fixed and coherent but in the process of projecting this view she comes to understand more fully and to accept the multiplicity of her identity. Periodically throughout the novel she has the experience of seeing her current "self" as in contradiction with her previous sense of identity (e.g., p. 80; pp. 96–97), and she feels learning to be "dangerous" because it threatens to "invalidate by its significance the whole of one's former life" (p. 81). But in these recognitions lie the seeds of her understanding that she exists in her actions, in her interpretations, and in the possibility for her to make use of multiplicity.

The split in narrative voice, then, is not an enactment of "schizoid" tendencies or madness. Her narrative division is a way of reclaiming wholeness in narrative agency rather than expressing madness. By the end of the novel she is able to acknowledge that the earlier emphasis on her helplessness and dislocation as cause for madness was put forth as a kind of self-justification, the plea of helplessness: "Poor helpless Jane, abandoned, afraid, timid, frigid, bereft" (p. 242). Instead of being actual, the helplessness and madness—the schizoid self—are narrative constructs of a woman seeking clearer self-awareness. She says now, "Looking back, with the wisdom of my present knowledge, I could well claim to have been perfectly well adjusted all the time" (p. 243). Such a reinterpretation is not a denial of her previous experience but rather an alternative assessment of it, accomplished through shifting the narrative lens by which to construe her experience: she can see herself as acting in terms of her own needs, not succumbing to external forces.

At the same time, this narrative process leads her to an ability to claim her love without being subsumed in it, to see it as a part of her life but not as her self-definition. In her concluding series of narrative switches after James is nearly killed in their attempted holiday to Norway, she inverts the dominant narrative paradigms before claiming her final first-person voice. The "she" here (pp. 213–19) takes on the qualities of guilt and self-questioning, and the "I" takes on the belief in love.

> I was hoping that in the end I would manage to find some kind of unity. I seem to be no nearer to it. But at the beginning I identified myself with distrust, and now I cannot articulate my suspicions, I have relegated them to that removed, third person. I identify myself with love, and I repudiate those nightmare doubts. (P. 220)

This inversion is not a permanent shifting of the voices but rather an indication of her increasing accommodation to complexity, her willingness to continually "rethink it all, in terms of what I now know myself to be" (p. 244).

The final section of the novel, then, is an "I" narrative based precisely on this recognition of change and the incapacity of narrative to contain lived experience. In this section, she offers multiple hypotheses about her experience and its recalcitrance to form. She searches "for an elegant vague figure that would wipe out all the conflict, all the bitterness, all the compromise that is yet to be endured" (p. 247),[22] but knows that there "isn't any conclusion. A death would have been the answer, but nobody died" (p. 248). In some sense, she provides an alternate conclusion—a birth—in her assertion of narrative control, but a birth is more obviously a beginning and her beginning here is intertwined in far more complexity than she allowed into her opening narrative scheme: she has gone back to writing poetry for publication despite James's dislike of this activity; she has organized the practical affairs of her life; she has a limited but, for the moment, ongoing relationship with James. Her admiration for the waterfall at Goredale Scar retains the love of beautiful form that she felt for James's card trick and that she exhibits still more powerfully in her own commitment to poetry. As she says, "It is all so different from what I expected. It is all so much more cheerful" (p. 251). But her double conclusion—in "scotch and dust" on the weekend trip with James and in the postscript addition of her thrombic clot—reemphasizes the complexity of experience and its recalcitrance to form.

Jane does not feel that she has resolved the complexities that initially led her to try to structure her experience into narrative. But she does see more clearly her own participation in the human tension between autonomy and relationality. She is no longer likely to yield up her autonomy to the drowning of love or sex and yet she has not denied her sexuality either.[23] The entire complex narrative process has given her not only access to her own experience but also the possibility of taking responsibility for herself: in Gilligan's terms she has learned to "care" for herself as well as others. No longer contained in an image of "thirteenth-century love," she is the "I" at the center of the narrative, claiming autonomous control over her experience.

The problem of how to "represent" women's lives is, then, central to *The Waterfall*. Bound by cultural assumptions about female sexuality, Jane's "she" sections participate in the femininity text, and many readers respond by resenting her narrative entrapment in romance and female objectification. But Jane herself is not bound. For she is the agent of the self-conscious narration and personal multiplicity by which she represents her experience outside the femininity text and eludes those cultural assumptions. Thus other readers respond positively to her claiming of narrative control. In the interaction between the two texts, however, we can see her greatest subversion and her strongest assertion of self-definition. As both "she" and "I," as the voice that names the "she" in order to free herself from entextualization and the voice that speaks through the "I" as interpretive agent, Jane is able to claim a far more complex selfhood; and in her narrative, readers are able to read through fragmentation and denial toward possibility and wholeness.

II

Like *The Waterfall*, Doris Lessing's *The Golden Notebook* has a complicated relationship to literary feminism. Some feminists argue that it relies on a traditional view of women and especially of female sexuality; in this view, the novel is bound into the femininity text within which women must define themselves in relationship to men. At the same time, other feminists have found in this novel the powerful characterization of female experiences rarely available in novels and an effective criticism of a male-dominant society. As an extremely complex novel, *The Golden Notebook* can provide some evidence for both positions; indeed, both positions are important to a feminist analysis of the novel. But neither is entirely adequate to the novel's complexity or to its possibilities for subversive representation: though both the critique and the approbation are warranted, the real power of the novel lies in its formal capacity to set these views in dialectical relationship.[24]

Unlike *The Waterfall, The Golden Notebook* does not project its concerns with heterosexual sex and romantic love into an initially definable section of the text: the opening "she" narrative—the first "Free Women" section—seems itself prepared at least to raise questions about male-female relationships. Nevertheless, the femininity text has a clear presence in the novel and it is to this that many feminist critics have responded negatively, especially as it is evident in the view of female sexuality and the apparent lack of self-responsibility in its protagonist. Agate Nesaule Krouse, for example, argues that though *The Golden Notebook* has some feminist elements, it is "quite traditional and sexist in the treatment of the sexuality of women and the underlying definitions of 'real women' and 'real men.'"[25] Ellen Morgan recognizes in the novel significant perceptions from a feminist point of view, but centers her analysis on "Lessing's failure to come to terms with female authenticity."[26] And Elaine Showalter argues that "Lessing's heroines systematically . . . avoid responsibility for their own feelings."[27] Lessing herself became irritated when reviews of the novel centered on feminist issues and in one interview remarked, to the dismay of many feminists, "I'm impatient with people who emphasize the sexual revolution. I say we should all go to bed, shut up about sexual liberation, and go on with important matters."[28] Apparently confirming feminist objections, she seems to be speaking of sexuality in very traditional terms and to be asserting that women's lives in themselves are not "important matters."

The evidence for the critique can be drawn primarily from the personal sexual experiences of Anna and her self-fictionalization, Ella, both of whom seem very dependent on men and a destructive notion of romantic love. In "Free Women," for example, Anna presents herself to Molly as nearly incapacitated by Michael's departure: "when I really face it I don't think I've really got over Michael. I think it's done for me."[29] Or in the yellow notebook, Ella thinks, "My deep emotions, my real ones, are to do with my relationship with a man. One man" (p. 314); and she enacts this view through a painful obsession with Paul. Even in the final blue notebook, Anna shapes her life in response to a man, focusing, as she says, on "the pleasure of looking after a man" (p. 605) and concerned that this will disappear when Saul leaves her.

Further evidence for the critique can be found in the novel's descriptions of female sexuality. Ella's assertion that "Integrity is the orgasm" (p. 325) is often cited, as is the description of orgasm that Anna writes in the yellow notebook.

> A vaginal orgasm is emotion and nothing else, felt as emotion and expressed in sensations that are indistinguishable from emotion. The vaginal orgasm is a dissolving in a vague, dark generalized sensation like being swirled in a warm whirlpool . . . there is only one real female orgasm and that is when a man, from the whole of his need and desire, takes a woman and wants all her response. Everything else is a substitute and a fake, and the most inexperienced woman feels this instinctively. (Pp. 215–16)

The evocation of Freudian definitions of "adult" female sexuality, the insistence on heterosexuality, the judgment as to "right" and "wrong" orgasms, the implication that there are physiological distinctions for individual emotional preferences—all of these are decidedly troubling to a feminist perspective.

Similarly troubling is Anna's revulsion toward her own body in the crucial Golden Notebook: "I realised my body was distasteful to me. . . . I sat on my bed and I looked at my thin white legs and my thin white arms, and at my breasts. My wet sticky centre seemed disgusting, and when I saw my breasts all I could think of was how they were when they were full of milk, and instead of being pleasurable, it was revolting" (p. 612). The disgust is not just toward physicality but specifically toward femaleness: her body's sexual and reproductive capacities provide a powerful impetus toward her own self-dislike.

Even the novel's conclusion is implicated in a need for feminist critique. In the "Free Women" conclusion, Molly marries and Anna decides to do marriage counseling: a capitulation to the status quo given the criticisms of marriage that the novel offers elsewhere. And in what some see as a similar capitulation, the end of the Golden Notebook is only reached through Anna's dependence on Saul, her inability to act for herself, her passivity as she waits for him to leave rather than claiming her own rights.

In the configuration among such observations, it is indeed possible to see a lack of self-responsibility and a failure of authentic selfhood in Anna's characterization. Even in the broader patterns of the novel, one can identify a repeated turning to men to provide structure or meaning to a woman's life and an apparent acceptance of sex-role stereotypes as women are the nurturers, men the actors. By all of these criteria, Anna seems irremediably trapped within the grid of cultural expectations. As Alice Bradley Markow identifies it, the "pathology of feminine failure" among Lessing's protagonists is a function of such entrapment: "they do not feel a need to assume responsibility for themselves, and they are deeply but wrongly committed to romantic love."[30] Similarly, Morgan's conclusion says that The Golden Notebook's "overriding weakness" is "alienation from the authentic female perspective"—a perspective that is "smeared by the censor in Lessing."[31] According to this view, "the censor in Lessing," then, enacts Lessing's own inability to escape the values of the dominant culture, her own entrapment in the femininity text.

But if this is so, much has escaped the censor, even at the level of direct description. It is at this level that the feminist approbation of the novel usually claims its ample evidence: the sheer wealth of experience drawn from women's lives. From the beginning of the novel, we identify a female world: "The two women were alone in the London flat" (p. 3). In this very opening, we recognize the novel's commitment to examining women's lives, at least to some extent in relation to each other, rather than to men. Molly and Anna are reminiscent of Chloe and Olivia in the laboratory, reminiscent of the vision that Virginia Woolf called for in A Room of One's Own: a world of female friendship, "that vast chamber where nobody has yet been."[32] For Anna and Molly are not only alone but also talking of the multiple commitments in their lives: each other, friends, lovers, family, politics, work. In this opening, we recognize, as well, the novel's commitment to seeing women as serious, thinking, responsible beings in connection with significant human problems.

And we recognize its commitment to acknowledging women's sexual experience, both emotional and physical. All of these commitments are evident from the novel's first section and persist throughout the novel; all of these commitments provide ample basis for the response of those many women who read the novel, share it with friends, find in it the basis for offering to each other the initial feminist response: "me too."

This affirmation of shared experience, this "me too," is in some sense itself the overt representational concern of the novel's "Free Women" sections: the explicit focus on Molly's and Anna's need to test their own perceptions, beginning with the first scene as it vividly presents the conversation of two adult women, renewing their friendship after an extended separation from each other. This scene then establishes an important concern for the rest of the novel and for its representational possibilities: the tension between mutuality and distance in the Molly-Anna friendship. As Elizabeth Abel notes, this friendship predominates in the "Free Women" sections whereas heterosexual relationships predominate in the notebooks; these sections can be seen as Anna's narrative assessment of the importance of female friendships in her own experience and more particularly her exploration of a female-specific version of the tension between bonding and separation, inclusion and autonomy. But even apart from this tension—a tension that Abel casts as a psychoanalytic question of ego boundaries[33]—these sections give us a powerful characterization of women's need to claim both similarity to and difference from each other. Anna and Molly's conversation itself is the assessment of the commonality that many women readers seek in the novel: the shared world view based on women's experiences, the tensions of dominance and subordination in the midst of shared perceptions, the conversational dynamics grounded simultaneously in vulnerability and ironic self-protection, the ability to voice and interpret their differences and similarities. The "*odd, isn't it?*" that Lessing calls "the characteristic note of the intimate conversations they designated gossip" (p. 3) and that also functions in their shared recognition of the life choices they have made when they separate at the end (p. 666), itself bodies forth the tension of shared awareness and ironic withholding of self. It also identifies the representational need evident in the novel's treatment of female friendships: to agree on a version of the world.

The characterization of experiences shared by many women is

also present in the novel's representation of motherhood, another experience that is rarely available in novel reading. Though mothers are certainly characters in many novels, they are rarely themselves the primary actors or the defining point of view. As the narrator, Anna does claim this point of view, and through it she is able to characterize experiences that are part of many women's lives. She describes the extraordinary warmth of feeling in the wakening rituals and the bedtime rituals with Janet. She describes the tension among her roles as mother, lover, and worker. She describes her anxiety at being unable to "play" with Janet and the recognition that she can't always "feel" the connection, "That's my child, my flesh and blood" (p. 233). She describes the ongoing concern with the kind of adult she wants Janet to be and the recognition that Janet will grow up in her own ways, different from her mother. She describes the great difficulty associated with being responsible for a child—"The control and discipline of being a mother came so hard to me"—and acknowledges at the same time the pleasures evolving from that discipline: "when I close Janet's door behind me, and see her sitting up in bed, her black hair wild, in elf-locks, her small pale face (mine) smiling, the resentment vanishes under the habit of discipline, and almost at once becomes affection" (p. 334). And she describes the initial dissolution of identity when the role and discipline of motherhood are no longer required in Janet's absence.

Drawing on the actual experience of motherhood, Anna describes, as well, the kind of knowledge of human growth that often derives from that experience. As she says to Tommy in "Free Women," "When a woman looks at a child she sees all the things he's [or she's] been at the same time. When I look at Janet sometimes I see her as a small baby and I *feel* her inside my belly and I see her as various sizes of small girl, all at the same time" (p. 269). From this observation she draws her vision of "Everything in a sort of creative stream" (p. 269); that is, her experience as mother has given her a perception of both the complex multiplicity of a human being and the interconnectedness of human life. In the blue notebook, she writes as well of the deeply felt knowledge of human value and human mortality: "I was filled with an emotion one has, women have, about children: a feeling of fierce triumph: that against all odds, against the weight of death, this human being exists, here, a miracle of breathing flesh" (p. 332).

In Anna's narrative assessment of her own experience as mother, her descriptive control thus makes it possible to reveal both its difficulties and its satisfactions, to reveal much of the complexity of what we have learned from Adrienne Rich to call the experience of motherhood as compared to the institution of motherhood. Neither romanticized nor disparaged, the experience is made present: significant but not all-encompassing, central to her own life as a woman, but not definitional of womanhood.

In Anna's narrative, women's physiological experiences are, similarly, made present without being cast as definitional. I suggested in chapter 3 that since, in conventional terms, women are often defined by their bodies, the honest literary characterization of biological experiences is both difficult and important. This was Woolf's concern, too, when she identified a powerful need for herself as a woman writer: "telling the truth about my own experiences as a body."[34] And this is again a concern to which Lessing responds overtly in giving narrative description to Anna's physical experiences, as, for example, of menstruation. Describing her own response, both emotional and physiological, Anna gives form to inchoate sensations and identifies both her commonality with other women and her simultaneous recognition that women's experiences of menstruation are not all alike: "Now, sitting on the bus, I feel the dull drag at my lower belly. Not bad at all. Good, if this first pang is slight, then it will all be over in a couple of days. Why am I so ungrateful when I suffer so little compared to other women?—Molly, for instance, groaning and complaining in enjoyable suffering for five or six days" (p. 340). But more than that, she acknowledges the difficulty of breaking free from cultural norms as they function to take away women's own experiences: "And I read recently in some review, a man said he would be revolted by the description of a woman defecating. I resented this; because, of course, what he meant was, he would not like to have that romantic image, a woman, made less romantic. But he was right, for all that. I realise it's not basically a literary problem at all" (p. 340). Rather, the literary problem of representing female experiences is closely tied to the cultural problem of seeing women beyond the accepted images. But she has described her bodily experience, even if she has had to do so in a language partially bound into the femininity text.

In her political and work life, too, Anna insists on the complexity of her life as a woman, as she both describes her experience and assesses its relationship to cultural expectations. She tells of her participation as a young woman in the Communist party and of the intertwining of politics and sexuality in the group dynamics. She tells of her experiences with co-workers and the impinging of gender perceptions on those interactions. She tells of her work responding to letters written by distressed people—mostly women—and of her tensions of sympathy with them. She tells of her interactions in the role of "lady writer" and her relationship to her writing, past and present. Here too the experience of the woman reader is likely to be both a recognition that this literary experience is rare and that it speaks of the kinds of experiences women do share in their work lives: assumptions about appropriate female behavior, claims made upon their nurturant capacities, the need to insist upon the seriousness of the commitment to their work life as well as their capacities for meaningful action in public concerns.

The list of distinctively female experiences is long and could go on. In all of these experiences, Lessing has given Anna the capacity to "name" her own reality and thus to reopen cultural generalizations about the lives of women. These are the experiences that drew such strong response from readers who felt their own experiences resonating with the novel's particularity.[35] These too are some of the experiences that lie behind the approbation of those feminists who see the novel as a positive expression of female experience. In this view, a novel that makes female experience *present* and characterizes women's lives in such a way that women readers can say "me too" is a novel of considerable value to a feminist perspective.

My own initial response to the novel was itself very much congruent with the feminist approbation; even when I saw the legitimacy of the feminist critique, I was somehow not prepared to relinquish that initial value of experiential "naming." But this straightforward claiming of the value of female experience did not resolve for me the tension in feminist criticism between critique and approbation. The question still remained: how is a novel that does express a number of rather conventional and sexist attitudes toward women nonetheless able to avoid entrapment within the femininity text? How is *The Golden Notebook* in fact able to give powerful representation to women's lives, to subvert the premises of representation in order to represent women's lives?

At the beginning of my consideration of *The Golden Notebook*, I answered this question by asserting that the novel's power for feminist representation resides in its formal capacity to set the two broad critical responses in dialectical relationship: critique and approbation informing and redirecting each other. I think this is possible, indeed necessary, because the novel itself is extremely self-conscious about the problems of representation. Though we can find and cite sections of the novel that either meet or fail to meet some feminist "standard," these sections are meaningful only as they are set in relationship to each other and to the novel as a whole.

In my consideration of a feminist poetics of the novel, I suggested two unifying concerns for feminist novel criticism: a concern with lived experience and a skepticism about the representational capacity of traditional novelistic form. Because *The Golden Notebook* is overtly structured on both of these concerns, rather than on the experiential concern alone, it requires of its critics a response to its self-conscious form as an integral part of its experiential concerns. It is, then, not a question of identifying which authentic experience has escaped the "censor in Lessing." Rather it is a question of recognizing how the novel's form itself takes into account the cultural expectations for women, sometimes even representing *through* those expectations, at the same time that its own critique of novelistic form subverts those expectations. Through subversive representation, female authenticity is revealed *as* the capacity to critique, the capacity to define and redefine for oneself.

In an introduction to the novel, Lessing points out what I see as two key factors in the novel's dialectical capacity for feminist representation. Most obvious is the centrality of a woman perceiver; as Lessing asserts, the novel assumes that the "filter which is a woman's way of looking at life has the same validity as the filter which is a man's way."[36] This is the assumption behind feminist analysis in general; it is, as well, the assumption implicit in a female narrating "I." By placing Anna at the subjective center of the novel, Lessing initially valorizes her perceptions and thence her experiences. But equally crucially, the novel, as Lessing says, speaks "through the way it [is] shaped."[37] Through its formal complexity—its linear evolution of a third-person narrative, framed and broken by the voice of an "I" that is itself multiple and fragmented—the novel takes on the capacity to critique the novelistic conventions within which women have been entrapped; through its multiple voice, it characterizes the narrator-protagonist as a woman able to escape and subvert even the patterns of cultural expectation that she herself sometimes articulates; through the agency of form as well as voice, she eventually becomes a woman able to claim both her sexuality and her autonomy.

The process by which Anna Wulf arrives at this sense of self differs substantially from Jane Gray's interaction with the culture text of femininity. Anna parodies some expressions of the femininity text in her experiments with literary pastiche, but she does not directly engage this cultural view of entextualized woman. Instead she acts through the writing of the novel as a woman interpreting her personal experience and her social context, speaking directly as a woman as she overtly rejects novelistic conventions. In the narrowest sense, Lessing's rejection of reviews that center on feminism is appropriate: the novel does not argue a feminist position or even center exclusively in female experiences; instead it examines broadly the crises of twentieth-century society and the problems of characterizing those crises in novelistic form. But since Anna places herself, as female, at the center of the novel, draws overtly on her own experience, and watches the self-projection play out her roles in the notebooks and especially in the "Free Women" sections, the novel becomes more complexly feminist than is possible in any attempt simply to describe female experience.

The complexity of her "filter"—her interpretive capacity and her use of form as access to voice—is, then, what gives Anna the simultaneous capacity to represent and to subvert the premises of representation, to characterize her own experience without being bound into the femininity text. In my speculations on a feminist poetics of the novel, I identified the general shifts in novelistic conventions that I see as crucial for developing the possibility of subversive representation and for freeing a female protagonist from traditional expectations: the view of plot as explanatory hypothesis subject to alteration and resisting closure; the view of character as defined through action, choice, and perception rather than qualities; the view of reality as subject to interpretation; and the view of thematic coherence as one construction among many. In speaking through its form, The Golden Notebook exemplifies all of these shifts in novelistic conventions; in speaking through a female protagonist, it uses them to develop a powerful characterization of complex female experience and a complex female selfhood.

From the proliferation of information by which the novel has its base in formal realism, Anna lays preliminary claim to the power to represent and the power to subvert the premises of representation—and thence to the possibility of an altered view of reality. As her own narrator she has from the beginning claimed the capacity of both description and critique: as agent of selection and description, she can actively disrupt anticipations of the femininity text. This capacity results not only from her simple selection of what will be included, but also and more crucially from her means of presentation. My attempt merely to document the presence of female experience has already led me to suggest the associated and inseparable critique of cultural views of female experience. In part because she is using the self-reflective journal form, in part because of the self-projection that is possible in her third-person narratives, and in part simply because of the way she uses a "woman's filter," each specifically female experience brings with it the awareness of associated cultural expectations. The representation of female friendship is also the representation of the stresses on those friendships. The representation of motherhood is inseparable from the knowledge that motherhood is both a role learned through self-discipline and a source of acquired ways of seeing human experience. The representation of the physiological experience of menstruation is embedded in its emotional significance: as a basis of commonality among women and as an experience that is culturally obscured by romantic images of women. The representation of women's work life is not merely a description of a particular activity but also the acknowledgment that work life, too, is embedded in a cultural context that requires a double commitment for women: trying to accomplish a task while negotiating the cultural images and expectations of women.

The novel's representation of reality is, then, grounded in the tension between subjective perception and shared awareness. In the absence of cultural certainty, it claims the centrality of subjective experience at the same time that it uses the subjective as a way to identify what is shared. In one of her general statements about art, Anna suggests the power of personal experience: "the flashes of genuine art are all out of a deep, suddenly stark, undisguisable private emotion" (p. 349). As Lessing says in the introduction, "Writing about oneself, one is writing about others" (p. xiii). But one must first be able to identify the subjective, particularly in the instance of experiences that are culturally obscured or denied—e.g., women's experiences.

In this regard, the blue notebooks have a privileged position among the notebooks Anna keeps: it is here that she attempts to characterize most directly and specifically her personal and emotional life as a woman, and it is from the last blue notebook that she moves into the Golden Notebook. Her attempt on 17 September 1954 in the blue notebook to write down everything of one day's occurrences is particularly revealing, for it provides a wealth of specificity: her reactions to menstruation, her sensory pleasure in cooking, her choices of clothing, her daily activities. It provides as well an attempt to understand her complex configuration of emotions— guilt, happiness, anguish—and finally a realization that such an attempt is both inevitably false and yet a genuine effort. She also experiences in this section the specifically female basis for the novel's structural complexity. Her fragmentation is seen to be grounded in the multiple demands upon her, from lover, daughter, comrades; and her need for structural critique is seen to derive from the deeply engrained emotions that are culturally attributed to women and at war within her—guilt, happiness, relational responsibility, anger. Though her conversation about fragmentation with Michael in this section is cast in political terms, her own experiencing of the preparation for her breakdown is clearly rooted, as well, in her interaction with female experiences: the stress of multiple roles in a social context that reinforces guilt and frustration rather than the capacity to act. From the attempt to describe personal reality, she claims the capacity to interpret and communicate. The inclusion of rarely named female experiences opens those experiences to a new interaction with the available interpretive schemata and participates in the interpretive openness of the novel.

It is in the personal account of the blue notebook, as well, that Anna defines humanism as residing in the tension between the individual and the collective: "humanism stands for the whole person, the whole individual, striving to become as conscious and responsible as possible about everything in the universe" (p. 360). The problem, as she assesses it, is the problem of modern complexity and its attendant fragmentation of the individual; but though the dominant commitment here is to socialism, the belief is also closely bound to the pressures on her identity as a woman. The tension in pushing autonomy and relationality to such extremes, similar to the effort of the "game" in the later blue notebook (p. 588), reveals the congruity of her political views and her personal tensions: as she feels she is here coming to the end of "a stage of my life" (p. 353), both the political and the personal seem to threaten destruction of a "coherent self" by a chaotic external reality. As the demands made on her threaten to overwhelm, she suffers the powerful sense of being cut loose from human connections. Her placing of herself in a social and political context thus suggests both the female specific and the generally human tension and it makes her experiences as a woman integral to her understanding of reality.

The definition of character in action, choice, and perception is also implicit in the structure of the novel, for the narrating "I" is a perceptual "filter" that refuses any external definition and chooses form as well as event. Not only is Anna the narrative agent of the individual "stories" of which the novel is composed, but she is also the agent of its architecture: the "I" who structures the interaction among the notebooks and between "Free Women" and the notebooks, not the Anna or even the "I" who is recorded in any one of the narratives. She uses each of the four notebooks as a relatively unified structuring of her experience—an explanatory hypothesis that distorts but functions in conjunction with the other notebooks to remind her, and us, of its distortion. In identifying her various roles—writer of a previous novel (black), political activist (red), creator of new stories (yellow), and relational woman in daily experience (blue)—they also reveal the multiplicity of her selfhood. Because, as she notes, the written-down self is "lifeless" (p. 571), she is not found in any of the notebooks or in her novelistic self-projection in "Free Women"; she is found only in the agency of their interaction. Her self-consciousness as a narrator gives her the added complexity of a character who is her own creator, a self in process.

Anna's eventual breakdown, then, enacts the tensions in her view of self and reality, the fragmentation that is central to her narrative, and the strength she is finally able to claim from a rejection of the concept of coherent identity. At first, she forestalls the collapse through self-compartmentalization into the four notebooks, but she comes to feel split up rather than assisted by this process: the note-books become self-dividers rather than multiple hypotheses about the self. The final blue notebook and its inheritor, the Golden Note-book, show her letting go of ready external definitions—the struc-turing of time, the naming capacity of language, the social roles of mother and colleague, the linear narrative process, and the claim to unified and single selfhood. She merges and doubles in ka-leidoscopic interplay with memory, imagined film, dream. As the attempt to narrate an entire day proved a falsification—the attempt shaped the actual living and the writing inevitably called for selec-tion, sequence, causality—so the progression in the final notebooks must finally yield a letting go of all coherences. In the interaction between these two obverse narrative experiences and their respec-tive threats to her self in the world, we can see the need both to represent and to subvert the premises of representation. She needs narrative form but she needs, also, to escape the falsification of imposed coherence.

Anna's eventual capacity to let go of coherence as a way to claim wholeness is, in part, developed through her own understanding of narrative complexity and the disruption of form. And her capacity to represent this experience to a reader of the novel depends upon the reader's active participation in the disruption of form. Of particular significance in this process is the novel's overall rejection of the-matic coherence—structural preparation for Anna's redefined self-hood—and crucial, as well, to the reader's recognition of her agency. As I have insisted repeatedly, the narrating "I" is the basis of agency and redefined selfhood, but Anna's subversion of the narrative con-ventions of coherence gives added complexity to her representation in the novel's simultaneous refusal and subversion of the traditional agent of coherence: the omniscient narrator.

Naturally the convention of omniscience is immediately refused in any first-person narration. But the novel's initial pretense to om-niscient voice gives added power to this refusal and eventually gives power to the capacity of the first-person voice to represent. Unless readers read the novel's introduction first, we presumably enter the first "Free Women" section with that sense of security available in omniscient narration. At the time of the first shift in narrative voice, we do not lose much of that security because the omniscient narrator in "Free Women" has just told us that Anna was looking at her notebooks. We certainly do not experience the explosive and immediate disruption that occurs when Jane Gray first claims her "I" in her narrative. But we experience at least an interference in the ease of reading simply in the changing of the narrative dimension; as J. M. Lotman explains it, " 'point of view' is an element of literary structure which we become aware of as soon as there is a possibility of switching in the course of the narrative."[38] The notebooks, then, make us aware of the narrative voice and thence of the possibility of switching other dimensions in our initial assumptions of coherence.

As we read on through the notebooks, the original uneasiness derived from shifting the point of view continues to grow. We notice that apparent "facts" in the novel are in conflict: that Willi in the black notebook is Max in the blue notebook; that Richard is said to have sons in "Free Women" and daughters in the blue notebook; and even that Tommy, who is seen in "Free Women" to have blinded himself in a suicide attempt and entered into complicated emotional interdependence with Marion, is seen in the blue notebook to become a conscientious objector, marry a sociologist, and settle into a middle-class version of socialism. As we strain to reconcile these discrepancies, we are increasingly aware of the threat of incoherence: there is no omniscience to be trusted.

We strain, as well, to accommodate and reconcile the novel's multiple sections: an "omniscient" section and four different notebooks, each with its own initial claim to coherence. But even within each of the notebooks we must accommodate shifts in focus, tone, or method. Experience is increasingly seen as fractured in its presentation as story or multiple stories: data, dream, newspaper clippings. Even the designated theme of each notebook is disrupted. The black notebook, supposed to be concerned with Anna Wulf the writer, includes personal stories from her past, current narratives about negotiations with a number of movie and television agents, various exercises in literary parody, explicit observations about the nature of literary form, and eventually a series of newspaper clippings about Africa. Similarly, the other notebooks are at best loosely unified by their designations. The blurring and overlapping of supposed thematic unities thus reinforces our growing uneasiness about the trustworthiness of the narrative voice.

As we progress through the novel, this uneasiness increases in response to narrative complexity. We try to correlate large amounts

of memory constructed into narrative with our evolving understanding of "present" events; we look for ways to twine together the
separate strands from each of the four notebooks; we try to deter-
mine how to reconcile discrepancies of "fact." The confusion grows
as the novel progresses until in the Golden Notebook we arrive at
the line which sends us reeling back to the beginning of the novel:
"The two women were alone in the London flat" (p. 639). With this,
we experience the completed explosion of coherence and the crum-
bling of the entire structure we may have built up: the realization
that the Anna of the notebooks is not a character in the "Free Wom-
en" novel—she is its author, and the agent of our confusion. Evolving as it does from an uneasiness that has been growing throughout
the novel, this most overt denial of omniscience is even more dis-
turbing to the reader than was Jane Gray's abrupt shift of narrative
voice from "she" to "I." Rather than being a simple change of point
of view, this recognition is the decisive refusal of coherence and the
establishment of alternative wholeness. Lessing says that in the
"Free Women" sections, she was "really trying to express [her]
sense of despair about writing a conventional novel."[39] The denial
of coherence that evolves out of the initial "Free Women" is precisely such an expression: a conventional novel with its omniscient
voice and thematic coherence cannot adequately characterize the
complexity of lived experience. But the agency of the narrating "I"
takes on the interpretive authority over her own experience. As
agent of our confusion, Anna's narrative voice is the only encompassing reality in the novel.

The "I" is then present precisely in the agency of voice: not voice
as linguistic subject but voice as active interpreter. Despite the difficulty of interpretation and the impossibility of omniscience, the
claim to interpretive agency remains central. In voice resides the
resistance to chaos through a recognition that form is necessary
even if it does falsify. Just as the complexity of reality is the initial
justification for there being four notebooks and the eventual justification for Anna's breakdown, so the need to create form remains the
justification for writing in the notebooks and for the structure of the
novel as a whole. Writing down the events of her day, Anna feels "as
if I had saved that day from chaos" (p. 476). It is precisely chaos that
takes over when she can no longer retain a sense of the meaning of
words and the possibility of giving her days form, and it is "the

burden of re-creating order out of the chaos that my life had become" (p. 619) that she feels during her period of madness. Both necessary and inadequate, narrative structure is a predominant agent of our perception. As John L. Carey interprets the novel, "Reality thus comes to be understood as a complex interplay of objective and the subjective ordering of that experience by the artist. Life and art are seen as a single unit impossible to split."[40] But even more pervasively, the interaction of information and interpretation is a function of all human living, not only the effort of the artist: narrative, in art or in daily "reality," is portrayed as a powerful—if distorting—means by which lived experience is understood.

Even overt statements about thematic coherence then become challenges to coherence rather than claims to it: assertions about experiential complexity rather than novelistic unity. The first thing Anna says in the novel identifies the impossibility of unity: "the point is, that as far as I can see, everything's cracking up" (p. 3). Anna's response to Molly a little later in the first "Free Women" section—"Men. Women. Bound. Free. Good. Bad. Yes. No. Capitalism. Socialism. Sex. Love . . ." (p. 44; Lessing's ellipsis)—identifies the pervasive resistance to unity. The statement, to which Lessing's introduction points as a "theme," is based precisely in a refusal of resolution, the impossibility of thematic coherence despite the recognition that each of these concepts has thematic significance. This thematic dialectic implies, in Lessing's words, that "we must not divide things off, must not compartmentalize" (p. x).

In order to characterize the thematic tensions without compartmentalizing, Lessing must simultaneously reveal them and deny their individual coherence. Thus, words and concepts and narrative forms must be made to critique themselves if we are to overcome the problem that Anna identifies as a contemporary one in the black notebook: it is possible to read the same story as "parody, irony or seriously" because of "the fragmentation of everything . . . [and] the thinning of language against the density of our experience" (p. 302). In its effort both to assess the fragmentation and to avoid compartmentalizing, the novel must raise a number of central thematic concerns but must also continue to defy thematic coherence as it denies a consistent perspective.

The complexity of the novel's structure as a dialectic between form and formlessness is a central concern in a number of perceptive analyses of the novel as a modernist or postmodernist statement: as Betsy Draine argues in her illuminating analysis, "Chaos and form are inextricably bound to one another in a dialectical process."[41] More crucial for my analysis, however, is the particular usefulness of the disruption of form and coherence for a portrayal of women's lives as they escape the femininity text, the dialectic of chaos and form as a redefinition of representation.

The specific importance of subverting the premise of coherence is evident in the novel's initially straightforward "representation" of women's lives. Because the "conventional novel" within the novel—i.e., "Free Women"—does not immediately seem bound into the femininity text, its difficulty in portraying an autonomous woman becomes an especially acute reminder of the need to subvert its expectations: its progression in isolation shows the particular dangers of the convention of coherence, attended as it usually is by the convention of omniscience. Read without interruption by the notebooks, these sections show Anna as unable to claim even her own feminist statements. Without the disruptive recognition of the notebooks, Anna of a coherent "Free Women" is somehow crippled, guilt-ridden in her inability to find socially efficacious action, cynical about what she terms "welfare work," yet finally unable to escape traditional expectations of women's lives, bound by both her dependence on men and her need as a woman to be acting on other people's behalf. Despite the contemporary context and the explicit attempts to resist cultural norms, she is still bound by the expectations, both novelistic and cultural, that she will be an "Angel in the House," even when she tries to move out of the house and into a larger social world. The frequent play with the word "free" in these sections only underlines the ways in which Anna is "bound": the title can only be ironic as it emphasizes the impossibility of freedom in a male-dominant social context.

Even more to the point is the recognition of the power of a coherent structure to subdue the disruptive statements within such a structure: whatever criticism may be offered within the conventional novel are subject to embeddedness in a thematic coherence by which freedom is illusory. Dependent on narrative omniscience we cannot achieve sufficient distance to escape the sense of inevitability in the femininity text.

This power of anticipated coherence to control our reading of women's lives thus defines the need and value of disrupting novelistic coherence. Because the novel's structure undermines our trust in the omniscient voice of "Free Women," we are led to see the falsity of its wholeness. Because coherence itself is questioned and subverted, we are led to identify alternative ways to interpret Anna's experience outside the femininity text; and she is led to a narrative claiming of that experience. *The Golden Notebook* asserts the ability of language to convey shared awareness—"representation"—at the same time it subverts the culturally defined limits of coherence; subverts, that is, a central premise of representation.

The multiplicity of theme then becomes not only a critique of false coherence or "compartmentalizing," but also a way to include opposing perceptions of women's lives: "Men. Women. Bound. Free. Good. Bad. Yes. No. Capitalism. Socialism. Sex. Love." In a conventional novel—even in "Free Women"—the protagonist must make choices between the opposing categories. Indeed, the feminist critiques I cited earlier seem to rest rather heavily on the perception that Anna has made the "wrong" choices among these categories; not surprisingly these critiques rely as well on statements taken primarily from the conventional narratives and bound by expectations of coherence. By contrast, the novel as a whole—form in dialectic with formlessness—is able to recognize the powerful constraints on women's lives as present even in their own choices and values, at the same time that it acknowledges their conflicting capacity to live the dialectical interaction between freedom and constraint.

Within the disrupted coherence, then, the critique of the novelistic conventions of plot are similarly denials of uniformity of perception and hence of any linearly bound direction for women's lives. As we have no unified and trustworthy narrative perspective, so we have no expectations of continuous plot, no assumptions that women's lives are necessarily consistent with the symbolic systems of the dominant culture. To assist in the critique of the conventions, the novel everywhere reminds us that narrative is a structuring and thus a falsification. The yellow notebook with its story of Ella and Julia and Paul plays against the stories of Anna and Molly and Michael in the blue notebook and in "Free Women." Anna's views of her novel *The Frontiers of War* play against her record of memories in the black notebook. Her recorded conversations with Mother

Sugar play against her other assessments of her life. The past intrudes on the present and refuses to retain consistent shape. Time is fractured and narrative continuity is questioned.

The efforts we make to reconcile the elements of this complex structure not only make us aware of the inadequacy of the conventional novel; they also make us aware of the incompleteness of any narrative structure. As Lessing says, "it's always a lie . . . Because you can't get life into it—that's all there is to it—no matter how hard you try."[42] The experience of madness in the Golden Notebook emphasizes such a recognition.

> The fact is, the real experience can't be described. I think, bitterly, that a row of asterisks, like an old-fashioned novel, might be better. Or a symbol of some kind, a circle perhaps, or a square. Anything at all, but not words. The people who have been there, in the place in themselves where words, patterns, order, dissolve, will know what I mean and the others won't. (Pp. 633–34)

The madness is then an extension of the chaos of life throughout the novel. The circle and the square, the speaking through forms and symbols, provide the pattern of the novel and the knowledge that words and narrative structure cannot fully convey "life."

With such criticism comes the specific criticism of narrative teleology. In the yellow notebook, Anna speculates about how she is structuring the story of Paul and Ella.

> The trouble with this story is that it is written in terms of analysis of the laws of dissolution of the relationship. . . . I don't see any other way to write it. As soon as one has lived through something, it falls into a pattern. . . . That is why all this is untrue. Because while living through something one doesn't think like that at all. (Pp. 227–28)

She rejects the idea of telling just two days at either end of the affair because selection and teleology would inevitably govern even that narrative: "I would still be instinctively isolating and emphasising the factors that destroyed the affair. It is that which would give the thing its shape. Otherwise it would be chaos" (p. 228). Her conclusion—"Literature is analysis after the event" (p. 228)—is precisely the rationale for criticizing narrative form as it is pulled toward the ending that governs selection and emphasis. As Anna gives tele-ological form to Ella's affair with Paul, she makes Ella's dependence on men an explicit component of the narrative structure. As she critiques the teleology of narrative form, she thus also identifies the effectiveness for women of a form not bound by teleology: the de-pendence that is a part of the femininity text can be seen as a part of the teleological form that binds rather than as a permanent compo-nent of a woman's identity.

Anna's use of the yellow notebook, then, in many ways makes overt the falsification of experience that provides the structure for the conventional novel: it is not that the experience is the same but that the awareness of narrative falsification automatically raises questions about the structure of "Free Women" as well and finally about the patterning inherent in all narrative. At the same time, the yellow notebook reminds us of the way in which art informs life as well as life informing art. Through using Ella as a parallel by which to interpret her own experience in the yellow notebook and similar-ly using the self-projected character in "Free Women," Anna comes to understand the intertwining of form and chaotic experience, of art and life. By the final entries in the yellow and blue notebooks, she is no longer certain which precedes which: event or narrative, experience or fictional form. She understands that they exist in powerful interaction.

From these recognitions Anna is able to develop the full sense of alternative female selfhood as both character and narrator: a self not bound by the novelistic conventions of character and not bound by the cultural conventions of femininity. She claims the distinctive empirical presence of a narrating "I" as she also makes clear the complexity of that "I": Anna Freeman, Anna Wulf, Ella, Ella-Anna—all of these but not any one of them. She claims the con-tinuity of her lived experience, connecting past with present, and yet she acknowledges the possibility of alternative strands of causality leading to new understandings. She claims the centrality of memory in her sense of self and yet she understands that her memory is itself an interpretation. She sees the power of roles in her presentation of herself to other people—the comrade, the writer, the friend—but she uses these roles to assess her complexity rather than to bind her within character traits. Through the complex narrative structuring of her experience, she becomes the "filter" through which we see the modern world, the perceptual agent of her own experience in resistance to the containment of cultural definitions.

Lessing suggests that the Golden Notebook is where we ought to look for the central meaning of the novel (p. x), but because it seems so like the final blue notebook, readers are not always certain what its significance might be. In my view, its centrality resides not so much in its full confrontation with the possibility of madness as in the dialectic by which that confrontation takes place: Anna's assessment of her life experiences in the tension between the madness of being multiple personalities and the barrenness of life as "conventionally, well-made films . . . glossy with untruth" (p. 619). From this specific version of the dialectic between formlessness and form, she takes for herself the capacity she earlier gave to her character Ella: "the belief that anything is possible"; a vision shared with "people who deliberately try to be something else, try to break their own form as it were" (p. 466). She claims, as well, the opening onto a future of altered possibility that she also attributed to Ella.

> I've got to accept the patterns of self-knowledge which mean unhappiness or at least a dryness. But I can twist it into victory. A man and a woman—yes. Both at the end of their tether. Both cracking up because of a deliberate attempt to transcend their own limits. And out of the chaos, a new kind of strength. (P. 467)

As the boundaries between fiction and life blur, Anna almost becomes Ella's projected character: claiming, through the relationship with Saul, the capacity to transcend her own limits and finally to structure her experience and her selfhood with a new kind of strength in the unfinished dialectic of the entire novel.

It is through the recognition of this dialectic that Anna is eventually able to reclaim her sanity and elude the threat of her own male-dependent inclinations, as well as the threat of fragmentation. In the fourth blue notebook, she thinks of herself as "in the middle of . . . a period" which she will later assess retrospectively: "I was an Anna who invited defeat from men without even being conscious of it. (But I am conscious of it. And being conscious of it means I shall leave it all behind me and become—but what?)" (p. 480). Through such recognitions as this, she opens her sexual identity toward the future; she prepares her recognition of Saul's contribution to her growth in the Golden Notebook; and she claims the fundamental capacity to grow and change. When Saul gives her the opening line of her novel, he prefaces it by saying, " 'There are the two women you are, Anna' " (p. 639). What she takes from that is not the perception that she has two personalities—she has been continually confronting her capacity for multiple selfhood. Rather she takes the fruitfulness of narrative projection as a way of understanding and assessing her experiences as a woman. She writes the novel much beyond the conventional novel because she understands the value of narrative interpretation at the same time that she has found a way to guard against the dangers of narrative entrapment. Her self-projection is not the coherent projection of romantic and sexual identity enacted by Jane Gray, but it is self-projection nonetheless: multiple self-projection in the novel's dialectical structure, complex wholeness in the narrative understanding of personal and sexual identity.

It is, then, in that act of self-narration that Anna is able to claim her authenticity despite the continuing pressures of cultural femininity even in her own thinking. I agree with Morgan that *The Golden Notebook* reveals "the peculiar problem of the woman writer working in a climate of assumptions and sympathies about women and sex roles which do not support female authenticity."[43] But unlike Morgan, I do not think this climate has been able to deny Anna her authenticity; rather I think its denials have forced her into a complex redefinition of narrative conventions in order to characterize her experiences as a woman and claim her authenticity. As she strives to assess her own identifiably female experience, despite cultural silencing, she finds in the multiplicity of her narrative voice the affirmation of her autonomy.

Because Anna's experiences are presented in the context of a complex narrative structure, they are not fixed in their representation but are instead automatically subject to reinterpretation. As her use of narrative form insists that both reality and selfhood are multidimensional and that our explanations of experience are hypotheses not absolutes, so she is herself not bound by the premises of representation. If, in this context, she offers explanations not shared by other women, she has also made immediately available the perception that explanations are subject to change. Through the novel's form—through Anna's fragmented selfhood and complex structuring process—Lessing is thus able to draw the reader into the fruitfulness of an epistemological process rather than the confinement of a female ontology.[44] Anna does, indeed, characterize some of her experiences in the context of cultural expectations, but rather than enclosing her within those expectations, her narrative opens for her the possibility of complex selfhood and continued growth.

In "The Small Personal Voice," Lessing writes of what she values in the nineteenth-century novel: "the warmth, the compassion, the humanity, the love of people," and she identifies the need for the writer to feel "responsibility, as a human being, for the other human beings he [or she] influences."[45] These are the values from which her general interest in realism derives: "I define realism as art which springs so vigorously and naturally from a strongly held view of life that it absorbs symbolism."[46] The currently dominant definitions of human beings present one of the problems for writing such a novel, but Lessing asserts that an alternative is possible, rejecting the view of "the isolated individual unable to communicate" and the view of the "collective [hu]man with a collective conscience" in favor of something in between, "hard to reach and precariously balanced."[47]

These are, I believe, the views of the human being, of the novel, and of artistic responsibility that she is addressing in *The Golden Notebook:* the individual who is fragmented and alone but working toward a responsible place in the human community, the individual balancing autonomy and inclusion through developing a strongly held, but not fixed, view of life. The character she creates is in the process of creating herself through the recognition that identity needs to be an active process rather than a fixed construct that is likely to shatter. That character is also a woman, and one of the fixed constructs she rejects is an external definition of how she is to be female and one of the elements of her balance is her femaleness. Through seeing herself as "the position of women in our time" (p. 579), Anna claims her commonality with other women; through her self-narration, she learns to critique and resist the cultural constraints on her identity as woman.

Like her author, Anna Wulf is concerned with the possibilities of the novel in the modern world. Near the beginning of the first black notebook she writes despairingly of the contemporary novel as lacking an essential novelistic quality: "the quality of philosophy" (p.

61). And she explains why she will "never write another novel": "I am incapable of writing the only kind of novel which interests me: a book powered with an intellectual or moral passion strong enough to create order, to create a new way of looking at life. It is because I am too diffused" (p. 61). Yet what she does in the course of structuring her own experience in multiple ways, building on her personal experiences as a woman and her complex visions of the larger society, is find a way to *use* that diffusion to empower a way of looking at life.

In *The Golden Notebook*, Doris Lessing, through Anna Wulf, reopens the novelistic conventions in such a way that it is possible to see a communicating individual identifying her responsible place within the collective. Though Anna is nearly destroyed by her overwhelming awareness of both the needs of other people and her own isolation, she responds instead by taking on both of these recognitions in her role as writer—writer of the novel we read, not just of the "Free Women." She is not herself "free" but she is capable of self-definition, through this writing, as a strong autonomous woman for whom being female and being a writer are not in irremediable conflict. Like Jane Gray, she finds in the narrative act a way to use her culturally imposed fragmentation and claim the wholeness of her adult womanhood.

Through the self-fragmentation of their narrator-protagonists, both *The Golden Notebook* and *The Waterfall* are, then, able to show us new possibilities in the complexity of women's lives. Just as *The Waterfall* shows a capacity of female narrative beyond "a feminine aesthetic," so the "new kind of mimesis" in *The Golden Notebook* is grounded in the representational possibilities of female narrative. Indeed, the two novels share a capacity to characterize perceptions of female experience in resistance to the expectations of the dominant culture, to represent by subverting the premises of representation. The power of those characterizations lies in the interpretive agency of the narrative voice as it insists that perception and information interact to structure experience. Through such a recognition, women's capacity for autonomy is affirmed and female experience is opened to the possibilities of ongoing change.

CHAPTER 7

Women's Stories, Women's Lives:
The Novel, the Reader, and Cultural Change

Del Jordan, Claudia MacTeer, Violet Clay, Hagar Shipley, Jane Gray, Anna Wulf—each in her own way addresses a conflict central to many women's lives: to claim female "identity" or to claim autonomy. Each is threatened by the novelistic and cultural expectations of femininity, the pressure to relinquish self-definition in order to be acceptably female; each experiences the tension between sexuality and autonomy, body and mind, love and self-definition. But none of these protagonists remains bound by the imposed conflict. Instead, they all find ways to shift the narrative descriptions of their lives and thereby to redefine events and reinterpret experiences. In narrating their lives as women, they learn to see differently physical experiences such as menstruation and childbirth and cultural ones such as growing up female and being defined by expectations of passivity and nurturance. For each of them, self-narration becomes a way to claim her own possibilities for wholeness.

The "liberation" of these protagonists is, in part, an effect of renewed thematic concerns with female experience, but it can not be accomplished without an accompanying renewal of the novel's formal resources. Through reinterpreting the evolving capacities of novelistic narrative, their authors find new possibilities for reinterpreting women's lives. They find, in a kind of dialogue between realism and modernism, the resources by which to represent women's lives without being bound by the premises of representation: a reorganization of personal memory and subjective experience; a fragmentation of character as one way to separate the cultural from the personal; a treatment of the past as partially indeterminate; a joining of female selfhood with the lives of other women; a use of multiple narrative lines; and a refusal of closure.

These narrative qualities are not, however, presented to us as novelistic "devices" in an author's experimental form; they are, instead, integral to the character's own reclamation of voice and experience. As their own narrators, the characters are manifest in the acts of narrative choice itself. And because they premise their stories on the express recognition that narrative is always a temporary explanation subject to reinterpretation, they are able to retain the humanly central commitment to narrative even as they elude objectification in a male culture text. As they tell their lives, no longer bound by the old stories, they simultaneously redefine our notions of how stories work; as they give narrative definition to their complex humanity—telling *new* stories—they reveal, as well, new ways for women to live lives.

Women's stories, women's lives: the juxtaposition itself raises an old question of literary criticism. What is the relationship between literature and life? In focusing on female characters, I have been concerned primarily with how novels can represent the lives of women and why women's novels need to subvert the conventional premises of representation in order to reveal new possibilities in women's lives. But the relationship between literature and life is not unidirectional, not a simple matter of how "life" is represented in literature. It is also a matter of how literature interacts with "life," how novels affect the lives of readers. Indeed, it is through this concern that feminist literary criticism most fully identifies its commitment to cultural change, what Annette Kolodny calls its "overriding commitment . . . to a radical alteration . . . in the nature of [human] experience."[1]

Feminist critics may, then, share with Jonathan Culler a view that as a poetics, the study of literature becomes "a study of the conditions of meaning and thus a study of reading,"[2] but we must also see the study of reading as a part of the larger commitment to cultural change. For to study only the conditions of meaning is to focus exclusively on interpretation and to strip literature of its power for the reader beyond the actual encounter with the text. This is, in fact, the limitation that Jane Tompkins identifies as a problem throughout contemporary reader-response criticism: its focus on interpretation, like that of New Criticism, neglects concern with the power of language and literature in moral and pragmatic concerns.[3] Though Tompkins, ironically, ignores feminist criticism completely, her projection for criticism's future is precisely the effort of most feminist critics: to make central the "perception of language as a form of power."[4] In this effort, feminist criticism insists that the study of reading extend the analysis of the *conditions* of meaning to the analysis of the *effects* of meaning and of meaning making: not only the structures of language and idea or even of characters' lives, but also the importance of those structures for readers' lives.

Despite the recent surge of interest in reader response, we do not have much empirical evidence about the actual process of reading or its effects. Thus my concluding considerations here will be more speculative than decisive. But I would like, at least, to suggest the part the novel reader might play in the processes of feminist change and the importance that a first-person narrative might have for enhancing the reader's part. For, as I see it, the fullest participation of the novel in feminist change derives from the reader, especially the woman reader, who might find through the reading of novels the growing edge of her own humanity, extending beyond available roles and categories and into a renewed future. As she learns from female characters new ways to interpret her own and other women's experiences, she helps to reshape the culture's understanding of women and participates in the feminist alteration of human experience.

One of the most immediate needs of women readers is also one of the most immediate effects of reading novels by and about women: the need not to be alone with one's own experiences and perceptions. Historically excluded from many other forms of social consensus, women have found in novel reading an important means of gauging their own experience.[5] Margaret Drabble's observation— "Most of us read books with this question in mind: what does this say about my life?"[6]—has special pertinence for women readers as their roles have been often held in isolation from most public ways of assessing commonality. Nancy Burr Evans draws on her personal need to find "a female hero, a woman like myself," when she identifies the importance of women writers: "a sense that I was not alone in my feelings . . . , which is so crucial in grasping the very real function of women writers for women themselves."[7] This need is not the need propounded by the psychiatrist in the article that so distresses Del Jordan—the need to "personalize" everything. Rather it is the need to escape the confines of the purely personal: to find, in the acknowledgment of shared experiences, a confirmation or clarification of what has been culturally denied or trivialized.

Doris Lessing argues that it is only possible to be a writer "because one represents, makes articulate, is continuously fed by, numbers of people who are inarticulate, to whom one belongs, to whom one is responsible."[8] For Lessing, the very capacity to write derives from this recognition that large numbers of people share experiences that have not been adequately voiced. But the process is interactional, for the very voicing of experience itself creates a new communal awareness. As I noted in chapter 6, Lessing was both surprised and confirmed by the intensity of reader response to the "private" perceptions she included in *The Golden Notebook*. Similarly, if more prosaically, Erica Jong identifies an interaction with women readers as a basis for her own growing capacity to write of female experience.

> From the courage the women's movement gave me and from the reinforcement I received from grateful and passionate readers, I learned the daring to assume that my thoughts, nightmares, and daydreams were the same as my readers'. I discovered that whenever I wrote a fantasy I thought was wholly private, bizarre, kinky—(the fantasy of the Zipless Fuck in *Fear of Flying* is perhaps the best example of this)—I invariably discovered that thousands of other people had experienced the same private, bizarre, and kinky fantasy.[9]

Whatever one may think of "the Zipless Fuck," the voicing of private thoughts and perceptions has tremendous potency: only through developing the courage of shared perceptions can women evolve new possibilities for interpreting experience and living lives in resistance to cultural expectations.[10] This is one crucial effort of novel reading for women.

As feminist concern with reader response begins with this sense of shared experience, literary criticism parallels a general concern of feminist scholarship: to develop the recognition of commonality in women's lives and to remove individual women from a sense of personal isolation. Just as feminist psychologists seek to identify previously hidden commonality in women's feelings, thoughts, and actions, just as feminist historians seek that commonality in women's past, so feminist literary critics and female readers in general seek commonality in the fictional treatment of women's lives.

Because it is by convention permeated by actual social experience, the novel form, in fact, has a particular readiness for such examination, despite its fictionality. Susan Lanser's explanation of two kinds of novelistic expectations gives an initial indication of how this is possible: *"formal realism* . . . [involving] specific details about the historical world" and *"evaluative illocutions* . . . : commentary and assertions about events, states, beings, values, problems, and ideas that have meaning in the historical world."[11] Through attachment of novelistic description to places and events in the historical world, the novel has an immediate capacity to include information specifically related to women's lives. The conventions of formal realism make permissible the presentation of an object world invoking specifically female experiences, such as the cultural trappings of femininity, the physical phenomena of childbirth, or the sensual expression of female sexuality; in the narratives of protagonists like Del Jordan or Jane Gray, readers can identify experiences that parallel their own. Similarly, through evaluative illocutions, also meaningful in the historical world, the novel can even directly challenge assumptions made about the lives of women. Direct commentary from a female-centered perspective or even an overtly feminist one opens onto women readers' experiences and evaluations in the social world and enables a responding recognition of female commonality. When Jane Eyre says that women "need exercise for their faculties, and a field for their efforts as much as their brothers do," the woman reader is able to respond with an acknowledgment of her own needs and desires.

These capacities of the novel are emphasized by a third set of conventions, which Lanser also identifies: "the conventions of naturalization that govern novel-reading."[12] The material of the historical world evident in the novelistic world encourages the reader's inclination to see the latter as also "real" and to place it in relation to her own experience, to test its congruity or incongruity with her own sense of the world in which she lives. In a consideration of the mimetic function of the novel, Robert Alter argues that readers persist in "testing our own perceptions of reality against [novels]."[13]

By a similar process, readers are also able to test novelistic perceptions against perceptions of reality. From this interaction, the reader gains a greater sense of participation in a human community. As a narrator-protagonist finds in self-narration new ways to include specifically female experiences, the woman reader finds in the novel a possible way to overcome her isolation—through the very naming of those experiences—and thus a way to develop, with other women, shared recognition of their own experiences.

The development of community—based, as Lessing says, on a novelist talking "as an individual to individuals, in a small personal voice"[14]—is particularly powerful when the author gives to her character a personal voice as well. The "I" invites not only a very basic identification of reader with character, but also a more complicated suggestion of interaction. In the immediate presence of a first-person narrator—in Violet Clay's direct address to the reader or in the private interactions of Hagar Shipley's interior monologue or in Jane Gray's and Anna Wulf's overt comments on narrative structure—the reader enters into a communicative pattern that becomes an initial basis of community. Edward Said claims that the need for community is a general condition for creating narrative fiction: "In the community formed among reader, author, and character, each desires the company of another voice."[15] The overt manifestation of voice in first-person narration draws on this general narrative condition as it responds to the feminist need to gain mutual support in overcoming the silencing imposed by male dominance. As reader, character, and author form an interacting triad of subjective presences, their shared experiences become the basis for developing shared perceptions.

But to claim only the possibilities for immediate commonality is to see the novel as exclusively a document of the historical world; the novel, after all, is primarily a fictional work. As such, its relationship to individual readers has an additional importance, growing out of the understanding of narrative as interpretive agent. Speaking as a reader, Drabble suggests how novel reading participates in her own interpretations of experience: "I find out about living and about the values of living—and a lot of my beliefs in life and my feelings about people and what to do—from reading novels. . . . They give you guidelines on familiar, unfamiliar people."[16] Christa Wolf's narrator in *A Model Childhood* claims a similar interpretive centrality for literary understanding: "I believe that the mechanism which deals with the absorption and processing of reality is formed by literature."[17]

This interpretive relationship between life and literature grows out of the value of shared perception but has much more complex implications for women readers. Just as women authors and female characters have historically had difficulty in developing new plots and understandings of women's lives, so women readers have been implicated in the same claims of old narrative patterns. When women readers test their perceptions about reality against the possibilities available in realist novels, they may well be seeing their lives in relation to the cultural assumptions of the eighteenth or nineteenth century, a male-dominant sexual ideology that persists in the premises of representation and in many of the symbolic systems of the twentieth century. If they seek in novels a "mechanism" for processing their own experience, they risk reading their lives toward the formal telos of marriage or painful isolation, premature death. Like Rachel Brownstein, they risk finding in novels the support for "becoming a heroine," rather than for feminist self-definition.[18]

The "mechanism," however, need not be a constraining grid for the reader, any more than for author or character: like the novel itself, which has continually evolved new capacities for interpreting characters' lives in relation to a social context, the experience of *reading* novels is also interactional. Novels become, in Said's phrase, "speculative instruments" by which readers "engage their own narrative histories."[19] Reading, in other words, is not merely a matter of testing the fit between a novel and one's own experience or reshaping one's experience to merge into the available patterns; rather it is a way of reassessing experience toward the possible formation of new patterns.

The need to reassess is a second area of concern that feminist literary criticism shares with general feminist analysis; in addition to identifying the commonality of female experiences, feminist analysis seeks ways to redefine the meaning of those experiences. This is the process by which Adrienne Rich, in *Of Woman Born*, resees "our physicality as a resource, rather than a destiny."[20] This is the process by which feminist psychologists have reexamined female experience to account for the fact that women are anomalous in achievement research.[21] This is the process that has led them, as well, to redefine competence to include women's realistic assessment of "the interpersonal strategies and skills necessary for success in a particular setting" and thus to recognize the competence already evident in women if the appropriate interpretation is available.[22] This is the process of developing new interpretive frameworks by which to give substance to the crucial feminist commitment to consciousness raising. In sum, this is the process by which feminist scholarship helps us to see women's lives with new sight.

The distinctive capacity of the novel to participate in this feminist commitment again resides in the dialogic capacity of its narrative conventions, here in interaction with the reader. Like the author writing, the reader reading employs available conventions as interpretive strategies for making sense of the novel. But those conventions also participate in the interpretive power of the novel as "mechanism" for processing her own experience. As the novel's old conventions of plot, character, reality, and coherence have endangered the autonomy of female characters, so they have endangered the autonomy of female readers by shaping readers' cognitive strategies and causal attributions for interpreting their own experience. In my introduction, I cited, as support for new novelistic understandings of female experience, Fredric Jameson's statement that "lived reality alters . . . in function of the 'model' through which we see and live the world."[23] The same statement suggests a parallel importance of novelistic conventions by which readers, like characters and authors, "see and live the world." This, then, becomes the most crucial importance of female characters' new understandings of their lives through new novelistic conventions: as the characters and their authors reshape conventions of realism, these conventions interact with women readers' own experience to become new cognitive strategies for reassessing their lives as women.

Although we lack concrete information about the specific cognitive processes involved in reading or how they relate to living, we can derive from work in other disciplines a general awareness of how the novel as speculative instrument has the potential to shape a reader's response to her own world. From E. H. Gombrich's work on representational painting, we can take the crucial recognition that both anticipation and memories of previous images have a powerful suggestive effect when we look at an image: we often see what we expect to see, even when the image itself in a different context yields a different suggestion.[24] As cognitive psychologists have demonstrated, language works in similar ways, making experience either visible or invisible: "the *names* of objects—the words most frequently used to denote them—become incorporated into the anticipatory schemata by which the objects themselves are perceived."[25] Even more than images or words alone, novelistic narrative, conveyed as it is in words "thoroughly and subtly steeped in memory both public and private"[26] and shaped to incorporate images and patterns from the culture at large, bears a still more complex cultural weight of memory and anticipation. But like repeated images and words, narrative, too, has the capacity to transmit new shapes for future anticipation. As words invoke memories, both cultural and personal, the absence of words creates gaps in the anticipatory schemata by which we interpret meaning; the absence of narrative forms fosters blindness to fuller understandings of women's lives. But just as the broader conventions of representation invoke memories of previous ways of completing narrative patterns, so the redefinition of novelistic conventions in contemporary feminist novels creates a new set of anticipations for the reading of lives. In this way, the reader's assimilation of novelistic form as a part of her own perceptual response can become a new capacity to see her own experience differently.

This cognitive connection between novels and lived experience gives to readers their most dynamic place in the interaction between novels and lives.[27] For if women have historically learned many of the ways we have interpreted our lives from the narrative schemata of novels, which have in part participated in a male-dominant discourse, we can also gain from novels new insights into the narrative processes of constructing meaning and hence the possibilities of constructing meaning differently. And in recognizing how those conventions function in our lives as well as in literature, we become better able to shift experiential perceptions through the process labeled "defamiliarization" by the Russian Formalists: to become conscious of conventions is to see "reality" differently. As I said in chapter 2, the history of the realist novel is itself tied to the breaking down of conventional assumptions. In playing upon narrative conventions, the novel can thus be made doubly fruitful for developing new ways of understanding lives: not only as cognitive instrument but also as re-cognitive instrument. The "historic function" of narrative mimesis as "the secular 'decoding' of those preexisting . . . narrative paradigms"[28] makes it a form especially available to the feminist critique and revision of the narratives that structure women's lived experience.

To make my speculations on reading more concrete, I want to suggest how this process might work in relation to the persistent cultural paradigm for femininity: women, if appropriately female—that is, relational, expressive, passive—will not be competent and self-defined. From this gender stereotype spring the traditional character traits and plot choices for female characters; in service of this gender stereotype women in novels are placed in the midst of domestic social reality and bounded by a novelistic coherence of erotic and familial concerns. This same stereotype also implicates women outside novels in the limitations of femininity as it yields a possible "motive to avoid success"[29] or at least undermines their confidence "on achievement-related issues."[30] This stereotype even governs the possibilities for how women are perceived by others and how they perceive themselves. As Kay Deaux demonstrates in her work on women and the attribution process, the explanations that we choose for human behavior, like our interpretations of images and words and novels, are "directly related to the prior assumptions and the expectations." Women's failure, for example, will be "more often attributed to lack of ability" than men's; and both women's success and men's failure will be attributed to temporary causes.[31] This becomes, as Deaux concludes, a "vicious cycle" by which women are confirmed in a feeling of inadequacy and men are confirmed in a feeling of adequacy.[32] Self-stereotypes are supported by cultural stereotypes: women, simply by being female, tend to be perceived and to perceive themselves as relatively incompetent, unable to perform adequately the tasks that contribute to a sense of adulthood.

The cultural problem faced by women readers has much in common with the problems encountered by female protagonists: how to break out of this "vicious cycle," how to change the negating perceptions of women by the culture at large and by women themselves. Like the complex "liberation" of female protagonists, this change in the lives of women readers cannot be accomplished simply on the individual level nor can it be accomplished in isolation from broad patterns of cultural change. But through the novel's complex possibilities of interpretive interaction, women readers, like female protagonists, can also gain support for escaping this "vicious cycle."

Novels of female self-definition thus do more than "represent" the available possibilities in women's lives. They do more, even, than create new "role models." They take an *active* role in the broader patterns of cultural change, first by enacting their own redefinition of personal attribution processes and then by giving substance to readers' alternative interpretations of femaleness. As characters find for themselves new patterns of attribution beyond the stereotypes, they simultaneously help to create for readers the alternative memories and anticipations by which cognitive processes project narrative resolutions and gender-based generalizations. Having observed and participated in the redefinition of selfhood by characters like Claudia MacTeer or Anna Wulf, women readers begin to develop an attribution process that makes accomplishment an explicit capacity of a woman in relation to her human community. As they recognize each protagonist's active responsibility for her own accomplishment—Del Jordan as writer, Violet Clay as painter, Jane Gray as poet, or even Hagar Shipley as woman of complex courage facing death—women readers gain support for resisting the old attributions of female inadequacy. They learn to recognize female strength, accomplishment, and responsibility; and they learn to identify the shared cultural constraints that often make female "failure"—like Pecola Breedlove's madness—a function of cultural denial rather than personal inadequacy.

Through integrating new novelistic possibilities into their own cognitive strategies, readers then gain the resources for new attributions even about their own previous experience. Wolfgang Iser argues that reading not only gives us new experience but also leads us to restructure our previous experience;[33] in the terms I have set out, which are similar to Iser's, the cognitive schema that the novel assists readers in developing will prompt a rereading of the available information from their own personal past and help them to create an alternative interpretation of previous experiences and actions.[34] In working through Hagar Shipley's re-cognition of her past experiences toward seeing her as life-affirming and both strong and sexual, readers develop the ability to perceive differently the human capacities expressed in their own personal past and present. In continually reassessing the multiple narrative paradigms by which Del Jordan keeps her identity flexible or Claudia MacTeer joins and separates herself from the people around her, readers develop a capacity to find female complexity and possibility in their own past experience. And in the process of defining and assessing Jane Gray's participation in the love story—and recognizing all the ways in which Jane emerges from her defensive strategies into her capacities to act for herself as poet and mother as well as lover—readers learn to perceive latent capacities in their own lives as well.

For the development of such cognitive strategies, the first-person novel again has special fecundity for the reader's involvement. Because it is centered in the perceiver as narrative agent, first-person narration also makes "procedures . . . its subject"[35] and thus becomes a visible paradigm for the entire interpretive process: the female narrator-protagonist exemplifies the cognitive acts by which readers can similarly construct narrative interpretations of their own experience. In all of the novels I have examined, the narrator-protagonists also engage readers in the *re*interpretive process: as narrators hypothesize and then reject conventional explanations of their behavior, readers are drawn into the process by which narrative hypotheses are developed and altered in interaction with experiential evidence. Through participating in the narrative constructions of literary characters, readers become better prepared to develop new narrative constructions of their own experience.

Such participation is further encouraged by texts that disrupt our conventional expectations, texts that, in Iser's phrase, suspend *"good continuation"* and therefore lead the reader through perpetual formation and abandonment of perceptual images.[36] Iser associates a high proportion of "blanks" with modernist texts and accurately points out the correlation between the experience of reading Joyce or Beckett and the experience of indeterminacy in lived experience: "This experience corresponds to the openness of the world, and so the serial variations constantly turn definitive, current, and given world views into mere possibilities of how the world can be experienced."[37] Though their narrative strategies vary, all of the novels I have examined make use of some suspension of "good continuation" and draw the reader into such an epistemological involvement. Their blanks, their disruptions of narrative continuity, are not only crucial for breaking down narrative assumptions and expectations but also crucial for drawing the reader into narrative participation. The woman reader's active participation in meaning making leads her to question her own perceptual constructions.

But because these novels are grounded in the shared awareness of the problems of gender, they raise ontological concerns even as they insist on epistemological questioning: they lead the woman reader to question not only how she interprets her own experience but also what that experience is. To do both, the texts do not totally relinquish the expectations of continuity, of signification, of social reality, but rather invoke expectations of meaning in the reader's pragmatic experience, especially in her gendered experience; as I have suggested, the female experiences characterized in the novels extend beyond the novels' boundaries to the extraliterary world of the reader. These novels, therefore, call upon both the involvement that Roland Barthes calls "writerly"—that is, the reader's active participation in producing the text, as encouraged by gaps and indeterminacies—and the involvement he calls "readerly"—that is, a commitment to narrative, nomination, and signification.[38] Through such a balance—what I have called a dialogue between realism and modernism—these novels are able to draw readers into an examination of their lives as women without becoming programmatic scripts for how those lives should be lived: they illuminate possibilities and processes without insisting on ideological solutions.

The recognitions in readers' own lives, then, also participate in an evolving ability to read the novels differently. Though readers can and do see Violet Clay as passive, Jane Gray as helpless, or Anna Wulf as overdependent on male approval (and the novels can be seen to support these views), the novels also provide evidence for alternative character paradigms of strength, agency, and self-definition. The process of readers' interaction with their own narrative histories as well as with those of the characters emphasizes the importance of process and change: identities are not fixed by defining traits but rather subject to multiple interpretations. Readers join authors in developing alternative novelistic conventions by which to read the capacities of both characters and self.

Through active involvement in interpreting the narrator-protagonist's life, the reader thus learns to interpret and reinterpret her own experience as a woman.[39] Sandra Gilbert's distinction between the critic and the reader is a particularly apt description of the process: the critic, she says, tends "to embalm or reify life"; through the text, the *reader*, however, sees life as "a series of studies, and studies dissolve into life."[40] The woman reader or feminist critic, seeking in novels for ways to interpret her own experience, is ultimately reading her "own self," using the novel as what Proust called "a kind of optical instrument" for discerning otherwise unavailable perceptions of herself.[41] The interaction between narrative schemata and lived experience, which I made central to my feminist poetics of the novel, becomes the process by which readers as well as writers and characters identify new possibilities for women's lives.

The emphasis in my poetics and in my textual analyses has been the recognition that novelistic conventions are not fixed but are instead subject to redefinition. For women readers, as well as women writers and female characters, the need to integrate newly available information—in this case, the specific information of female experience that doesn't "fit" the expectations of femininity—leads to the recognition that old conventions are inadequate. As women writers and readers begin to perceive their own experience differently, they develop new cognitive strategies that participate in developing new novelistic conventions for female experience. These conventions, in turn, make perceptually available—make *visible*—new awareness of lived experience, so that readers and writers can see both novels and lives differently. As new anticipatory schemata, altered novelistic conventions continue to generate new recognitions from the available information; the new information continues to alter the novelistic conventions as employed by both writer and reader. In broad terms, the role of the reader is at the fulcrum point of this interaction: women's novels alter women's lives; women's lives alter women's novels.

At that fulcrum point, women readers are able to draw new understandings from novels and to understand novels with new insight as they reinterpret their own lives. The cycle is unending but it is a progressive cycle rather than a vicious one, as long as we avoid the reification of both novelistic conventions and gender stereotypes. Just as feminist work in attribution theory has shown us the distorting power of gender stereotypes in our interpretive processes, so can our changes in attribution and interpretation, in turn, begin to alter our gender stereotypes. As women readers develop new cognitive strategies through our novel reading, we do change our assumptions and expectations; we do change our causal attributions; and eventually we contribute, as well, to cultural changes in gender stereotypes.

In the introductory chapter of this book, I indicated that a central problem for women in the novel is the encoding process by which women in novels cannot be both female and autonomous. As I have said, this split in literary characterization, in fact, reflects the presence of the "pervasive and persistent sex-role stereotypes" in the culture at large.[42] But the narrator-protagonists' capacity for complex self-definition in the six novels I have considered at length, and in a growing number of other novels by women, shows a powerful resistance to those sex-role stereotypes, a resistance by which women readers can understand their own complexity as well.

As the autonomous woman in literature becomes a shaping force for the autonomous woman in life, we can see in the novel a power beyond the "mirroring" of life, a power to open the eyes and understandings of its readers, a power to participate in cultural change. No longer trapped within stories of the past, women can learn—are learning—to create new stories for the future, to live new lives in the present. No longer forced by narrative expectation or cultural assumption to choose between femaleness and autonomy, women can begin to identify in their lived experiences the possibilities for altering the constraints on their lives, the possibilities for claiming human wholeness.

Notes

1. Joanna Russ, "What Can a Heroine Do? Or Why Women Can't Write," in *Images of Women in Fiction: Feminist Perspectives*, ed. Susan Koppelman Cornillon (Bowling Green, Ohio: Bowling Green University Popular Press, 1972), p. 9.
2. Nancy K. Miller, *The Heroine's Text: Readings in the French and English Novel, 1722–1782* (New York: Columbia University Press, 1980), esp. pp. 157 and 175.
3. See Carolyn Heilbrun, *Reinventing Womanhood* (New York: Norton, 1979), esp. pp. 71ff.; and Patricia Meyer Spacks, *The Female Imagination* (New York: Avon Books, 1976), passim.
4. See Michelle Zimbalist Rosaldo's anthropological generalization: "women, as wives, mothers, witches, midwives, nuns, or whores, are defined almost exclusively in terms of their sexual functions." "Woman, Culture, and Society: A Theoretical Overview," in *Woman, Culture and Society*, ed. Michelle Zimbalist Rosaldo and Louise Lamphere (Stanford: Stanford University Press, 1974), p. 31. See also Sherry Ortner's important analysis of the basis of women's cultural position, "Is Female to Male as Nature Is to Culture?" also in *Woman, Culture, and Society*, pp. 66–87.
5. This awareness is pervasive in feminist criticism. For social scientific documentation, see especially Inge K. Broverman et al., "Sex-Role Stereotypes: A Current Appraisal," and Matina S. Horner, "Toward an Understanding of Achievement-Related Conflicts in Women," both in *Women and Achievement: Social and Motivational Analyses*, ed. Martha T. Shuch Mednick, Sandra Schwartz Tangri, and Lois Wladis Hoffman (New York: John Wiley and Sons, 1975), pp. 32–47 and 206–20. Broverman's assessment of the research findings provides a succinct statement of the overall problem: "If women adopt the behaviors specified as desirable for adults, they risk censure for their failure to be appropriately feminine; but if they adopt the behaviors that are desig-

nated as feminine, they are necessarily deficient with respect to the general standards for adult behavior" (p. 45).

6. Simone de Beauvoir, *The Second Sex*, trans. H. M. Parshley (1952; reprint, New York: Vintage, 1974), p. 758.

7. Adrienne Rich, "When We Dead Awaken: Writing as Re-Vision," in *On Lies, Secrets and Silence* (New York: Norton, 1979), pp. 42–44. See also Suzanne Juhasz's analysis of this dilemma in *Naked and Fiery Forms: Modern American Poetry by Women, A New Tradition* (New York: Harper, 1976), esp. pp. 1–3.

8. Rich, *Of Woman Born: Motherhood as Experience and Institution* (1976; reprint, New York: Bantam, 1977), p. 154.

9. For a psychoanalytic perspective (which I do not share) see Jane Flax's analysis of gender expectations regarding nurturance and autonomy: "The Conflict Between Nurturance and Autonomy in Mother-Daughter Relationships and Within Feminism," *Feminist Studies* 4, no. 2 (June 1978): 171–89.

10. I adopt the term from J. M. Lotman, "Point of View in a Text," trans. L. M. O'Toole, in *New Literary History* 6, no. 2 (1975): 341.

11. See Miller's distinction between the ambitious and the erotic plots; "Emphasis Added: Plots and Plausibilities in Women's Fiction," *PMLA* 96, no. 1 (January 1981): 36–48, esp. p. 40.

12. Virginia Woolf, *To the Lighthouse* (New York: Harcourt, Brace and World, 1927), e.g., pp. 75, 238.

13. Woolf, "Professions for Women," in *Collected Essays* (New York: Harcourt, Brace and World, 1967), 2:285.

14. Ibid., p. 288.

15. Sandra M. Gilbert and Susan Gubar, *The Madwoman in the Attic: The Woman Writer and the Nineteenth-Century Imagination* (New Haven: Yale University Press, 1979), p. 3.

16. Although contemporary advocates of *l'écriture féminine* seek in the resources of the female body a special capacity for inscribing femininity, this process can only be accomplished subversively, if at all; within current cultural assumptions, it cannot, at any rate, be a parallel claim to authoritative grounding. See, e.g., Hélène Cixous, "The Laugh of the Medusa," trans. Keith Cohen and Paula Cohen, in *Signs* 1, no. 4 (Summer 1976): 875–93.

17. As should become clear in my overall argument, I am not suggesting that feminism requires women to claim autonomy at the expense of human interconnectedness; rather I am arguing for the value of female autonomy, in the context of human community, as a part of women's need to resist externally imposed definitions. It is very likely that male-centered novels suffer a somewhat parallel problem in the difficulty of portraying expressiveness as integral to maleness, but the problem is less difficult to overcome because of the cultural assumption that maleness can include whatever is "generally human" as well as what is specifically male.

18. For an explanation of these two forms as central to the history of the novel, see Mikhail M. Bakhtin, *The Dialogic Imagination: Four Essays,* ed. Michael Holquist, trans. Caryl Emerson and Michael Holquist (Austin: University of Texas Press, 1981), esp. pp. 388–96.

19. Although I share Rachel Blau DuPlessis's view that in twentieth-century female *Künstlerromane* "the figure of the female artist counters the modernist tradition of exile, alienation, and refusal of social roles," I am also convinced that this possibility can only evolve from a complex confrontation with an enforced cultural split between femaleness and author-ity. See *Writing beyond the Ending: Narrative Strategies of Twentieth-Century Women Writers* (Bloomington: Indiana University Press, 1985), p. 101.

20. Fredric Jameson, *The Prison-House of Language: A Critical Account of Structuralism and Russian Formalism* (Princeton, N.J.: Princeton University Press, 1974), p. 14.

21. Jameson's phrase, in *The Political Unconscious: Narrative as a Socially Symbolic Act* (Ithaca, N.Y.: Cornell University Press, 1981), p. 77.

22. Gilbert and Gubar offer this apt descriptive phrase for the process by which women are textually encoded as objects (p. 248).

23. Russ identifies science fiction as one of the few available plot strategies available to women writers (p. 18). See also DuPlessis on "speculative consciousness"—utopian and futuristic—as an important narrative strategy for twentieth-century women writers (pp. 178–97).

24. DuPlessis, p. 197.

25. Bonnie Zimmerman, "Exiting from Patriarchy: The Lesbian Novel of Development," in *The Voyage In: Fictions of Female Development,* ed. Elizabeth Abel, Marianne Hirsch, and Elizabeth Langland (Hanover, N.H.: University Press of New England, 1983), pp. 244–45.

26. Ibid., p. 246.

27. Catharine Stimpson, "Zero Degree Deviancy: The Lesbian Novel in England," *Critical Inquiry* 8, no. 2 (Winter 1981): 363–79.

28. Zimmerman, p. 250.

29. Ibid., p. 257.

30. Heilbrun, "A Response to *Writing and Sexual Difference,*" *Critical Inquiry* 8, no. 1 (Summer 1982): 810.

31. See DuPlessis for a fruitful consideration of a number of significant narrative strategies by which women writers have been able to "write beyond the ending."

32. The label derives from Bakhtin, whose overall understanding of the novel is vital to my own analysis.

CHAPTER 2

1. Terry Eagleton, *Literary Theory: An Introduction* (Minneapolis: University of Minnesota Press, 1983), p. 204.

2. Ibid., p. 210.

3. Ibid., p. 212.
4. Annette Kolodny, "Dancing through the Minefield: Some Observations on the Theory, Practice and Politics of a Feminist Literary Criticism," *Feminist Studies* 6, no. 1 (Spring 1980): 1–25; and Elaine Showalter, "Feminist Criticism in the Wilderness," *Critical Inquiry* 8, no. 2 (Winter 1981): 179–205.
5. Elizabeth Abel, "Editor's Introduction: Writing and Sexual Difference," *Critical Inquiry* 8, no. 2 (Winter 1981): 174.
6. Showalter, "Towards a Feminist Poetics," in *Women Writing and Writing about Women,* ed. Mary Jacobus (New York: Barnes and Noble, 1979), p. 39. See pp. 37–40 for her analysis of why feminist criticism cannot simply adopt and revise such male-defined theories as Marxism and structuralism. In "Feminist Criticism in the Wilderness," Showalter reassesses the "impasse," suggesting that it was "actually an evolutionary phase" (p. 181).
7. Mary Jacobus, "The Difference of View," in *Women Writing and Writing about Women,* p. 14.
8. For a discussion of this evolution, see Showalter, "Feminist Criticism in the Wilderness," especially pp. 182ff.
9. Showalter explains her introduction of this term in "Towards a Feminist Poetics," p. 25.
10. Abel, p. 174.
11. Kolodny, p. 20.
12. Showalter, "Feminist Criticism in the Wilderness," p. 205.
13. Margaret Homans, " 'Her Very Own Howl': The Ambiguities of Representation in Recent Women's Fiction," *Signs* 9, no. 2 (Winter 1983): 186.
14. Ibid., p. 204.
15. For a feminist linguistic approach rejecting either/or positions on language and claiming a "communicationally oriented alternative theory," see Deborah Cameron, *Feminism and Linguistic Theory* (London: Macmillan, 1985), esp. p. 93.
16. Homans, p. 205.
17. See, e.g., Kolodny, "A Map for Rereading: Or, Gender and the Interpretation of Literary Texts," *New Literary History* 11, no. 3 (1980): 451–67; Sandra Gilbert and Susan Gubar, *The Madwoman in the Attic: The Woman Writer and the Nineteenth-Century Imagination* (New Haven: Yale University Press, 1979); and Showalter, "Feminist Criticism in the Wilderness."
18. My view of the human importance of narrative is pervasively indebted to Frank Kermode, *The Sense of an Ending: Studies in the Theory of Fiction* (New York: Oxford University Press, 1967). In the face of more recent work in narratology, this work retains its interest as it affirms the human and dynamic rather than the structural and static elements of narrative. For an important recent effort to restore considerations of narrative to a more dynamic awareness of human needs, see Peter

Brooks, *Reading for the Plot: Design and Intention in Narrative* (Oxford: Oxford University Press, 1984).

19. Doris Lessing, *The Golden Notebook* (1962; reprint, New York: Bantam, 1973), p. 363.

20. Ulric Neisser, *Cognition and Reality: Principles and Implications of Cognitive Psychology* (San Francisco: W. H. Freeman, 1976), p. 182.

21. Barbara Hardy, "An Approach Through Narrative," in *Towards a Poetics of Fiction*, ed. Mark Spilka (Bloomington: Indiana University Press, 1977), p. 31.

22. Louis Mink, "Narrative Form as Cognitive Instrument," in *The Writings of History: Literary Form and Historical Understanding*, ed. Robert H. Canary and Henry Kozicki (Madison: University of Wisconsin Press, 1978), pp. 129–49.

23. Ibid., p. 133.

24. Robert Alter, *Partial Magic: The Novel as a Self-Conscious Genre* (1975; reprint, Berkeley: University of California Press, 1978), p. 64.

25. Fredric Jameson, *The Political Unconscious: Narrative as a Socially Symbolic Act* (Ithaca, N.Y.: Cornell University Press, 1981), p. 13. Cf. also Christa Wolf's impassioned conviction that "Storytelling is humane and achieves humane effects" and "Storytelling is the assignment of meaning." *Cassandra: A Novel and Four Essays*, trans. Jan Van Heurck (London: Virago, 1984), pp. 173–74.

26. Susan Sniader Lanser, *The Narrative Act: Point of View in Prose Fiction* (Princeton, N.J.: Princeton University Press, 1981), p. 65.

27. Northrop Frye, *The Anatomy of Criticism* (1957; reprint, Princeton, N.J.: Princeton University Press, 1971), p. 97.

28. J. Paul Hunter, "The Loneliness of the Long-Distance Reader," *Genre* 10 (Winter 1977): 481.

29. Walter Reed, "The Problem with a Poetics of the Novel," in *Towards a Poetics of Fiction*, p. 64.

30. Ibid., p. 65.

31. Cf., for example, Frye, pp. 95–98.

32. Mikhail M. Bakhtin, *The Dialogic Imagination: Four Essays*, ed. Michael Holquist, trans. Caryl Emerson and Michael Holquist (Austin: University of Texas Press, 1981), p. 61. Subsequent references will be indicated within the text.

33. Hunter, p. 459.

34. See, for example, Ellen Moers, *Literary Women: The Great Writers* (Garden City, N.Y.: Anchor Books, 1977), p. 182. See, too, Ian Watt's suggestion that the "rise of the novel . . . would seem to be connected with the much greater freedom of women in modern society." *The Rise of the Novel: Studies in Defoe, Richardson and Fielding* (1957; reprint, Berkeley: University of California Press, 1965), p. 138.

35. Carol Pearson and Katherine Pope, *The Female Hero in American and British Literature* (New York: R. R. Bowker and Co., 1981), p. 11; see also pp. 6–7 on the conservatism of popular literary forms.

36. See Showalter, "Women Writers and the Double Standard," in *Woman in Sexist Society: Studies in Power and Powerlessness*, ed. Vivian Gornick and B. K. Moran (1971; reprint, New York: New American Library, 1972), pp. 452–79.

37. Nancy K. Miller, *The Heroine's Text: Readings in the French and English Novel, 1722–1782* (New York: Columbia University Press, 1980), p. 158.

38. Myra Jehlen, "Archimedes and the Paradox of Feminist Criticism," *Signs* 6, no. 4 (Summer 1981): 600. Although I disagree with a number of her major conclusions, I find Jehlen's analysis provocative and much more complex than my use of it here implies.

39. Ann Barr Snitow, "The Front Line: Notes on Sex in Novels by Women, 1969–1979," *Signs* 5, no. 4 (Summer 1980): 705. Snitow also concludes that women novelists will continue to find "social realism" a fruitful form (p. 718).

40. See Bakhtin, especially p. 367.

41. Walter Benjamin, "The Storyteller," in *Illuminations*, trans. Harry Zohn (New York: Schocken, 1969), p. 87.

42. Watt, "Serious Reflections on *The Rise of the Novel*," in *Towards a Poetics of Fiction*, p. 102.

43. Edward Said, *Beginnings: Intention and Method* (Baltimore: Johns Hopkins University Press, 1975), p. 141.

44. See Hunter, esp. p. 471.

45. Mary Poovey, "*Persuasion* and the Promises of Love," in *The Representation of Women in Fiction*, ed. Carolyn G. Heilbrun and Margaret R. Higonnet (Baltimore: Johns Hopkins University Press, 1983), p. 172.

46. Jehlen, p. 595.

47. Bakhtin speaks repeatedly of the novel's distinctive capacity to criticize itself (e.g., pp. 6, 49, and 412).

48. I share Eagleton's view that a concern for "the experience of the human subject" is participant in the political basis of feminist criticism because "sexism and gender roles are questions which engage the deepest personal dimensions of life" (p. 149).

49. Jehlen, p. 600.

50. Lessing, *A Small Personal Voice*, ed. Paul Schlueter (New York: Alfred A. Knopf, 1974), p. 21.

51. Jonathan Culler, Introduction to Tzvetan Todorov, *The Poetics of Prose*, trans. Richard Howard (Ithaca, N.Y.: Cornell University Press, 1977), pp. 10 and 12.

52. Roland Barthes, "An Introduction to the Structural Analysis of Narrative," trans. Lionel Diusit, in *New Literary History* 6, no. 2 (1975): 238.

53. Gilbert and Gubar, p. xi.

54. Ibid., pp. 67 and 71.

55. Lanser, p. 100.

56. Gilbert and Gubar, p. 73.

57. Showalter, "Feminist Criticism in the Wilderness," pp. 201 and 204.
58. Nancy K. Miller, "Emphasis Added: Plots and Plausibilities in Women's Fiction," *PMLA* 96, no. 1 (January 1981): 36.
59. Clifford Geertz, *The Interpretation of Cultures* (New York: Basic Books, 1973), p. 220. Kolodny also draws on Geertz's definition of ideologies; see "Dancing through the Minefield," p. 24. See also Showalter's use of cultural anthropologists, especially Edwin Ardener, in "Feminist Criticism in the Wilderness."
60. Neisser, p. 14.
61. Ibid., see diagram, p. 21.
62. See Henry D. Herring's theory of constructivist criticism as a process that focuses on the "cognitive strategies created in the work." "Constructivist Interpretation: An Alternative to Deconstruction," *Bucknell Review* 29, no. 2 (1985): 32–46. Also see his argument that literature provides us with a way of "understanding, reinforcing or revising the constructive scheme that currently guides our action." "Literature, Concepts, and Knowledge," *New Literary History* (forthcoming). I am indebted throughout to Herring's application of cognitive psychology to the understanding of literature.
63. George Levine, *The Realistic Imagination: English Fiction from Frankenstein to Lady Chatterley* (Chicago: University of Chicago Press, 1981); Alter.
64. For an extended treatment of this historical break, see the essay titled "Epic and Novel: Toward a Methodology for the Study of the Novel," Bakhtin, pp. 3–40.
65. See Sherry Ortner's anthropological analysis of women's cultural position as "both under and over (but really simply outside of) the sphere of culture's hegemony." "Is Female to Male as Nature Is to Culture?" in *Woman, Culture and Society*, ed. Michelle Zimbalist Rosaldo and Louise Lamphere (Stanford: Stanford University Press, 1974), pp. 66–87, esp. p. 86.
66. For a powerful reading of this pattern, see Gilbert and Gubar, pp. 3–44.
67. Following Bakhtin, I recognize that "novelization" evolved gradually and was evident well before the development of what we generally recognize as the genre of the novel. See especially "From the Prehistory of Novelistic Discourse," pp. 41–83.
68. Virginia Woolf, "Modern Fiction," in *Collected Essays* (New York: Harcourt, Brace and World, 1967), 2:106.
69. Cf. Gillian Beer, "Beyond Determinism: George Eliot and Virginia Woolf," in *Women Writing and Writing about Women:* "The eschewing of plot as an aspect of her feminism" (p. 95).
70. Cf. Carolyn A. Durham's argument that women's experimental uses of narrative form, as evident in Marie Cardinal, are different from the New Novel because they are concerned with lived experience. "Feminism and Formalism: Dialectical Structures in Marie Cardinal's *Une Vie pour deux*," *Tulsa Studies in Women's Literature* 4, no. 1 (Spring 1985):

94. I am indebted to Durham for insights in conversation on the novel and its experimental forms, as well as on feminism.

71. For analysis of more specific "codes" that can be grouped into these areas, see Barthes, "An Introduction to the Structural Analysis of Narrative," and his analysis of Balzac in *S/Z*, trans. Richard Miller (New York: Hill and Wang, 1974); see, too, Jonathan Culler's summary of structuralist codes in *Structuralist Poetics: Structuralism, Linguistics and the Study of Literature* (Ithaca, N.Y.: Cornell University Press, 1976), pp. 202–38. For a less static perspective on literary conventions as they interact with social context, see Raymond Williams, *Marxism and Literature* (Oxford: Oxford University Press, 1977), pp. 173–79; his assessment of the interaction between narrative conventions of causation is particularly suggestive (pp. 176–77).

72. Alain Robbe-Grillet, *For a New Novel: Essays on Fiction*, trans. Richard Howard (New York: Grove Press, 1965), p. 168.

73. Ibid., pp. 160 and 161.

74. Alter, p. 64.

75. Mink, p. 145. Cf. also Culler's analysis of the "double logic" of narrative, by which both event and plot claim priority, thus creating "a certain self-destructive force in narrative." "Story and Discourse in the Analysis of Narrative," in *The Pursuit of Signs: Semiotics, Literature, Deconstruction* (Ithaca, N.Y.: Cornell University Press, 1981), pp. 169–87, esp. p. 187.

76. Hayden White, "The Value of Narrativity in the Representation of Reality," in *On Narrative*, ed. W. J. T. Mitchell (Chicago: University of Chicago Press, 1981), p. 10.

77. The phrase is Alter's; see "Mimesis and the Motive for Fiction," in *Images and Ideas in American Culture*, ed. Arthur Edelstein (Hanover, N.H.: University Press of New England, 1979), p. 113.

78. White, "The Historical Text as Literary Artifact," in *The Writing of History*, p. 49.

79. Culler, *Structuralist Poetics*, p. 209.

80. See Rachel Blau DuPlessis, *Writing beyond the Ending: Narrative Strategies of Twentieth-Century Women Writers* (Bloomington: Indiana University Press, 1985). DuPlessis also gives Woolf a central position in her valuable analysis of women's narrative strategies in the twentieth century.

81. Kieran Egan, "What Is a Plot?" *New Literary History* 9, no. 3 (Spring 1978): 462.

82. Donald Marshall, "Plot as Trap, Plot as Mediation," in *The Horizon of Literature*, ed. Paul Hernadi (Lincoln: University of Nebraska Press, 1982), pp. 71–96.

83. Kermode, *The Sense of an Ending*, p. 39.

84. Kermode, "Secrets and Narrative Sequence," in *On Narrative*, p. 83.

85. Margaret Laurence, *The Diviners* (1974; reprint, Toronto: Bantam Books, 1975), p. 60.

86. Roger Fowler, *Linguistics and the Novel* (1977; reprint, London: Methuen, 1979), p. 32.
87. Culler, *The Pursuit of Signs*, p. 33; see also *Structuralist Poetics*, pp. 230–37.
88. Lucien Goldmann, *Towards a Sociology of the Novel*, trans. Alan Sheridan (London: Tavistock, 1977), p. 134.
89. *Structuralist Poetics*, p. 231.
90. Fowler, pp. 36–37.
91. Ibid., p. 128.
92. See Woolf, "Mr. Bennett and Mrs. Brown," in *Collected Essays* (New York: Harcourt, Brace and World, 1967), 1:319–37.
93. Elizabeth Ermath, "Fictional Consensus and Female Casualties," in *The Representation of Women in Fiction*, pp. 1–18. For Ermath's assessment of the relationship between consensus and realism, see *Realism and Consensus in the English Novel* (Princeton, N.J.: Princeton University Press, 1983).
94. See Geertz, especially chaps. 1–3.
95. Jean-Paul Sartre, *Search for a Method*, trans. Hazel E. Barnes (New York: Vintage Books, 1968), p. 152.
96. This is Robert Anchor's suggestion for what will happen if contemporary realism makes effective use of the possibilities evident in postmodernist literature. "Realism and Ideology: The Question of Order," *History and Theory* 22, no. 2 (May 1983): 119.
97. Jean E. Kennard, "Convention Coverage or How to Read Your Own Life," *New Literary History* 13, no. 1 (Autumn 1981): 84, 71, and 71–72, respectively.
98. Adrienne Rich, "When We Dead Awaken: Writing as Re-Vision," in *On Lies, Secrets and Silence* (New York: Norton, 1979), p. 33.
99. Poovey, p. 178.

CHAPTER 3

1. Christa Wolf, *Cassandra: A Novel and Four Essays*, trans. Jan Van Heurck (London: Virago, 1984), p. 298. Subsequent references will be indicated within the text.
2. The phrase, again, is Mikhail M. Bakhtin's, *The Dialogic Imagination: Four Essays*, ed. Michael Holquist, trans. Caryl Emerson and Michael Holquist (Austin: University of Texas Press, 1981), p. 37.
3. See Ian Watt, *The Rise of the Novel: Studies in Defoe, Richardson and Fielding* (1957; reprint, Berkeley: University of California Press, 1965), esp. pp. 135 and 138.
4. Watt, p. 113.
5. Evidence for this can be found in the infrequency with which most current literary theory even mentions feminist criticism and the near total absence of women from a book like Frank Lentricchia's *After the New Criticism* (Chicago: University of Chicago Press, 1980), which

gives an otherwise notable assessment of critical movements in the preceding two decades. Recent indicators suggest that this pattern of marked neglect may be changing, though the evidence for such a possible shift is as yet insufficient.

6. Lynn Z. Bloom, "Promises Fulfilled: Positive Images of Women in Twentieth-Century Autobiography," in *Feminist Criticism: Essays on Theory, Poetry and Prose*, ed. Cheryl L. Brown and Karen Olson (Metuchen, N.J.: Scarecrow Press, 1978), p. 331.

7. Ibid., p. 325.

8. Ibid., p. 330.

9. Mary G. Mason, "The Other Voice: Autobiographies of Women Writers," in *Autobiography: Essays Theoretical and Critical*, ed. James Olney (Princeton, N.J.: Princeton University Press, 1980), pp. 207–35.

10. Suzanne Juhasz, "Towards a Theory of Form in Feminist Autobiography: Kate Millett's *Flying* and *Sita; Maxine Hong Kingston's *The Woman Warrior*," in *Women's Autobiography*, ed. Estelle C. Jelinek (Bloomington: Indiana University Press, 1980), pp. 221–37.

11. Estelle C. Jelinek, "Introduction: Women's Autobiography and the Male Tradition," in *Women's Autobiography*, pp. 1–20.

12. See Kim Chernin, *In My Mother's House: A Daughter's Story* (1983; reprint, New York: Harper and Row, 1984) and Maxine Hong Kingston, *The Woman Warrior: Memories of a Girlhood Among Ghosts* (New York: Vintage, 1977). See my analysis of Kingston, "*The Woman Warrior*: Claiming Narrative Power, Recreating Female Selfhood," in *The Faith of a (Woman) Writer*, ed. Alice Kessler-Harris and William McBrien (New York: Greenwood Press, 1985).

13. Hayden White, "The Value of Narrativity in the Representation of Reality," in *On Narrative*, ed. W. J. T. Mitchell (Chicago: University of Chicago Press, 1981), p. 19.

14. Louis Mink, "Narrative Form as Cognitive Instrument," in *The Writing of History: Literary Form and Historical Understanding*, ed. Robert H. Canary and Henry Kozicki (Madison: University of Wisconsin Press, 1978), p. 136.

15. Doris Lessing, *The Golden Notebook* (1962; reprint, New York: Bantam, 1973), p. 363.

16. See White, "The Historical Text as Literary Artifact," in *The Writing of History*, p. 49.

17. Lessing, p. 363.

18. See Kate Millett's conversation with Lessing, quoted in *Flying* (New York: Alfred A. Knopf, 1974), p. 357.

19. Margaret Homans, " 'Her Very Own Howl': The Ambiguities of Representation in Recent Women's Fiction," *Signs* 9, no. 2 (Winter 1983): 203.

20. Adrienne Rich, "Taking Women Students Seriously," in *On Lies, Secrets and Silence* (New York: Norton, 1979), p. 245.

21. Sandra M. Gilbert and Susan Gubar, *The Madwoman in the Attic: The*

Woman Writer and the Nineteenth-Century Imagination (New Haven: Yale University Press, 1979), p. 63; quoted in Judith Kegan Gardiner, "On Female Identity and Writing by Women," *Critical Inquiry* 8, no. 2 (Winter 1981): 347.

22. Gardiner, p. 348.

23. Ibid., p. 349.

24. Elizabeth Abel, "Narrative Structure(s) and Female Development: The Case of *Mrs. Dalloway*," in *The Voyage In: Fictions of Female Development*, ed. Elizabeth Abel, Marianne Hirsch, and Elizabeth Langland (Hanover, N.H.: University Press of New England, 1983), p. 164.

25. Abel, "(E)Merging Identities: The Dynamics of Female Friendship in Contemporary Fiction by Women," *Signs* 6, no. 3 (Spring 1981): 413–35. See also the subsequent interchange between Gardiner and Abel, pp. 436–44.

26. Annis Pratt, *Archetypal Patterns in Women's Fiction* (Bloomington: Indiana University Press, 1981), p. 6.

27. Ibid., e.g. pp. 34–35.

28. Ibid., see especially chap. 8.

29. Gillian Beer, "Beyond Determinism: George Eliot and Virginia Woolf," in *Women Writing and Writing about Women*, ed. Mary Jacobus (New York: Barnes and Noble, 1979), p. 91.

30. The importance of multiplicity for female character or selfhood is evident in a number of feminist analyses, e.g., Sandra M. Gilbert, "Costumes of the Mind: Transvestism as Metaphor in Modern Literature," *Critical Inquiry* 7, no. 2 (Winter 1980): 391–417, esp. p. 394; Hélène Cixous, "The Character of 'Character,'" trans. Keith Cohen, *New Literary History* 5, no. 2 (Winter 1974): 383–402; Jane Gallop, *The Daughter's Seduction: Feminism and Psychoanalysis* (Ithaca, N.Y.: Cornell University Press, 1982), esp. p. xii. Because of my commitment to conscious processes and to issues of representation, however, my own perspective differs markedly from the poststructuralist approaches predominating in critics like Cixous and Gallop, as well as from the general psychoanalytic view that women experience ego "boundary confusion" that often underpins these views of female selfhood. For the latter perspective see, for example, Nancy Chodorow, *The Reproduction of Mothering: Psychoanalysis and the Sociology of Gender* (Berkeley: University of California Press, 1978), p. 110 and passim.

31. Janet Varner Gunn, *Autobiography: Toward a Poetics of Experience* (Philadelphia: University of Pennsylvania Press, 1982), p. 8.

32. James Olney, "Autobiography and the Cultural Moment: A Thematic, Historical, and Bibliographical Introduction," in *Autobiography: Essays Theoretical and Critical*, p. 25.

33. The association of definable, recorded reality with author and of "action-being-made" with actor is Edward Said's characterization of the tension in Conrad between "two conflicting modes of existence." *Beginnings: Intention and Method* (Baltimore: Johns Hopkins University Press, 1975), p. 106.

34. Roland Barthes, *Writing Degree Zero*, trans. Annette Lavers and Colin Smith (1968; reprint, New York: Hill and Wang, 1981), p. 35.

35. Ulric Neisser, *Cognition and Reality: Principles and Implications of Cognitive Psychology* (San Francisco: W. H. Freeman, 1976), pp. 104–5; emphasis added.

36. Gardiner, p. 349.

37. For an overview of gender schema theory, see Sandra Lipsitz Bem, "Gender Schema Theory and Its Implications for Child Development: Raising Gender-aschematic Children in a Gender-schematic Society," *Signs* 8, no. 4 (Summer 1983): 598–616. For a somewhat different perspective, see Janet T. Spence's argument that "gender-related phenomena are multidimensional." "Changing Conceptions of Men and Women: A Psychologist's Perspective," in *A Feminist Perspective in the Academy: The Difference It Makes*, ed. Elizabeth Langland and Walter Gove (Chicago: University of Chicago Press, 1983), pp. 130–46, esp. p. 146.

38. Though I do not share Nancy Chodorow's psychoanalytic premises, my concern is very similar to hers when she suggests the problem of difference: "To speak of difference as a final irreducible concept and to focus on gender differences as central is to reify them and to deny the reality of these *processes* which create the meaning and significance of gender." "Gender, Relation, and Difference in Psychoanalytic Perspective," in *The Future of Difference*, ed. Hester Eisenstein and Alice Jardine (Boston: G. K. Hall with Barnard College Women's Center, 1980), p. 16.

39. Marcel Proust, *Swann's Way*, trans. C. K. Scott Moncrieff (New York: Vintage, 1970), p. 15.

40. Roy Schafer, "Narration in the Psychoanalytic Diaglogue," in *On Narrative*, p. 31.

41. Christa Wolf, *A Model Childhood*, trans. Ursula Molinaro and Hedwig Rappolt (New York: Farrar, Straus and Giroux, 1980), pp. 4 and 10.

42. See, for example, Gardiner's view that male and female memory differ because of the difference in the way "oedipal repression operates" for women as compared to men. "The (US)es of (I)dentity: A Response to Abel on '(E)Merging Identities,'" *Signs* 6, no. 3 (Spring 1981): 441.

43. Jean-Paul Sartre, *Search for a Method*, trans. Hazel E. Barnes (New York: Vintage Books, 1968), p. 91.

44. See, for example, Simone de Beauvoir, *The Second Sex*, trans. H. M. Parshley (1952; reprint, New York: Vintage, 1974), p. 741; and Sartre, pp. 167 and 181.

45. Carol Gilligan, "In a Different Voice: Women's Conceptions of Self and Morality," in *The Future of Difference*, p. 281. See also her more extended analysis of women's sense of self and its relationship to choice. *In a Different Voice* (Cambridge: Harvard University Press, 1982).

46. Cf. Neisser, p. 182; cf. also Sartre's argument that "subjectivity is neither everything nor nothing" (p. 33).

47. Kingston, p. 5.
48. Cf. Michelle Zimbalist Rosaldo's statement that "women . . . are defined almost exclusively in terms of their sexual functions" and must therefore "either deny their physical bodies or circumscribe their dangerous sexuality." "Woman, Culture and Society: A Theoretical Overview," in *Woman, Culture and Society,* ed. Michelle Zimbalist Rosaldo and Louise Lamphere (Stanford: Stanford University Press, 1974), p. 31.
49. Lessing, *A Proper Marriage* (1952; reprint, New York: New American Library, 1970); see especially her departing conversation with her daughter Caroline in which she tells her "I'm setting you free" (p. 340).
50. Kingston, p. 10.
51. Gilbert and Gubar, p. 34.
52. See, e.g., Lois Wladis Hoffman, "Early Childhood Experiences and Women's Achievement Motives," in *Women and Achievement: Social and Motivational Analyses,* ed. Martha T. Shuch Mednick, Sandra Schwartz Tangri, and Lois Wladis Hoffman (New York: John Wiley and Sons, 1975), p. 134.
53. Jerome S. Bruner, *On Knowing: Essays for the Left Hand* (Cambridge, Mass.: Belknap Press, 1980), p. 44.
54. Robin R. Vallacher, "An Introduction to Self Theory," in *The Self in Social Psychology,* ed. Daniel M. Wegner and Robin R. Vallacher (New York: Oxford University Press, 1980), p. 23.
55. Grace Baruch, Rosalind Barnett, and Caryl Rivers, *Lifeprints: New Patterns of Love and Work for Today's Women* (New York: McGraw-Hill, 1983), p. 140, cf. p. 197.
56. Paul John Eakin, "Malcolm X and the Limits of Autobiography," in *Autobiography: Essays Theoretical and Critical,* p. 193.
57. Jean Baker Miller, *Toward a New Psychology of Women* (1976; reprint, Boston: Beacon Press, 1977), p. 119.

CHAPTER 4

1. Patricia Meyer Spacks, *The Female Imagination* (New York: Avon, 1976), p. 166.
2. Ellen Morgan, "Humanbecoming: Form and Focus in the Neo-Feminist Novel," in *Images of Women in Fiction: Feminist Perspectives,* ed. Susan Koppelman Cornillon (Bowling Green, Ohio: Bowling Green University Popular Press, 1972), p. 184.
3. For their treatment of *The Voyage Out,* see Elizabeth Abel, Marianne Hirsch, and Elizabeth Langland, "Introduction," in *The Voyage In: Fictions of Female Development,* ed. Abel, Hirsch, and Langland (Hanover, N.H.: University Press of New England, 1983), pp. 3–4.
4. Jerome Buckley, *Season of Youth: The Bildungsroman from Dickens to Golding* (Cambridge: Harvard University Press, 1974), p. 17.
5. Georg Lukacs, "Wilhelm Meister's Years of Apprenticeship," in *The*

Theory of the Novel, trans. Anna Bostock (Cambridge: M.I.T. Press, 1977), p. 132.

6. Abel, Hirsch, and Langland, p. 14.

7. Virginia Woolf, *The Voyage Out* (1915; reprint, New York: Harcourt, Brace and World, 1948), p. 302.

8. Ibid., p. 315.

9. Carol Gilligan, *In a Different Voice* (Cambridge: Harvard University Press, 1982), p. 63.

10. Robert Kegan, *The Evolving Self: Problem and Process in Human Development* (Cambridge: Harvard University Press, 1982), esp. pp. 108–9.

11. See Sandra M. Gilbert and Susan Gubar, *The Madwoman in the Attic: The Woman Writer and the Nineteenth-Century Imagination* (New Haven: Yale University Press, 1979), pp. 259–61.

12. Abel, Hirsch, and Langland, p. 15.

13. Charlotte Brontë, *Jane Eyre* (New York: Signet, 1960), p. 256. Subsequent references will be indicated within the text.

14. *Villette* seems to enact the human tension in the opposite direction; though Lucy Snowe achieves a relational context and an autonomous identity in the novel—again in the first-person voice—she ends the novel with a powerful sense of isolation.

15. See J. R. Struthers, "Reality and Ordering: The Growth of a Young Artist in *Lives of Girls and Women*," *Essays on Canadian Writing* 3 (Fall 1975): 32–46.

16. Alice Munro, *Lives of Girls and Women* (1971; reprint, New York: Signet, 1974), p. 166. Subsequent references will be indicated within the text.

17. Munro, interview in Graeme Gibson, *Eleven Canadian Novelists* (Toronto: Anansi, 1973), p. 251.

18. Roland Barthes, *Writing Degree Zero*, trans. Annette Lavers and Colin Smith (1968; reprint, New York: Hill and Wang, 1981), p. 36.

19. An extended use of first-person plural is difficult to sustain. For a recent and generally very effective example—four girls growing up together on their grandmother's farm—see Joan Chase, *During the Reign of the Queen of Persia* (New York: Harper and Row, 1983).

20. Struthers uses this address as an argument for "the direct influence of Joyce on Munro" (p. 33); I see no reason that should suggest influence since this sort of geographical self-placement is frequent among children.

21. Munro in Gibson, p. 258.

22. Cf. Helen Hoy's statement that "these visions, internally coherent and explicitly identified as independent worlds, in most cases vie with each other for the exclusive right to define experience. In the end none has ultimate authority; each is clearly presented as one reality in the context of others." " 'Dull, Simple, Amazing and Unfathomable': Paradox and Double Vision in Alice Munro's Fiction," *Studies in Canadian Literature* 5 (Spring 1980): 110.

23. See, e.g., Signe Hammer, *Daughters and Mothers: Mothers and Daughters* (New York: Signet, 1976), p. 14.

24. Hallvard Dahlie, "The Fiction of Alice Munro," *Ploughshares* 4, no. 3 (1978): 69.

25. See, e.g., Elizabeth Higginbotham, "Two Representative Issues in Contemporary Sociological Work on Black Women," in *But Some of Us Are Brave: Black Women's Studies,* ed. Gloria T. Hull, Patricia Bell Scott, and Barbara Smith (Old Westbury, N.Y.: Feminist Press, 1982), pp. 93–98; Debra R. Kaufman and Barbara L. Richardson, *Achievement and Women: Challenging the Assumptions* (New York: Free Press, 1982), p. 39; Lena Wright Myers, "Black Women and Self-esteem," in *Another Voice,* ed. Marcia Millman and Rosabeth Kanter (New York: Anchor, 1975), pp. 240–50; and Peter J. Weston and Martha T. Shuch Mednick, "Race, Social Class, and the Motive to Avoid Success in Women," in *Women and Achievement: Social and Motivational Analyses,* ed. Martha T. Shuch Mednick, Sandra Schwartz Tangri, and Lois Wladis Hoffman (New York: John Wiley and Sons, 1975), pp. 231–38.

26. See Higginbotham.

27. Toni Morrison quoted in Bettye J. Parker, "Complexity: Toni Morrison's Women: An Interview Essay," in *Sturdy Black Bridges: Visions of Black Women in Literature,* ed. Roseann P. Bell, Bettye J. Parker, and Beverly Guy-Sheftall (Garden City, N.Y.: Anchor Press, 1979), p. 256.

28. Hortense Spillers, "The Politics of Intimacy: A Discussion," in *Sturdy Black Bridges,* p. 105.

29. Gilbert and Gubar, p. 36.

30. Morrison, *Sula* (1973; reprint, New York: Bantam, 1975), p. 80.

31. Ibid.

32. Barbara Smith, "Toward a Black Feminist Criticism," in *But Some of Us Are Brave,* p. 167.

33. Morrison, *The Bluest Eye* (1970; reprint, New York: Pocket Books, 1972), p. 9. Subsequent references will be indicated within the text.

34. *Sula,* p. 103.

35. Morrison, interview in Maggie Lewis, "Toni Morrison: Writing from the Inside Out," *Christian Science Monitor,* April 23, 1981.

36. Ibid.

37. Mary Burgher, "Images of Self and Race in the Autobiographies of Black Women," in *Sturdy Black Bridges,* p. 118.

38. Mary Helen Washington, "Teaching *Black-Eyed Susans:* An Approach to the Study of Black Women Writers," in *But Some of Us Are Brave,* p. 212.

CHAPTER 5

1. Louis O. Mink, "Everyman His or Her Own Annalist," in *On Narrative,* ed. W. J. T. Mitchell (Chicago: University of Chicago Press, 1981), p. 238.

2. Frank Kermode's comment on Jean-Paul Sartre, in *The Sense of an*

Ending: Studies in the Theory of Fiction (New York: Oxford University Press, 1967), p. 150.

3. Frank Lentricchia, *After the New Criticism* (Chicago: University of Chicago Press, 1980), p. 297 (emphasis added).

4. A slightly different version of this analysis of *Violet Clay* originally appeared as "Narrating the Self: The Autonomous Heroine in Gail Godwin's *Violet Clay*," *Contemporary Literature* 24, no. 1 (Spring 1983): 66–85.

5. Gail Godwin, *Violet Clay* (1978; reprint, New York: Warner Books, 1979), p. 11. Subsequent references will be indicated within the text.

6. Katha Pollit, "Her Own Woman," *New York Times Book Review*, May 21, 1978, p. 11.

7. Ibid.

8. Susan Lorsch, "Gail Godwin's *The Odd Woman:* Literature and the Retreat from Life," *Critique: Studies in Modern Fiction* 20, no. 2 (1978): 21.

9. Godwin, *The Odd Woman* (1974; reprint, New York: Warner Books, 1980), p. 49.

10. Ian Watt, *The Rise of the Novel: Studies in Defoe, Richardson and Fielding* (1957; reprint, Berkeley: University of California Press, 1965), pp. 21–22.

11. Kermode, p. 39.

12. *The Odd Woman*, p. 151 and p. 50.

13. Godwin, "Towards a Fully Human Heroine: Some Worknotes," *Harvard Advocate*, Winter 1973, pp. 26–28.

14. Ibid., p. 28.

15. Ibid.

16. A version of this analysis was presented at the Twentieth Century Literature Conference, University of Louisville, February 1983.

17. Margaret Atwood, *Survival: A Thematic Guide to Canadian Literature* (Toronto: Anansi, 1972), p. 205.

18. George Woodcock, *The World of Canadian Writing* (Seattle: University of Washington Press, 1980), p. 57.

19. Ibid., p. 58.

20. Margaret Laurence, *The Stone Angel* (1964; reprint, New York: Bantam, 1981), p. 261. Subsequent references will be indicated within the text.

21. Laurence, "Living Dangerously . . . by Mail," in *Heart of a Stranger* (1976; reprint, Toronto: McClelland and Stewart, 1981), p. 203. In this essay Laurence also traces the process by which she arrived at the present title (pp. 203–4).

22. Roy Schafer, "Narration in the Psychoanalytic Dialogue," in *On Narrative*, p. 31.

23. Simone de Beauvoir, *The Second Sex*, trans. H. M. Parshley (1952; reprint, New York: Vintage, 1974), p. 645.

24. Harriet Blodgett, "The Real Lives of Margaret Laurence's Women," *Critique: Studies in Modern Fiction* 23, no. 1 (1981): 8.

25. Laurence identifies as the novel's dominant theme the "theme of survival . . . the preservation of some human dignity and in the end of some human warmth and ability to reach out and touch others." "A Place to Stand On," in *Heart of a Stranger*, p. 6. Cf. also her statement that in *The Stone Angel*, "the theme had changed to that of survival, the attempt of the personality to survive with some dignity, toting the load of excessive mental baggage that everyone carries, until the moment of death." "Ten Years' Sentences," in *Margaret Laurence: The Writer and the Critics*, ed. William New (Toronto: McGraw-Hill Ryerson, 1977), p. 17.

26. In saying this, I am in some disagreement with William H. New's statement that Hagar is a tragic and isolated figure; see "Introduction to *The Stone Angel*," in *Margaret Laurence: The Writer and the Critics*, p. 138. I am in general agreement with Patricia Morley's view that the "closing chapters chronicle Hagar's gradual reconciliation with her world and herself." See *Margaret Laurence* (Boston: Twayne, 1981), p. 80.

27. Laurence, "Time and the Narrative Voice," in *Margaret Laurence: The Writer and the Critics*, p. 157.

28. See Victor Turner's definition of narrative as "knowledge . . . emerging from action, that is, experiential knowledge." "Social Dramas and Stories about Them," in *On Narrative*, p. 63.

29. Beauvoir, p. xxxiii.

CHAPTER 6

1. The difference between femininity and experiential femaleness has been central to feminist literary criticism. See, for example, Susan Koppelman Cornillon, "The Fiction of Fiction," in *Images of Women in Fiction: Feminist Perspectives*, ed. Cornillon (Bowling Green, Ohio: Bowling Green University Popular Press, 1972), pp. 113–30.

2. Simone de Beauvoir, *The Second Sex*, trans. H. M. Parshley (1952; reprint, New York: Vintage, 1974), p. 758.

3. Nadine Gordimer, *Burger's Daughter* (1979; reprint, New York: Penguin Books, 1980), p. 4.

4. Christa Wolf, *The Quest for Christa T.*, trans. Christopher Middleton (New York: Farrar, Straus and Giroux, 1979), e.g., pp. 169, 170, 174. See also *A Model Childhood*, trans. Ursula Molinaro and Hedwig Rappolt (New York: Farrar, Straus and Giroux, 1980).

5. Ellen Cronan Rose, "Feminine Endings—and Beginnings: Margaret Drabble's *The Waterfall*," *Contemporary Literature* 21, no. 1 (Winter 1980): 89–90.

6. See Joan Mannheimer's argument that Jane, "through her experience of various doubles, discovers the boundaries of the self and achieves a meaningful independence of her varied reflections." "Margaret Drabble and the Journey to the Self," *Studies in the Literary Imagination* 11, no.

2 (1978): 135. Mannheimer argues not only that Lucy acts as a double, but also that the literary tradition doubles her (p. 137) and that the novel's narrative structure "implies that the self as subject arises from the felt necessity to distinguish self from the other" (p. 139). In my argument Jane is not so much distinguishing self from other as continually reassessing her experience in an open-ended definition of self.

7. Virginia K. Beards makes a different kind of argument, also centered in an exclusive focus on Jane's sexuality: "Drabble writes of a female destroyed by her physiology and culture and rejects the cliché that eros is the way to happiness." "Margaret Drabble: Novels of a Cautious Feminist," *Critique* 15, no. 1 (1973): 43.

8. Margaret Drabble quoted in Nancy S. Hardin, "An Interview with Margaret Drabble," *Contemporary Literature* 14, no. 3 (Summer 1973): 292.

9. Ibid., p. 293.

10. Ibid., pp. 283–84.

11. Elizabeth Fox-Genovese, "The Ambiguities of Female Identity: A Reading of the Novels of Margaret Drabble," *Partisan Review* 46 (1979): 239.

12. See Bernard Bergonzi's entry on Drabble in *Contemporary Novelists*, ed. James Vinson (New York: St. Martin's Press, 1976), pp. 373–74.

13. Drabble quoted in Hardin, p. 292.

14. Drabble, *The Waterfall* (1969; reprint, New York: Popular Library, 1977), p. 89. Subsequent references will be indicated within the text.

15. See, for example, Rose's argument that "Jane's task as woman and as artist is the same: to acknowledge the existence within her of the Other, and not simply to reconcile but to encompass that division" (p. 92).

16. Michael F. Harper's excellent analysis of Drabble as combining postmodernist recognitions with a realist commitment is, in general, similar to my view of Drabble, but his analysis of *The Waterfall* claims that "Jane is redeemed by her affair with James." "Margaret Drabble and the Resurrection of the English Novel," *Contemporary Literature* 23, no. 2 (1982): 162.

17. Carol Gilligan, *In a Different Voice* (Cambridge: Harvard University Press, 1982), pp. 150 and 131. For a contrasting view that Jane follows "her instinct for survival through love, against the moral code, into deceit and selfishness," see Valerie Grosvenor Myer, *Margaret Drabble: Puritanism and Permissiveness* (London: Vision Press, 1974), p. 25.

18. See Caryn Fuoroli's argument that this opening ironic interplay is evidence of Drabble's initial narrative control and the novel's "great, if unfulfilled potential." "Sophistry or Simple Truth? Narrative Technique in Margaret Drabble's *The Waterfall*," *Journal of Narrative Technique* 11, no. 2 (Spring 1981): 113.

19. See Virginia Woolf, *The Voyage Out* (1915; reprint, New York: Harcourt, Brace and World, 1948), chap. 25.

20. Nancy Chodorow, "Family Structure and Feminine Personality," in *Woman, Culture and Society*, ed. Michelle Zimbalist Rosaldo and

Louise Lamphere (Stanford: Stanford University Press, 1974), pp. 58 and 59.

21. See Jane Campbell on the use of literary analogies to structure the focus toward the narrative process rather than the experience. "Margaret Drabble and the Search for Analogy," in *The Practical Vision: Essays in Honor of Flora Roy*, ed. Jane Campbell and James Doyle (Waterloo, Ont.: Wilfrid Laurier University Press, 1977). See, too, Elaine Showalter's statement that because of her "connection to female tradition," as well as her treatment of female biosexual experiences, "Drabble is the most ardent traditionalist" among contemporary English women novelists. *A Literature of Their Own: British Women Novelists from Brontë to Lessing* (Princeton, N.J.: Princeton University Press, 1977), p. 304.

22. Rose sees Drabble's refusal of closure as a "feminine" ending in resistance to literary tradition (p. 95); by contrast, I think the refusal of closure is basically a modernist phenomenon, whose possibilities have always been present in the novel and whose expression has a special usefulness to women writers who wish to characterize women's lives in new ways.

23. I disagree with Beards's statement that *"The Waterfall* concludes with the protagonist's intense sense of isolation" (p. 43).

24. For a compatible view of the novel's dialectic between "an affirmative culture" and "the negating act of criticism," see Rachel Blau DuPlessis's brief but insightful comments on *The Golden Notebook* in *Writing beyond the Ending: Narrative Strategies of Twentieth-Century Women Writers* (Bloomington: Indiana University Press, 1985), pp. 101–3, esp. p. 101.

25. Agate Nesaule Krouse, "Toward a Definition of Literary Feminism," in *Feminist Criticism: Essays on Theory, Poetry and Prose*, ed. Cheryl L. Brown and Karen Olson (Metuchen, N.J.: Scarecrow Press, 1978), p. 279.

26. Ellen Morgan, "Alienation of the Woman Writer in *The Golden Notebook,"* in *Doris Lessing: Critical Studies*, ed. Annis Pratt and L. S. Dembo (Madison: University of Wisconsin Press, 1974), p. 55.

27. Showalter, p. 312.

28. Doris Lessing, "Doris Lessing at Stony Brook: An Interview by Jonah Raskin," in *A Small Personal Voice*, ed. Paul Schlueter (New York: Alfred A. Knopf, 1974), p. 71.

29. Lessing, *The Golden Notebook* (1962; reprint, New York: Bantam Books, 1973), p. 53. Subsequent references will be indicated within the text.

30. Alice Bradley Markow, "The Pathology of Feminine Failure in the Fiction of Doris Lessing," *Critique* 16, no. 1 (1974): 88.

31. Morgan, p. 63.

32. Virginia Woolf, *A Room of One's Own* (1929; reprint, New York: Harcourt, Brace and World, 1957), p. 88.

33. Elizabeth Abel, "(E)Merging Identities: The Dynamics of Female

Friendship in Contemporary Fiction by Women," *Signs* 6, no. 3 (Spring 1981): 430.

34. Woolf, "Professions for Women," in *Collected Essays*, (New York: Harcourt, Brace and World, 1967), 2:288.
35. See Kate Millett's conversation with Lessing quoted in *Flying* (New York: Alfred A. Knopf, 1974), p. 357.
36. Lessing, Introduction to *The Golden Notebook*, p. xi.
37. Ibid., p. xiv.
38. J. M. Lotman, "Point of View in a Text," trans. L. M. O'Toole, *New Literary History* 6, no. 2 (1975): 339.
39. Lessing in Florence Howe, "A Talk with Doris Lessing," in *A Small Personal Voice*, p. 81.
40. John L. Carey, "Art and Reality in *The Golden Notebook*," in *Doris Lessing: Critical Studies*, p. 24.
41. Betsy Draine, "Nostalgia and Irony: The Postmodern Order of *The Golden Notebook*," *Modern Fiction Studies* 26, no. 1 (Spring 1980): 32. See also, e.g., Herbert Marder, "The Paradox of Form in *The Golden Notebook*," *Modern Fiction Studies* 26, no. 1 (Spring 1980): 49–54; and Roberta Rubenstein, *The Novelistic Vision of Doris Lessing: Breaking the Forms of Consciousness* (Urbana: University of Illinois Press, 1979).
42. "A Talk with Doris Lessing," p. 82.
43. Morgan, pp. 62–63.
44. Cf. Judith Stitzel's statement that "I read Lessing not as a stimulus to think this or that but as a stimulus to thinking about thinking." "Reading Doris Lessing," *College English* 40, no. 5 (January 1979): 502.
45. Lessing, "The Small Personal Voice," in *A Small Personal Voice*, p. 6.
46. Ibid., p. 4.
47. Ibid., p. 12.

CHAPTER 7

1. Annette Kolodny, "Dancing through the Minefield: Some Observations on the Theory, Practice and Politics of a Feminist Literary Criticism," *Feminist Studies* 6, no. 1 (Spring 1980): 17.
2. Jonathan Culler, "Prolegomena to a Theory of Reading," in *The Reader in the Text*, ed. Susan R. Suleiman and Inge Crosman (Princeton, N.J.: Princeton University Press, 1980), p. 49.
3. Jane P. Tompkins, "The Reader in History," in *Reader Response Criticism: From Formalism to Post-Structuralism*, ed. Tompkins (Baltimore: Johns Hopkins University Press, 1980), pp. 201–32.
4. Ibid., p. 22. Many feminist critics have pointed to the value of reader-response criticism for a feminist perspective—e.g., Sandra M. Gilbert's allusion to the importance for feminist criticism of the "Age of the Reader." See "Life Studies, or, Speech After Long Silence: Feminist Critics Today," *College English* 40, no. 8 (April 1979): 862. Reader-response criticism, on the other hand, remains pervasively blind to

feminist criticism. Jean E. Kennard makes a similar point in "Convention Coverage or How to Read Your Own Life," *New Literary History* 13, no. 1 (Autumn 1981): 73 and 87.

5. Historically, this has been true especially of middle-class women, though the expansion of literacy and the accompanying expansion of the "middle class" have made this an important phenomenon across class boundaries in the twentieth century.

6. Margaret Drabble quoted in Judith Kegan Gardiner, "On Female Identity and Writing by Women," *Critical Inquiry* 8, no. 2 (Winter 1981): 355.

7. Nancy Burr Evans, "The Value and Peril for Women of Reading Women Writers," in *Images of Women in Fiction: Feminist Perspectives*, ed. Susan Koppelman Cornillon (Bowling Green, Ohio: Bowling Green University Popular Press, 1972), p. 310.

8. Doris Lessing, *A Small Personal Voice*, ed. Paul Schlueter (New York: Alfred A. Knopf, 1974), pp. 20–21.

9. Erica Jong, "Blood and Guts: The Tricky Problem of Being a Woman Writer in the Late Twentieth Century," in *The Writer on Her Work*, ed. Janet Sternburg (New York: W. W. Norton and Co., 1980), p. 178.

10. Similarly, Colette Dowling says that her need to write her nonfiction explanation of her own experience derived from a desire not "to be alone anymore. . . . I think then, as now, I was writing specifically to create a sense of communion with other women." *The Cinderella Complex: Women's Hidden Fear of Independence* (New York: Pocket Books, 1981), p. 170.

11. Susan Sniader Lanser, *The Narrative Act: Point of View in Prose Fiction* (Princeton, N.J.: Princeton University Press, 1981), p. 292. On formal realism, cf. George Levine, *The Realistic Imagination: English Fiction from Frankenstein to Lady Chatterley* (Chicago: University of Chicago Press, 1981): "From Defoe on, realistic narratives have depended on circumstantial particularity to establish verisimilitude" (p. 151); Ian Watt, *The Rise of the Novel: Studies in Defoe, Richardson and Fielding* (1957; reprint, Berkeley: University of California Press, 1965); and Jonathan Culler's concept of "descriptive residue" in *Structuralist Poetics: Structuralism, Linguistics and the Study of Literature* (Ithaca, N.Y.: Cornell University Press, 1976), p. 193.

12. Lanser, p. 292.

13. Robert Alter, "Mimesis and the Motive for Fiction," in *Images and Ideas in American Culture*, ed. Arthur Edelstein (Hanover, N.H.: University Press of New England, 1979), p. 109.

14. Lessing, p. 21.

15. Edward Said, *Beginnings: Intention and Method* (Baltimore: Johns Hopkins University Press, 1975), p. 88.

16. Drabble quoted in Nancy S. Hardin, "An Interview with Margaret Drabble," *Contemporary Literature* 14, no. 3 (Summer 1973): 279.

17. Christa Wolf, *A Model Childhood*, trans. Ursula Molinaro and Hedwig Rappolt (New York: Farrar, Straus and Giroux, 1980), pp. 368–69.

18. See Rachel M. Brownstein, *Becoming a Heroine: Reading about Women in Novels* (New York: Viking Press, 1982), although she also considers the ways in which the traditional heroine's novel instructs against the temptation to become a heroine; see especially pp. 295–96.
19. Said, p. 141.
20. Adrienne Rich, *Of Woman Born: Motherhood as Experience and Institution* (1976; reprint, New York; Bantam, 1977), p. 21.
21. See, for example, Debra R. Kaufman and Barbara L. Richardson, *Achievement and Women: Challenging the Assumptions* (New York: Free Press, 1982), especially chap. 1; and *Women and Achievement: Social and Motivational Analyses*, ed. Martha T. Shuch Mednick, Sandra Schwartz Tangri, and Lois Wladis Hoffman (New York: John Wiley and Sons, 1975).
22. Kaufman and Richardson, p. 31.
23. Fredric Jameson, *The Prison-House of Language: A Critical Account of Structuralism and Russian Formalism* (Princeton, N.J.: Princeton University Press, 1974), p. 14.
24. See E. H. Gombrich, *Art and Illusion: A Study in the Psychology of Pictorial Representation* (Princeton, N.J.: Princeton University Press, 1969), especially pp. 74–90.
25. Ulric Neisser, *Cognition and Reality: Principles and Implications of Cognitive Psychology* (San Francisco: W. H. Freeman, 1976), p. 165.
26. Robert Alter, *Partial Magic: The Novel as a Self-Conscious Genre* (1975; reprint, Berkeley: University of California Press, 1978), p. 234.
27. For a more complete exploration of the place of cognition in literary study, see the work of Henry D. Herring in two key articles: "Constructivist Interpretation: An Alternative to Deconstruction," *Bucknell Review* 29, no. 2 (1985): 32–46, and "Literature, Concepts, and Knowledge," *New Literary History*, forthcoming.
28. Jameson, *The Political Unconscious: Narrative as a Socially Symbolic Act* (Ithaca, N.Y.: Cornell University Press, 1981), p. 152.
29. Matina Horner, "Toward an Understanding of Achievement-Related Conflicts in Women," in *Women and Achievement*, pp. 206–20.
30. Kaufman and Richardson, p. 39.
31. Kay Deaux, "Sex: A Perspective on the Attribution Process," in *New Directions in Attribution Research*, vol. 1, ed. John H. Harvey, William John Ickes, and Robert F. Kidd (Hillsdale, N.J.: Lawrence Erlbaum Assoc., 1976), pp. 340–41; also Irene Hanson Frieze, "Women's Expectations for and Causal Attribution of Success and Failure," in *Women and Achievement*, pp. 158–71. I am indebted to Karla McPherson for pointing out Deaux's work and for informative conversations about the attribution process and about social psychology in general.
32. Deaux, p. 347.
33. Wolfgang Iser, *The Act of Reading: A Theory of Aesthetic Response* (1978; reprint, Baltimore: Johns Hopkins University Press, 1980), p. 132. Cf. Barbara Herrnstein Smith's statement that poetry can "trigger

memory," prompting us to recall experiences previously "selected out" by memory. *On the Margins of Discourse: The Relation of Literature to Language* (Chicago: University of Chicago Press, 1978), pp. 144–45.

34. Iser's view of reader and text as interactional is very similar to mine, though he sometimes sees the text as offering fixed schemata that cannot be affected by the reader's experience even though the reader's experience is altered by the text; e.g., "the reader's subjective contribution is controlled by the given framework. It is as if the schema were a hollow form into which the reader is invited to pour his [or her] own store of knowledge" (p. 143). This view seems more compatible with the unidirectional relationship between text and reader, schema and correction in a movement toward "accuracy," as is dominant in E. D. Hirsch's *The Aims of Interpretation* (1976; reprint, Chicago: University of Chicago Press, 1978), especially pp. 32–35.

35. J. Paul Hunter makes this point in "The Loneliness of the Long-Distance Reader," *Genre* 10 (Winter 1977): 483.

36. Iser, p. 186. Cf. also Linda Hutcheon's view that metafiction can "lure the reader into participating in the creation of a novelistic universe" and perhaps even into "direct political action." *Narcissistic Narrative: The Metafictional Paradox* (1980; reprint, New York: Methuen, 1984), p. 155.

37. Iser, p. 211.

38. For Barthes's distinction between "readerly" and "writerly," see *S/Z*, trans. Richard Miller (New York: Hill and Wang, 1974), pp. 4–5. See also *The Pleasure of the Text* (New York: Hill and Wang, 1974) for his extended celebration of the erotics of reading and reading as a suspension of signification. Cf. Iser's more sober preference for similar texts, such as *The Sound and the Fury* with its frequent "blanks" and "empty spaces" (p. 200).

39. Because of the complexity of reader involvement, first-person fiction probably has a greater impact on readers' lives than do most autobiographies—in addition to the capacity for more complex interaction with cultural asssumptions that I noted in chap. 3—despite the greater frequency of evidently strong women in autobiography, which Lynn Bloom points out. See "Promises Fulfilled: Positive Images of Women in Twentieth-Century Autobiography," in *Feminist Criticism: Essays on Theory, Poetry and Prose*, ed. Cheryl L. Brown and Karen Olson (Metuchen, N.J.: Scarecrow Press, 1978), pp. 330–31.

40. Gilbert, p. 853.

41. Marcel Proust, *The Past Recaptured*, quoted in Janet Varner Gunn, *Autobiography: Toward a Poetics of Experience* (Philadelphia: University of Pennsylvania Press, 1982), p. 90.

42. Inge K. Broverman et al., "Sex-Role Stereotypes: A Current Appraisal," in *Women and Achievement*, p. 36.

Bibliography

Abel, Elizabeth. "Editor's Introduction: Writing and Sexual Difference." *Critical Inquiry* 8, no. 2 (Winter 1981): 173–78.

———. "(E)Merging Identities: The Dynamics of Female Friendship in Contemporary Fiction by Women." *Signs* 6, no. 3 (Spring 1981): 413–35.

———. "Narrative Structure(s) and Female Development: The Case of *Mrs. Dalloway.*" In *The Voyage In: Fictions of Female Development*, edited by Elizabeth Abel, Marianne Hirsch, and Elizabeth Langland. Hanover, N. H.: University Press of New England, 1983.

Abel, Elizabeth, Marianne Hirsch, and Elizabeth Langland. "Introduction." In *The Voyage In: Fictions of Female Development*, edited by Abel, Hirsch, and Langland. Hanover, N. H.: University Press of New England, 1983.

Alter, Robert. "Mimesis and the Motive for Fiction." In *Images and Ideas in American Culture*, edited by Arthur Edelstein. Hanover, N.H.: University Press of New England, 1979.

———. *Partial Magic: The Novel as a Self-Conscious Genre.* 1975. Reprint. Berkeley: University of California Press, 1978.

Anchor, Robert. "Realism and Ideology: The Question of Order." *History and Theory* 22, no. 2 (May 1983): 107–19.

Atwood, Margaret. *Survival: A Thematic Guide to Canadian Literature.* Toronto: Anansi, 1972.

Bakhtin, Mikhail M. *The Dialogic Imagination: Four Essays.* Edited by Michael Holquist. Translated by Caryl Emerson and Michael Holquist. Austin: University of Texas Press, 1981.

Barthes, Roland. "An Introduction to the Structural Analysis of Narrative." Translated by Lionel Diusit. *New Literary History* 6, no. 2 (1975): 237–72.

———. *The Pleasure of the Text.* New York: Hill and Wang, 1974.

———. *S/Z.* Translated by Richard Miller. New York: Hill and Wang, 1974.

———. *Writing Degree Zero.* Translated by Annette Lavers and Colin Smith. 1968. Reprint. New York: Hill and Wang, 1981.

Baruch, Grace, Rosalind Barnett, and Caryl Rivers. *Lifeprints: New Patterns of Love and Work for Today's Women.* New York: McGraw-Hill, 1983.

Beards, Virginia K. "Margaret Drabble: Novels of a Cautious Feminist." *Critique: Studies in Modern Fiction* 15, no. 1 (1973): 35–47.

Beauvoir, Simone de. *The Second Sex.* Translated by H. M. Parshley. 1952. Reprint. New York: Vintage, 1974.

Beer, Gillian. "Beyond Determinism: George Eliot and Virginia Woolf." In *Women Writing and Writing about Women,* edited by Mary Jacobus. New York: Harper and Row, 1979.

Bem, Sandra Lipsitz. "Gender Schema Theory and Its Implications for Child Development: Raising Gender-aschematic Children in a Gender-schematic Society." *Signs* 8, no. 4 (Summer 1983): 598–616.

Benjamin, Walter. "The Storyteller." In *Illuminations.* Translated by Harry Zohn. New York: Schocken, 1969.

Bergonzi, Bernard. "Margaret Drabble." In *Contemporary Novelists,* edited by James Vinson. New York: St. Martin's Press, 1976.

Blodgett, Harriet. "The Real Lives of Margaret Laurence's Women." *Critique: Studies in Modern Fiction* 23, no. 1 (1981): 5–17.

Bloom, Lynn Z. "Promises Fulfilled: Positive Images of Women in Twentieth-Century Autobiography." In *Feminist Criticism: Essays on Theory, Poetry and Prose,* edited by Cheryl L. Brown and Karen Olson. Metuchen, N.J.: Scarecrow Press, 1978.

Brontë, Charlotte. *Jane Eyre.* New York: Signet, 1960.

Brooks, Peter. *Reading for the Plot: Design and Intention in Narrative.* Oxford: Oxford University Press, 1984.

Broverman, Inge K., et al. "Sex-Role Stereotypes: A Current Appraisal." In *Women and Achievement: Social and Motivational Analyses,* edited by Martha T. Shuch Mednick, Sandra Schwartz Tangri, and Lois Wladis Hoffman. New York: John Wiley and Sons, 1975.

Brownstein, Rachel M. *Becoming a Heroine: Reading about Women in Novels.* New York: Viking Press, 1982.

Bruner, Jerome S. *On Knowing: Essays for the Left Hand.* Cambridge, Mass.: Belknap Press, 1980.

Buckley, Jerome. *Season of Youth: The* Bildungsroman *from Dickens to Golding.* Cambridge: Harvard University Press, 1974.

Burgher, Mary. "Images of Self and Race in the Autobiographies of Black Women." In *Sturdy Black Bridges: Visions of Black Women in Literature,* edited by Roseann P. Bell, Bettye J. Parker, and Beverly Guy-Sheftall. Garden City, N.Y.: Anchor Press, 1979.

Cameron, Deborah. *Feminism and Linguistic Theory.* London: Macmillan, 1985.

Campbell, Jane. "Margaret Drabble and the Search for Analogy." In *The Practical Vision: Essays in Honor of Flora Roy,* edited by Jane Campbell and James Doyle. Waterloo, Ont.: Wilfrid Laurier University Press, 1977.

Carey, John L. "Art and Reality in *The Golden Notebook.*" In *Doris Lessing: Critical Studies,* edited by Annis Pratt and L. S. Dembo. Madison: University of Wisconsin Press, 1974.

Chase, Joan. *During the Reign of the Queen of Persia*. New York: Harper and Row, 1983.

Chernin, Kim. *In My Mother's House: A Daughter's Story*. 1983. Reprint. New York: Harper and Row, 1984.

Chodorow, Nancy. "Family Structure and Feminine Personality." In *Woman, Culture and Society*, edited by Michelle Zimbalist Rosaldo and Louise Lamphere. Stanford: Stanford University Press, 1974.

———. "Gender, Relation, and Difference in Psychoanalytic Perspective." In *The Future of Difference*, edited by Hester Eisenstein and Alice Jardine. Boston: G. K. Hall with Barnard College Women's Center, 1980.

———. *The Reproduction of Mothering: Psychoanalysis and the Sociology of Gender*. Berkeley: University of California Press, 1978.

Cixous, Hélène. "The Character of 'Character.'" Translated by Keith Cohen. *New Literary History* 5, no. 2 (Winter 1974): 383–402.

———. "The Laugh of the Medusa." Translated by Keith Cohen and Paula Cohen. *Signs* 1, no. 4 (Summer 1976): 875–93.

Cornillon, Susan Koppelman. "The Fiction of Fiction." In *Images of Women in Fiction: Feminist Perspectives*, edited by Susan Koppelman Cornillon. Bowling Green: Bowling Green University Popular Press, 1972.

Culler, Jonathan. Introduction to Tzvetan Todorov, *The Poetics of Prose*. Translated by Richard Howard. Ithaca, N.Y.: Cornell University Press, 1977.

———. "Prolegomena to a Theory of Reading." In *The Reader in the Text*, edited by Susan R. Suleiman and Inge Crosman. Princeton, N.J.: Princeton University Press, 1980.

———. *The Pursuit of Signs: Semiotics, Literature, Deconstruction*. Ithaca, N.Y.: Cornell University Press, 1981.

———. *Structuralist Poetics: Structuralism, Linguistics and the Study of Literature*. Ithaca, N.Y.: Cornell University Press, 1976.

Dahlie, Hallvard. "The Fiction of Alice Munro." *Ploughshares* 4, no. 3 (1978): 56–71.

Deaux, Kay. "Sex: A Perspective on the Attribution Process." In *New Directions in Attribution Research*, edited by John H. Harvey, William John Ickes, and Robert F. Kidd, Vol. 1. Hillsdale, N.J.: Lawrence Erlbaum Assoc., 1976.

Dowling, Colette. *The Cinderella Complex: Women's Hidden Fear of Independence*. New York: Pocket Books, 1981.

Drabble, Margaret. *The Waterfall*. 1969. Reprint. New York: Popular Library, 1977.

Draine, Betsy. "Nostalgia and Irony: The Postmodern Order of *The Golden Notebook*." *Modern Fiction Studies* 26, no. 1 (Spring 1980): 31–48.

DuPlessis, Rachel Blau. *Writing beyond the Ending: Narrative Strategies of Twentieth-Century Women Writers*. Bloomington: Indiana University Press, 1985.

Durham, Carolyn A. "Feminism and Formalism: Dialectical Structures in

Marie Cardinal's *Une Vie pour deux.*" *Tulsa Studies in Women's Literature* 4, no. 1 (Spring 1985): 83–99.

Eagleton, Terry. *The Function of Criticism: From the Spectator to Post-Structuralism.* London: Verso, 1984.

———. *Literary Theory: An Introduction.* Minneapolis: University of Minnesota Press, 1983.

Eakin, Paul John. "Malcolm X and the Limits of Autobiography." In *Autobiography: Essays Theoretical and Critical,* edited by James Olney. Princeton, N.J.: Princeton University Press, 1980.

Egan, Kieran. "What Is a Plot?" *New Literary History* 9, no. 3 (Spring 1978): 455–73.

Ermath, Elizabeth Deeds. "Fictional Consensus and Female Casualties." In *The Representation of Women in Fiction,* edited by Carolyn G. Heilbrun and Margaret R. Higonnet. Baltimore: Johns Hopkins University Press, 1983.

———. *Realism and Consensus in the English Novel.* Princeton, N.J.: Princeton University Press, 1983.

Evans, Nancy Burr. "The Value and Peril for Women of Reading Women Writers." In *Images of Women in Fiction: Feminist Perspectives,* edited by Susan Koppelman Cornillon. Bowling Green: Bowling Green University Popular Press, 1972.

Flax, Jane. "The Conflict Between Nurturance and Autonomy in Mother-Daughter Relationships and Within Feminism." *Feminist Studies* 4, no. 2 (June 1978): 171–89.

Fowler, Roger. *Linguistics and the Novel.* 1977. Reprint. London: Methuen, 1979.

Fox-Genovese, Elizabeth. "The Ambiguities of Female Identity: A Reading of the Novels of Margaret Drabble." *Partisan Review* 46 (1979): 234–48.

Frieze, Irene Hanson. "Women's Expectations for and Causal Attribution of Success and Failure." In *Women and Achievement: Social and Motivational Analyses,* edited by Martha T. Shuch Mednick, Sandra Schwartz Tangri, and Lois Wladis Hoffman. New York: John Wiley and Sons, 1975.

Frye, Joanne S. "*The Woman Warrior:* Claiming Narrative Power, Recreating Female Selfhood." In *The Faith of a (Woman) Writer,* edited by Alice Kessler-Harris and William McBrien. New York: Greenwood Press, 1985.

Frye, Northrop. *The Anatomy of Criticism.* 1957. Reprint. Princeton, N.J.: Princeton University Press, 1971.

Fuoroli, Caryn. "Sophistry or Simple Truth? Narrative Technique in Margaret Drabble's *The Waterfall.*" *Journal of Narrative Technique* 11, no. 2 (Spring 1981): 110–24.

Gallop, Jane. *The Daughter's Seduction: Feminism and Psychoanalysis.* Ithaca, N.Y.: Cornell University Press, 1982.

Gardiner, Judith Kegan. "On Female Identity and Writing by Women." *Critical Inquiry* 8, no. 2 (Winter 1981): 347–61.

———. "The (US)es of (I)dentity: A Response to Abel on '(E)Merging Identities.'" *Signs* 6, no. 3 (Spring 1981): 436–42.

Geertz, Clifford. *The Interpretation of Cultures*. New York: Basic Books, 1973.

Gibson, Graeme. *Eleven Canadian Novelists*. Toronto: Anansi, 1973.

Gilbert, Sandra M. "Costumes of the Mind: Transvestism as Metaphor in Modern Literature." *Critical Inquiry* 7, no. 2 (Winter 1980): 391–417.

———. "Life Studies, or, Speech After Long Silence: Feminist Critics Today." *College English* 40, no. 8 (April 1979): 849–63.

Gilbert, Sandra M., and Susan Gubar. *The Madwoman in the Attic: The Woman Writer and the Nineteenth-Century Imagination*. New Haven: Yale University Press, 1979.

Gilligan, Carol. *In a Different Voice*. Cambridge: Harvard University Press, 1982.

———. "In a Different Voice: Women's Conceptions of Self and Morality." In *The Future of Difference*, edited by Hester Eisenstein and Alice Jardine. Boston: G. K. Hall with Barnard College Women's Center, 1980.

Godwin, Gail. *The Odd Woman*. 1974. Reprint. New York: Warner Books, 1980.

———. "Towards a Fully Human Heroine: Some Worknotes." *Harvard Advocate*, Winter 1973, pp. 26–28.

———. *Violet Clay*. 1978. Reprint. New York: Warner Books, 1979.

Goldmann, Lucien. *Towards a Sociology of the Novel*. Translated by Alan Sheridan. London: Tavistock, 1977.

Gombrich, E. H. *Art and Illusion: A Study in the Psychology of Pictorial Representation*. Princeton, N.J.: Princeton University Press, 1969.

Gordimer, Nadine. *Burger's Daughter*. 1979. Reprint. New York: Penguin Books, 1980.

Gunn, Janet Varner. *Autobiography: Toward a Poetics of Experience*. Philadelphia: University of Pennsylvania Press, 1982.

Hammer, Signe. *Daughters and Mothers: Mothers and Daughters*. New York: Signet, 1976.

Hardin, Nancy S. "An Interview with Margaret Drabble." *Contemporary Literature* 14, no. 3 (Summer 1973): 273–95.

Hardy, Barbara. "An Approach Through Narrative." In *Towards a Poetics of Fiction*, edited by Mark Spilka. Bloomington: Indiana University Press, 1977.

Harper, Michael F. "Margaret Drabble and the Resurrection of the English Novel." *Contemporary Literature* 23, no. 2 (1982): 145–68.

Heilbrun, Carolyn G. *Reinventing Womanhood*. New York: Norton, 1979.

———. "A Response to *Writing and Sexual Difference*." *Critical Inquiry* 8, no. 4 (Summer 1982): 805–11.

Herring, Henry D. "Constructivist Interpretation: An Alternative to Deconstruction." *Bucknell Review* 29, no. 2 (1985): 32–46.

———. "Literature, Concepts, and Knowledge." *New Literary History*, forthcoming.

Higginbotham, Elizabeth. "Two Representative Issues in Contemporary Sociological Work on Black Women." In *But Some of Us Are Brave:*

Black Women's Studies, edited by Gloria T. Hull, Patricia Bell Scott, and Barbara Smith. Old Westbury, N.Y.: Feminist Press, 1982.

Hirsch, E. D., Jr. *The Aims of Interpretation*. 1976. Reprint. Chicago: University of Chicago Press, 1978.

Hoffman, Lois Wladis. "Early Childhood Experiences and Women's Achievement Motives." In *Women and Achievement: Social and Motivational Analyses*, edited by Martha T. Shuch Mednick, Sandra Schwartz Tangri, and Lois Wladis Hoffman. New York: John Wiley and Sons, 1975.

Homans, Margaret. " 'Her Very Own Howl': The Ambiguities of Representation in Recent Women's Fictions." *Signs* 9, no. 2 (Winter 1983): 186–205.

Horner, Matina S. "Toward an Understanding of Achievement-Related Conflicts in Women." In *Women and Achievement: Social and Motivational Analyses*, edited by Martha T. Shuch Mednick, Sandra Schwartz Tangri, and Lois Wladis Hoffman. New York: John Wiley and Sons, 1975.

Hoy, Helen. " 'Dull, Simple, Amazing and Unfathomable': Paradox and Double Vision in Alice Munro's Fiction." *Studies in Canadian Literature* 5 (Spring 1980): 100–115.

Hunter, J. Paul. "The Loneliness of the Long-Distance Reader." *Genre* 10 (Winter 1977): 455–84.

Hutcheon, Linda. *Narcissistic Narrative: The Metafictional Paradox*. 1980. Reprint. New York: Methuen, 1984.

Iser, Wolfgang. *The Act of Reading: A Theory of Aesthetic Response*. 1978. Reprint. Baltimore: Johns Hopkins University Press, 1980.

Jacobus, Mary. "The Difference of View." In *Women Writing and Writing about Women*, edited by Mary Jacobus. New York: Barnes and Noble, 1979.

Jameson, Fredric. *The Political Unconscious: Narrative as a Socially Symbolic Act*. Ithaca, N.Y.: Cornell University Press, 1981.

———. *The Prison-House of Language: A Critical Account of Structuralism and Russian Formalism*. Princeton, N.J.: Princeton University Press, 1974.

Jehlen, Myra. "Archimedes and the Paradox of Feminist Criticism." *Signs* 6, no. 4 (Summer 1981): 575–601.

Jelinek, Estelle C. "Introduction: Women's Autobiography and the Male Tradition." In *Women's Autobiography*, edited by Estelle C. Jelinek. Bloomington: Indiana University Press, 1980.

Jong, Erica. "Blood and Guts: The Tricky Problem of Being a Woman Writer in the Late Twentieth Century." In *The Writer on Her Work*, edited by Janet Sternburg. New York: W. W. Norton and Co., 1980.

Juhasz, Suzanne. *Naked and Fiery Forms: Modern American Poetry by Women, A New Tradition*. New York: Harper, 1976.

———. "Towards a Theory of Form in Feminist Autobiography: Kate Millett's *Flying* and *Sita*; Maxine Hong Kingston's *The Woman Warrior*." In *Women's Autobiography*, edited by Estelle C. Jelinek. Bloomington: Indiana University Press, 1980.

Kaufman, Debra R., and Barbara L. Richardson. *Achievement and Women: Challenging the Assumptions.* New York: Free Press, 1982.

Kegan, Robert. *The Evolving Self: Problem and Process in Human Development.* Cambridge: Harvard University Press, 1982.

Kennard, Jean E. "Convention Coverage or How to Read Your Own Life." *New Literary History* 13, no. 1 (Autumn 1981): 69–88.

Kermode, Frank. "Secrets and Narrative Sequence." In *On Narrative,* edited by W. J. T. Mitchell. Chicago: University of Chicago Press, 1981.

———. *The Sense of an Ending: Studies in the Theory of Fiction.* New York: Oxford University Press, 1967.

Kingston, Maxine Hong. *The Woman Warrior: Memories of a Girlhood Among Ghosts.* New York: Vintage, 1977.

Kolodny, Annette. "Dancing through the Minefield: Some Observations on the Theory, Practice and Politics of a Feminist Literary Criticism." *Feminist Studies* 6, no. 1 (Spring 1980): 1–25.

———. "A Map for Rereading: Or, Gender and the Interpretation of Literary Texts." *New Literary History* 11, no. 3 (1980): 451–67.

Krouse, Agate Nesaule. "Toward a Definition of Literary Feminism." In *Feminist Criticism: Essays on Theory, Poetry and Prose,* edited by Cheryl L. Brown and Karen Olson. Metuchen, N.J.: Scarecrow Press, 1978.

Lanser, Susan Sniader. *The Narrative Act: Point of View in Prose Fiction.* Princeton, N.J.: Princeton University Press, 1981.

Laurence, Margaret. *The Diviners* 1974. Reprint. Toronto: Bantam Books, 1975.

———. *Heart of a Stranger.* 1976. Reprint. Toronto: McClelland and Stewart, 1981.

———. *The Stone Angel.* 1964. Reprint. New York: Bantam, 1981.

———. "Ten Years' Sentences." In *Margaret Laurence: The Writer and the Critics,* edited by William New. Toronto: McGraw-Hill Ryerson, 1977.

———. "Time and the Narrative Voice." In *Margaret Laurence: The Writer and the Critics,* edited by William New. Toronto: McGraw-Hill Ryerson, 1977.

Lentricchia, Frank. *After the New Criticism.* Chicago: University of Chicago Press, 1980.

Lessing, Doris. *The Golden Notebook.* 1962. Reprint. New York: Bantam, 1973.

———. *A Proper Marriage.* 1952. Reprint. New York: New American Library, 1970.

———. *A Small Personal Voice,* edited by Paul Schlueter. New York: Alfred A. Knopf, 1974.

Levine, George. *The Realistic Imagination: English Fiction from Frankenstein to Lady Chatterley.* Chicago: University of Chicago Press, 1981.

Lewis, Maggie. "Toni Morrison: Writing from the Inside Out." *Christian Science Monitor,* April 23, 1981.

Lorsch, Susan. "Gail Godwin's *The Odd Woman:* Literature and the Retreat from Life." *Critique: Studies in Modern Fiction* 20, no. 2 (1978): 21–32.

Lotman, J. M. "Point of View in a Text." Translated by L. M. O'Toole. *New Literary History* 6, no. 2 (1975): 339–52.

Lukacs, Georg. *The Theory of the Novel*. Translated by Anna Bostock. Cambridge: M.I.T. Press, 1977.

Mannheimer, Joan. "Margaret Drabble and the Journey to the Self." *Studies in the Literary Imagination* 11, no. 2 (1978): 127–43.

Marder, Herbert. "The Paradox of Form in *The Golden Notebook*." *Modern Fiction Studies* 26, no. 1 (Spring 1980): 49–54.

Markow, Alice Bradley. "The Pathology of Feminine Failure in the Fiction of Doris Lessing." *Critique: Studies in Modern Fiction* 16, no. 1 (1974): 88–100.

Marshall, Donald G. "Plot as Trap, Plot as Mediation." In *The Horizon of Literature*, edited by Paul Hernadi. Lincoln: University of Nebraska Press, 1982.

Mason, Mary G. "The Other Voice: Autobiographies of Women Writers." In *Autobiography: Essays Theoretical and Critical*, edited by James Olney. Princeton, N.J.: Princeton University Press, 1980.

Mednick, Martha T. Shuch, Sandra Schwartz Tangri, and Lois Wladis Hoffman, eds. *Women and Achievement: Social and Motivational Analyses*. New York: John Wiley and Sons, 1975.

Miller, Jean Baker. *Toward a New Psychology of Women*. 1976. Reprint. Boston: Beacon Press, 1977.

Miller, Nancy K. "Emphasis Added: Plots and Plausibilities in Women's Fiction." *PMLA* 96, no. 1 (January 1981): 36–48.

———. *The Heroine's Text: Readings in the French and English Novel, 1722–1782*. New York: Columbia University Press, 1980.

Millett, Kate. *Flying*. New York: Alfred A. Knopf, 1974.

Mink, Louis O. "Everyman His or Her Own Annalist." In *On Narrative*, edited by W. J. T. Mitchell. Chicago: University of Chicago Press, 1981.

———. "Narrative Form as Cognitive Instrument." In *The Writing of History: Literary Form and Historical Understanding*, edited by Robert H. Canary and Henry Kozicki. Madison: University of Wisconsin Press, 1978.

Moers, Ellen. *Literary Women: The Great Writers*. Garden City, N.Y.: Anchor Books, 1977.

Morgan, Ellen. "Alienation of the Woman Writer in *The Golden Notebook*." In *Doris Lessing: Critical Studies*, edited by Annis Pratt and L. S. Dembo. Madison: University of Wisconsin Press, 1974.

———. "Humanbecoming: Form and Focus in the Neo-Feminist Novel." In *Images of Women in Fiction: Feminist Perspectives*, edited by Susan Koppelman Cornillon. Bowling Green: Bowling Green University Popular Press, 1972.

Morley, Patricia. *Margaret Laurence*. Boston: Twayne, 1981.

Morrison, Toni. *The Bluest Eye*. 1970. Reprint. New York: Pocket Books, 1972.

———. *Sula*. 1973. Reprint. New York: Bantam, 1975.

Munro, Alice. *Lives of Girls and Women.* 1971. Reprint. New York: Signet, 1974.

Myer, Valerie Grosvenor. *Margaret Drabble: Puritanism and Permissiveness.* London: Vision Press, 1974.

Myers, Lena Wright. "Black Women and Self-esteem." In *Another Voice,* edited by Marcia Millman and Rosabeth Kanter. New York: Anchor, 1975.

Neisser, Ulric. *Cognition and Reality: Principles and Implications of Cognitive Psychology.* San Francisco: W. H. Freeman, 1976.

New, William. "Introduction to *The Stone Angel.*" In *Margaret Laurence: The Writer and the Critics,* edited by William New. Toronto: McGraw-Hill Ryerson, 1977.

Olney, James. "Autobiography and the Cultural Moment: A Thematic, Historical, and Bibliographical Introduction." In *Autobiography: Essays Theoretical and Critical,* edited by James Olney. Princeton: Princeton University Press, 1980.

Ortner, Sherry B. "Is Female to Male as Nature Is to Culture?" In *Woman, Culture and Society,* edited by Michelle Zimbalist Rosaldo and Louise Lamphere. Stanford: Stanford University Press, 1974.

Parker, Bettye J. "Complexity: Toni Morrison's Women: An Interview Essay." In *Sturdy Black Bridges: Visions of Black Women in Literature,* edited by Roseann P. Bell, Bettye J. Parker, and Beverly Guy-Sheftall. Garden City, N.Y.: Anchor Press, 1979.

Pearson, Carol, and Katherine Pope. *The Female Hero in American and British Literature.* New York: R. R. Bowker and Co., 1981.

Pollitt, Katha. "Her Own Woman." *New York Times Book Review,* May 21, 1978, p. 11.

Poovey, Mary. "*Persuasion* and the Promises of Love." In *The Representation of Women in Fiction,* edited by Carolyn G. Heilbrun and Margaret R. Higonnet. Baltimore: Johns Hopkins University Press, 1983.

Pratt, Annis. *Archetypal Patterns in Women's Fiction.* Bloomington: Indiana University Press, 1981.

Proust, Marcel. *Swann's Way.* Translated by C. K. Scott Moncrieff. New York: Vintage, 1970.

Reed, Walter. "The Problem with a Poetics of the Novel." In *Towards a Poetics of Fiction,* edited by Mark Spilka. Bloomington: Indiana University Press, 1977.

Rich, Adrienne. *Of Woman Born: Motherhood as Experience and Institution.* 1976. Reprint. New York: Bantam, 1977.

———. *On Lies, Secrets and Silence.* New York: Norton, 1979.

Robbe-Grillet, Alain. *For a New Novel: Essays on Fiction.* Translated by Richard Howard. New York: Grove Press, 1965.

Rosaldo, Michelle Zimbalist. "Woman, Culture, and Society: A Theoretical Overview." In *Woman, Culture and Society,* edited by Michelle Zimbalist Rosaldo and Louise Lamphere. Stanford: Stanford University Press, 1974.

Rose, Ellen Cronan. "Feminine Endings—and Beginnings: Margaret Drab-ble's *The Waterfall.*" *Contemporary Literature* 21, no. 1 (Winter 1980): 81–99.

Rubenstein, Roberta. *The Novelistic Vision of Doris Lessing: Breaking the Forms of Consciousness.* Urbana: University of Illinois Press, 1979.

Russ, Joanna. "What Can a Heroine Do? Or Why Women Can't Write." In *Images of Women in Fiction: Feminist Perspectives,* edited by Susan Koppelman Cornillon. Bowling Green: Bowling Green University Popu-lar Press, 1972.

Said, Edward. *Beginnings: Intention and Method.* Baltimore: Johns Hopkins University Press, 1975.

Sartre, Jean-Paul. *Search for a Method.* Translated by Hazel E. Barnes. New York: Vintage Books, 1968.

Schafer, Roy. "Narration in the Psychoanalytic Dialogue." In *On Narrative,* edited by W. J. T. Mitchell. Chicago: University of Chicago Press, 1981.

Showalter, Elaine. "Feminist Criticism in the Wilderness." *Critical Inquiry* 8, no. 2 (Winter 1981): 179–205.

————. *A Literature of Their Own: British Women Novelists from Brontë to Lessing.* Princeton, N.J.: Princeton University Press, 1977.

————. "Women Writers and the Double Standard." In *Woman in Sexist Society: Studies in Power and Powerlessness,* edited by Vivian Gornick and B. K. Moran. 1971. Reprint. New York: New American Library, 1972.

————. "Towards a Feminist Poetics." In *Women Writing and Writing about Women,* edited by Mary Jacobus. New York: Barnes and Noble, 1979.

Smith, Barbara. "Toward a Black Feminist Criticism." In *But Some of Us Are Brave: Black Women's Studies,* edited by Gloria T. Hull, Patricia Bell Scott, and Barbara Smith. Old Westbury, N.Y.: Feminist Press, 1982.

Smith, Barbara Herrnstein. *On the Margins of Discourse: The Relation of Literature to Language.* Chicago: University of Chicago Press, 1978.

Snitow, Ann Barr. "The Front Line: Notes on Sex in Novels by Women, 1969–1979." *Signs* 5, no. 4 (Summer 1980): 702–18.

Spacks, Patricia Meyer. *The Female Imagination.* New York: Avon Books, 1976.

Spence, Janet T. "Changing Conceptions of Men and Women: A Psychol-ogist's Perspective." In *A Feminist Perspective in the Academy: The Difference It Makes,* edited by Elizabeth Langland and Walter Gove. Chicago: University of Chicago Press, 1983.

Spillers, Hortense. "The Politics of Intimacy: A Discussion." In *Sturdy Black Bridges: Visions of Black Women in Literature,* edited by Roseann P. Bell, Bettye J. Parker, and Beverly Guy-Sheftall. Garden City, N.Y.: Anchor Press, 1979.

Stimpson, Catharine. "Zero Degree Deviancy: The Lesbian Novel in En-gland." *Critical Inquiry* 8, no. 2 (Winter 1981): 363–79.

Stitzel, Judith. "Reading Doris Lessing." *College English* 40, no. 5 (January 1979): 498–504.

Struthers, J. R. "Reality and Ordering: The Growth of a Young Artist in *Lives of Girls and Women.*" *Essays on Canadian Writing* 3 (Fall 1975): 32–46.

Tompkins, Jane P. "The Reader in History." In *Reader Response Criticism: From Formalism to Post-Structuralism,* edited by Jane Tompkins. Baltimore: Johns Hopkins University Press, 1980.

Turner, Victor. "Social Dramas and Stories about Them." In *On Narrative,* edited by W. J. T. Mitchell. Chicago: University of Chicago Press, 1981.

Vallacher, Robin R. "An Introduction to Self Theory." In *The Self in Social Psychology,* edited by Daniel M. Wegner and Robin R. Vallacher. New York: Oxford University Press, 1980.

Washington, Mary Helen. "Teaching *Black-Eyed Susans:* An Approach to the Study of Black Women Writers." In *But Some of Us Are Brave: Black Women's Studies,* edited by Gloria T. Hull, Patricia Bell Scott, and Barbara Smith. Old Westbury, N.Y.: Feminist Press, 1982.

Watt, Ian. *The Rise of the Novel: Studies in Defoe, Richardson and Fielding.* 1957. Reprint. Berkeley: University of California Press, 1965.

———. "Serious Reflections on *The Rise of the Novel.*" In *Towards a Poetics of Fiction,* edited by Mark Spilka. Bloomington: Indiana University Press, 1977.

Weston, Peter J., and Martha T. Shuch Mednick. "Race, Social Class, and the Motive to Avoid Success in Women." In *Women and Achievement: Social and Motivational Analyses,* edited by Martha T. Shuch Mednick, Sandra Schwartz Tangri, and Lois Wladis Hoffman. New York: John Wiley and Sons, 1975.

White, Hayden. "The Historical Text as Literary Artifact." In *The Writing of History: Literary Form and Historical Understanding,* edited by Robert H. Canary and Henry Kozicki. Madison: University of Wisconsin Press, 1978.

———. "The Value of Narrativity in the Representation of Reality." In *On Narrative,* edited by W. J. T. Mitchell. Chicago: University of Chicago Press, 1981.

Williams, Raymond. *Marxism and Literature.* Oxford: Oxford University Press, 1977.

Wolf, Christa. *Cassandra: A Novel and Four Essays.* Translated by Jan Van Heurck. London: Virago, 1984.

———. *A Model Childhood.* Translated by Ursula Molinaro and Hedwig Rappolt. New York: Farrar, Straus and Giroux, 1980.

———. *The Quest for Christa T.* Translated by Christopher Middleton. New York: Farrar, Straus and Giroux, 1979.

Woodcock, George. *The World of Canadian Writing.* Seattle: University of Washington Press, 1980.

Woolf, Virginia. "Modern Fiction." *Collected Essays.* Vol. 2. New York: Harcourt, Brace and World, 1967.

———. "Mr. Bennett and Mrs. Brown." *Collected Essays.* Vol. 1. New York: Harcourt, Brace and World, 1967.

_____. "Professions for Women." *Collected Essays.* Vol. 2. New York: Harcourt, Brace and World, 1967.

_____. *A Room of One's Own.* 1929. Reprint. New York: Harcourt, Brace and World, 1957.

_____. *To the Lighthouse.* New York: Harcourt, Brace and World, 1927.

_____. *The Voyage Out.* 1915. Reprint. New York: Harcourt, Brace and World, 1948.

Zimmerman, Bonnie. "Exiting from Patriarchy: The Lesbian Novel of Development." In *The Voyage In: Fictions of Female Development,* edited by Elizabeth Abel, Marianne Hirsch, and Elizabeth Langland. Hanover, N.H.: University Press of New England, 1983.

Index

Abel, Elizabeth, 13, 28, 29, 62, 167
Achievement motive, 198
Adventure novel, 4
Agency: absent from female literary paradigms, 32; of character in implementing change, 42–43; of first-person narrator, 9, 10, 56–57, 65; of narrator in *The Bluest Eye*, 107–8; of narrator in *The Golden Notebook*, 172; of narrator in *Jane Eyre*, 82; of narrator in *Lives of Girls and Women*, 90–91; 96; of narrator in *The Waterfall*, 149, 154–63
Aging, female experience of, 72; in *The Bluest Eye*, 108; in *The Stone Angel*, 130, 132–34, 138
Alter, Robert, 20, 33, 38, 193
Angel in the House: as Virginia Woolf's ideological phantom, 3, 6; in *The Golden Notebook*, 180
Angelou, Maya, 53
Anger: as claim to subjectivity in *The Bluest Eye*, 101; legitimate for Hagar Shipley, 131, 134–37
Artist, identity as: in conflict with identity as woman, 3; in *Lives of Girls and Women*, 84, 87; in *Violet Clay*, 120–21, 123–24
Attribution: by narrator, 68; of qualities to characters, 42–43, 64; reader's causal, 196–99, 202–3
Atwood, Margaret, 130

Austen, Jane, v–vi, 25, 35, 160
Autobiography: theories of, 64; women's 53–55, 227n.39
Autonomy: claimed in *Violet Clay*, 112; claimed in *The Waterfall*, 149; difficult for female protagonist, 1, 5, 26, 28; human need for, 81; in context of community, 206n.17; in tension with relationality, 73–74; in tension in *The Bluest Eye*, 104–5, 107; in tension in *The Golden Notebook*, 175; in tension in *Jane Eyre*, 82; in tension in *Lives of Girls and Women*, 89, 91–93; in tension in *The Stone Angel*, 141; in tension in *The Waterfall*, 153, 163
Awakening, The (Chopin), 46

Bakhtin, Mikhail M., 22, 26, 27, 30, 35
Barth, John, 53
Barthes, Roland, 29, 65, 89, 201
Beauty. *See* Physical appearance
Beauvoir, Simone de, 2, 133, 142, 143–44
Beckett, Samuel, 53, 200
Beer, Gillian, 63
Benjamin, Walter, 25
Bennett, Arnold, 43
Bergonzi, Bernard, 148
Bildungsroman: dangers for female protagonist (in *The Bluest Eye*),